Evangelical Christianity and Democracy in Latin America

EVANGELICAL CHRISTIANITY
AND DEMOCRACY
IN THE GLOBAL SOUTH

Series Editor
Timothy Samuel Shah

Evangelical Christianity and Democracy in Latin America
Edited by Paul Freston

Evangelical Christianity and Democracy in Africa
Edited by Terence O. Ranger

Evangelical Christianity and Democracy in Asia
Edited by David H. Lumsdaine

Evangelical Christianity and Democracy in Global Perspective
Edited by Timothy Samuel Shah

Evangelical Christianity and Democracy in Latin America

Edited by

PAUL FRESTON

OXFORD
UNIVERSITY PRESS

2008

OXFORD
UNIVERSITY PRESS

Oxford University Press, Inc., publishes works that further
Oxford University's objective of excellence
in research, scholarship, and education.

Oxford   New York
Auckland   Cape Town   Dar es Salaam   Hong Kong   Karachi
Kuala Lumpur   Madrid   Melbourne   Mexico City   Nairobi
New Delhi   Shanghai   Taipei   Toronto

With offices in
Argentina   Austria   Brazil   Chile   Czech Republic   France   Greece
Guatemala   Hungary   Italy   Japan   Poland   Portugal   Singapore
South Korea   Switzerland   Thailand   Turkey   Ukraine   Vietnam

Copyright © 2008 by Oxford University Press, Inc.

Published by Oxford University Press, Inc.
198 Madison Avenue, New York, New York 10016

www.oup.com

Oxford is a registered trademark of Oxford University Press.

Library of Congress Cataloging-in-Publication Data
Evangelical Christianity and democracy in Latin America /
edited by Paul Freston.
    p. cm.—(Evangelical Christianity and democracy in the Global South)
Includes bibliographical references and index.
ISBN 978-0-19-517476-2; 978-0-19-530803-7 (pbk.)
1. Evangelicalism—Political aspects—Latin America.
2. Democracy—Religious aspects—Christianity.
3. Christianity and politics—Latin America.   I. Freston, Paul.
II. Series.
BR1642.L29E93 2006
322'.1098—dc22   2005031887

9 8 7 6 5 4 3 2 1

Printed in the United States of America
on acid-free paper

For
Vinay Kumar Samuel,
on the fortieth anniversary of his ordination to ministry
in the Church of South India
(1967–2007)

And for all the churches of Asia, Africa, and Latin America
it remains his joy to serve

Preface

The research project that generated this volume began as an effort in evangelical self-understanding. The globally minded and globally active International Fellowship of Evangelical Mission Theologians (INFEMIT), together with its research and study arm, the Oxford Centre for Mission Studies (OCMS), based in Oxford, England, undertook numerous efforts in the 1980s and 1990s to develop sophisticated evangelical analyses of a host of global issues, including modernity and modernization, market economics, population growth, and human disability.[1] Toward the end of the 1990s it occurred to INFEMIT's director, Indian theologian Vinay Samuel, that international evangelicalism itself merited a critical analysis, particularly because of its growing social and political prominence in the developing countries of the "global South" (i.e., Africa, Asia, and Latin America).

Evangelical politics merited analysis, Samuel believed, not only because evangelical political efforts were increasingly organized and consequential but also because their impact on global South politics seemed so varied and ambivalent. After all, some of the best known instances of evangelical politics include the military dictatorship of Efraín Ríos Montt in Guatemala in the early 1980s as well as the support many white evangelicals gave to apartheid in South Africa until the early 1990s. On the other hand, the evangelical wing of Kenya's Anglican Church proved to be authoritarian president Daniel arap Moi's most vocal critic in the 1980s and 1990s.

In this variety and ambiguity, global South evangelicals are not unlike their evangelical counterparts in the United States. Major political figures (such as former president Jimmy Carter, former senator Mark Hatfield, and former attorney general John Ashcroft) and movements (such as the Moral Majority and the Christian Coalition) convey the enormous growth and influence of American evangelical political activism over the last thirty years. But they also underscore evangelicals' deep differences in political philosophy, their divergent policy goals, and the uncertainty of their long-term political achievements.[2] The fact that American evangelicals have remained consistent and enthusiastic supporters of George W. Bush—a president otherwise deeply and increasingly unpopular both inside and outside the United States—only deepens the sense that global evangelicalism has bequeathed an ambiguous political legacy that evangelicals bear a special responsibility to scrutinize.[3]

To launch this project of critical self-understanding, Vinay Samuel gathered a small team of evangelical scholars, including myself, in 1997. For the necessary funding, we turned to the Pew Charitable Trusts, which had an impressive track record of supporting scholarship on, and by, evangelicals. Luis Lugo, head of Pew's Religion Program at the time, and Susan Billington Harper, program officer with the Religion Program, provided indispensable encouragement and guidance at this early stage. As a first step in Pew's support, they provided a seed grant to conduct a preliminary "mapping" of the basic patterns of evangelical political activism across the global South as well as the most promising avenues for long-term research on the subject. Paul Freston, an outstanding sociologist specializing in the study of pentecostalism in Brazil and a member of our team, agreed to produce this mapping, and in a few short months performed the major miracle of writing a booklength overview of evangelical politics in nearly thirty countries in Africa, Asia, and Latin America, complete with an exhaustive bibliography. Freston's study, first in manuscript form and later as a published monograph, became a constant point of reference as we designed the project and, later, as we conducted the research.[4] It also made a compelling case to our prospective funders that the subject deserved more systematic and sustained examination. So in June 1999, the Pew Charitable Trusts provided our INFEMIT research team with a generous grant to conduct field research on politically engaged evangelicals on three continents—Asia, Africa, and Latin America—over three years.

We focused our critical analysis of evangelical politics in these regions of the global South in two ways. First, we identified what seemed to be the most significant cases of evangelical political mobilization and influence in each region's most significant countries: Brazil, Mexico, Guatemala, Nicaragua, Chile, and Peru in Latin America; Nigeria, Kenya, South Africa, Mozambique, Zambia, and Zimbabwe in Africa; and China, India, Indonesia, South Korea, and the Philippines in Asia.

Second, to give our research a sharper analytical and evaluative edge, we decided to pay special attention to the relationship between evangelical politics and democracy in each region. How has the overall trend toward democratization in all the regions of the global South, especially during the "third wave" of democratization (1974–1991), given evangelicals new incentives and opportunities for political mobilization and influence?[5] And, more important for our critical purposes, what has been the impact of politically engaged evangelicalism on democratization? To what extent has it contributed to the inauguration and consolidation of democratic regimes? And in countries where democratic transitions have not occurred, to what extent have evangelicals promoted the norms and practices of democratic politics, whether at the local, regional, or national level? Conversely, to what extent have politically engaged evangelicals blocked, slowed, or otherwise undermined democratization in the global South?

Evangelicalism's impact on democratization compelled our attention not only because of our interest in assessing the level and quality of evangelical political activism. It also seemed worthy of study because democratization in the global South, despite dramatic advances, remained so limited and fragile—particularly insofar as democracy in its most robust and valid form requires not only free and fair elections but also effective respect for basic human rights and freedoms. Democracy in Asia, Africa, and Latin America needed all the help it could get, and we wanted to know how much help, if any, evangelicals were giving. Since the start of our research, just how much the overall social and economic development of the global South requires the establishment of more effective, transparent, and democratic governance has become even more painfully obvious. Yet in Asia and Africa in particular, according to a 2007 Freedom House report, democratization has stagnated or even reversed since 2005.[6]

Furthermore, recent studies of religion and democratization had included almost no broad, comparative treatment of evangelical influences. Numerous scholars noted the important roles Catholic and mainline Protestant churches played in democratic transitions throughout the global South during the "third wave" of democratization, particularly in the 1980s and early 1990s. Indeed, the pro-democratic activism of such churches continues to provoke scholarly and journalistic interest. The vocal opposition of Zimbabwe's Catholic bishops to the increasingly repressive regime of Robert Mugabe, for example, received considerable attention in the press in early 2007, notably in *The Economist*.[7] But mainstream scholarship on religion and democratization, whether focused on Africa, Asia, or Latin America, tended to ignore or downplay the burgeoning evangelical sector of global South Christianity.[8] Granted that bishops and archbishops, clergy and laity, as well as a globe-trotting Pope mobilized Catholic and mainline Protestant churches to battle authoritarian regimes and support democratic transitions throughout the global South, what about evangelical churches, denominations, and political parties? What about evangelical movements within mainline churches? After all, many of these churches in the global South, if not in their counterpart churches in Europe and North America, remain animated by the biblicist theology and missionary activism that are the hallmarks of evangelicalism.[9] Finally, we were eager to investigate the political contributions of the pentecostal subsector of evangelicalism in particular, which has become the most dynamic and demographically dominant force not only in global South evangelicalism but in global South Protestantism as a whole.

In addition, demographic trends recommended a focus on evangelical contributions to global South democratization. Whereas throughout the 1950s and 1960s leading scholars and other observers, such as Indian historian and diplomat K. M. Panikkar, predicted with breathtaking confidence and uniformity that Christianity in Asia and Africa would collapse once the coercive pressures of Western colonialism were removed, Christianity and especially Protestantism saw continuing expansion, not contraction, in the last decades of the twentieth century.[10] In Africa, for example, according to religion demographers David Barrett and Todd Johnson, Christians numbered 10 million in 1900 and 30 million in 1945, but then jumped to 144 million by 1970 and further to 411 million by 2005.[11] Africa's most dramatic Christian growth, in other words, occurred *after* decolonization. Protestantism in particular has seen significant postcolonial growth across the global South, more than doubling from about 4 percent of the overall global South population in 1970 to about 10 percent by 2000. In comparison, Roman Catholicism saw its overall share of the global South population increase by only a little more than one percentage point during the same thirty-year period, from 13 percent to 14 percent, and Islam's share also grew rather modestly, from 19 percent to 23 percent. As a result of this exponential growth, the Protestant proportion of the population in Latin America was six times greater at the end of the twentieth century than at the beginning of the twentieth century, in Asia ten times greater, and in Africa thirteen times greater.[12] No other major religious group came close to experiencing such a dramatic, sustained, and extensive demographic expansion across the global South during this period.

The most important driver and beneficiary of Protestantism's demographic expansion across the global South has clearly been evangelicalism— particularly, in recent years, in its pentecostal expressions. Within most of the global South's thriving mainline Protestant churches, evangelicalism is the dominant element, which of course is what increasingly separates Protestants from fellow Anglicans, Episcopalians, Methodists, Lutherans, and Presbyterians in Europe and North America, among whom, to put it plainly, a gospel of political inclusion has increasingly displaced a gospel of spiritual conversion. Evangelicalism is thus not a denominational category, as our research takes pains to emphasize. Evangelical Methodists in Mozambique may have far more in common with evangelical Presbyterians in South Korea or with evangelical pentecostals in Brazil than with fellow Methodists in Maine or Minnesota.

Evangelicalism in its Spirit-filled pentecostal form has proven particularly contagious, constantly spreading across otherwise well-defended ecclesiastical borders. Numerous Protestant churches in the global South, not to mention the Roman Catholic Church, have succumbed to pervasive "pentecostalization" in the form of highly successful charismatic movements, even as pentecostal denominations such as the Assemblies of God expand and multiply with remarkable velocity in virtually every corner of Asia, Africa, and Latin America. A ten-country public opinion survey of global pentecostalism conducted by the Pew Forum on Religion and Public Life in 2006 found that nearly half or more of all Protestants interviewed in Brazil, Chile, Guatemala, Nigeria, and Kenya were members of pentecostal churches, while more than a quarter of Protestants interviewed in South Africa, South Korea, Guatemala, and the Philippines were Protestant charismatics (i.e., people who identified with the pentecostal label or with pentecostal practice such as speaking in tongues but remained members of nonpentecostal churches).[13] In Latin America, for example, according to 2006 figures from the World Christian Database, pentecostals and charismatics now represent nearly 30 percent, or about 150 million, of the population of 560 million people, whereas they represented only about 4 percent in 1970.[14] When one considers that both pentecostal and nonpentecostal evangelicals generally have higher rates of religious observance than other Christians, the conclusion that evangelicalism has become the dominant form of Christian practice in much of the global South is inescapable.

Further arguing in favor of a focus on evangelicalism's contributions to democracy is an impressive body of recent research on the democratic potential of this burgeoning form of Protestantism. Distinguished sociologist David Martin and a number of other scholars have painted a picture of global South evangelicals in the late twentieth century reminiscent of Alexis de Tocqueville's picture of American Christians in the early nineteenth century: voluntarist, independent of the state, and assiduous practitioners of the "art of association."[15] In their churches and small prayer and Bible study groups, evangelicals carve out what Martin terms "autonomous social spaces" within which believers receive Word and Spirit directly, without priestly mediation, and are empowered to share them with others. Amid degradation and exploitation, they experience stability, dignity, and equality.[16] In addition, Martin and others document how conversion to evangelicalism involves the acquisition of a "Protestant ethic" that transforms drunken and indolent men into sober and responsible householders, which in turn provides their families with a modicum of economic stability.[17] As the pioneering sociologist of religion Peter Berger likes to say, "Max Weber is alive and well and living in Guatemala."[18]

In documenting these cultural, social, moral, and economic transformations, Martin and other scholars argue that they may well suggest that evangelicalism enjoys an intrinsic tendency to promote both the kind of moral and purposeful individualism and the kind of robust associational life that are conducive to democratization. But these somewhat tentative claims concerning evangelicalism's long-term democratic potential could and should be empirically tested, it seemed to us, against the actual political activism and performance of evangelicals across the global South. If the "evangelical ethic" really does promote the spirit of capitalism through microlevel moral and cultural change, does it also promote the spirit of democracy through macrolevel political change? The increasing number of cases of evangelical political activism in Asia, Africa, and Latin America enabled us to investigate whether evangelicals were living up to their democratic potential.

To direct the research on Latin American evangelicals and democracy that generated this volume, we turned to Paul Freston, who was a crucial element of our research project from its inception. Formerly a lecturer in sociology at the Federal University of São Carlos, Brazil, and now a professor of sociology at Calvin College in Grand Rapids, Michigan, Freston helped us assemble an outstanding team of Latin American scholars as well as one U.S. scholar to conduct field research in the key countries we had selected: Alexandre Brasil Fonseca on Brazil, Felipe Vázquez Palacios on Mexico, Darío López Rodriguez on Peru, Clay Matthew Samson on Guatemala, Roberto Zub on Nicaragua, and David Muñoz Condell on Chile.[19] In addition, University of Michigan political scientist Daniel Levine, a long-time student of religion and politics in Latin America, contributes a highly readable, personal, and illuminating postscript on evangelicals and politics in the region.

The insightful studies of these scholars probe the efforts of evangelicals throughout Latin America to translate their recent demographic expansion into political clout. According to 2005 figures from the World Christian Database, pentecostals alone represent 13 percent of the region's population, and nonpentecostal evangelicals may represent another 3 to 5 percent.[20] Consequently, the evangelical proportion of the population in several countries—notably, Guatemala, Nicaragua, Chile, and Brazil—approaches or exceeds 20 percent.[21] In some cases, such as Guatemala, Chile, and Peru, evangelical church leaders and politicians have used the community's growth to help establish and legitimate various dictatorships. At the same time, in these countries as well as in Brazil and Nicaragua, other evangelicals have opposed authoritarian governments of the left and right, participated in democratic transitions, and thrown themselves into the rough and tumble of electoral competition. Evangelicals have fielded hundreds of candidates in national elections across the region, involved millions of Latin Americans in democratic political processes, and formed numerous political parties and parliamentary bodies (such as the Evangelical Parliamentary Front in Brazil, which included 10 percent of parliamentarians until October 2006). Evangelicals who had clung to the motto "Believers don't mess with politics!" became increasingly robust democratic actors between 1980 and 2000. Such evangelical activism contributes to democratic consolidation by intensifying political competition and broadening political participation. However, evangelicalism's greatest contribution to democracy may be indirect. Even when evangelicals eschew direct political involvement, a number of Freston's scholars as well as Daniel Levine suggest that evangelical churches naturally function as "schools of democracy": their emphasis on lay leadership and participation imparts the skills and values necessary for effective civic leadership, cooperation, and mobilization in a democratic context.

However, these chapters also provide vivid accounts of the costs and limits of evangelical politics. In terms of costs, evangelicals who play the game of politics prove no less subject than others to its characteristic dynamics and temptations, including the corporatist pursuit of narrow group interests over and against the common good and participation in corrupt patron–client relations. Precisely where evangelicals vigorously seek their fair share of the political pie, in other words, the almost inevitable result is that "politics bites back," as Daniel Levine notes in his postscript. Evangelicals who seek to enhance their political recognition and influence by any means whatsoever soon see their integrity, reputation, *and* political influence suffer one setback after another. In Brazil, for example, a disproportionately large number of pentecostal and evangelical congress members were under investigation since early 2006 for a contract kickback scandal, and many were not reelected to office in the October 2006 elections.[22] As for limits, evangelical efforts to forge a united political front have failed in all the Latin American countries we examined. Evangelicals have seldom if ever rallied *en bloc* behind a particular political figure, party, or movement, evangelical or otherwise. And as the chapter on Mexico suggests, at least some evangelicals continue to be apolitical and impervious to all forms of political mobilization.

Though this research has in many ways been an exercise in evangelical self-criticism, it is important to note that many of the researchers who have been involved in it do not identify with evangelical Christianity. To conduct field research and produce the country case studies, we sought scholars who were based in the countries they were studying and who had ample experience investigating evangelicalism in these countries, regardless of whether they were "card-carrying" evangelicals, as it were. In a number of cases, the most impressive scholars we could find *were* evangelicals. But that was not the point. Precisely because we wanted to offer the evangelical world a non-distortive picture of evangelical politics in the global South, warts and all, our overriding criterion in selecting our research team was not theological correctness but a proven ability to provide intelligent access to the phenomenon at hand.

Just as our research was produced by a religiously diverse team of scholars, however, we expect that it will be of interest to a religiously diverse audience. Evangelicals and nonevangelicals alike have a stake in understanding the political intentions and influences of this burgeoning, global movement, especially when a growing number of studies are sounding the alarm about the political dangers of religion in general and evangelical religion in particular.[23] The politics of global evangelicalism can be understood at the most basic level, however, only if one pays close attention to the politics of global South evangelicalism, which accounts for the vast majority of the world's evangelicals. At the same time, our research is an essential starting point even for those with no particular interest in global evangelical politics per se but who seek a deeper understanding of, say, American or Canadian or British evangelical political activism. For one cannot distinguish the constant and characteristically evangelical features of any of these movements from contingent features arising from the accidents of time, place, and political opportunity without systematically comparing them with forms of evangelical activism prevalent elsewhere. "And what should they know of England who only England know?"[24] Understanding evangelical politics anywhere requires at least some familiarity with evangelical politics everywhere.

Our somewhat fanatical insistence on the cardinal importance of broad and comparative inquiry leads us to believe that this volume is best read in conjunction with its companion volumes on Asia and Africa. These three volumes were not generated by three separate projects, after all, but by one project motivated from the start by a common set of concerns and questions about the adequacy of evangelicalism's "political witness"—to use an evangelical phrase—in the countries of the global South. We developed common approaches to our key concepts, particularly evangelicalism and democracy, and we immersed ourselves in a common body of literature on religion and democratization. In the course of the project, there was significant interaction between the directors of the regional research teams, which encouraged significant intellectual cross-fertilization. And in June 2002, all the project participants gathered in Potomac, Maryland, to present our research to a distinguished gathering of scholars from around the world. The answers to the questions that launched our project lie in the totality of this cross-regional research and should not be inferred from any one volume or case study.

When seen in its totality, this body of research not only provides a broad survey of evangelical politics in nearly twenty countries but also offers insights into the wider trend that Peter Berger aptly terms the "desecularization of the world": the process whereby all the major religious communities—Islam, Hinduism, Buddhism, and Christianity—have surged in vitality and political influence from the early 1970s right up to the present, thus weakening the hold of secularist political regimes and ideologies throughout the world and filling otherwise secular public spaces everywhere with religious voices.[25] Just as no case of evangelical politics can be properly studied in isolation from other cases, no case of religion's global political resurgence can be properly understood apart from this broad spectrum of politically mobilized religions. Any minimally adequate understanding of the causes and consequences of the Islamic political resurgence, for example, requires rigorous comparison with other cases of religion's political resurgence. And perhaps no case provides a more apt comparison than the worldwide evangelical political upsurge. Evangelical Protestantism, like Islam, is an egalitarian, scripture-based religion without a central hierarchy that has achieved impressive global expansion and political influence largely through grassroots mobilization. Yet I am aware of no systematic and sustained attempt to compare these powerful forms of religious political activism, despite the fresh insights into both movements such a study would be bound to generate. Perhaps our research can facilitate this and other potentially fruitful comparisons between the world's politically resurgent religions.

In coordinating such a massive project over so many years, I have incurred almost innumerable and certainly unrepayable debts. David Battrick, Darin Hamlin, Matthew Fesak, and Anne Fontenau provided crucial support as the project was launched in 1999 and early 2000. David Fabrycky, Laura Fabrycky, Scott Bond, and particularly Dawn Haglund offered various forms of assistance, with Dawn Haglund taking on the monumental task of organizing numerous research workshops throughout the world as well as the project's large international conference in June 2002. In this massive undertaking, Eric Naus and Cara Farr were a tremendous and cheerful help. At a later stage, Sarah Mehta and Stephen Joyce offered invaluable assistance. Abey George helped coordinate the arduous task of organizing and cleaning up the references for all three volumes, assisted admirably by Laura Fabrycky.

In the last two years, no single person has contributed more to the seemingly endless task of preparing the volumes for publication than Rachel Mumford. She happily immersed herself in the minutiae of each volume to an extent that would have driven lesser mortals insane. I can explain this only by her repeated affirmation that she made the project her own. I cannot thank her enough. Working closely with Rachel Mumford, Patricia Barreiro contributed her tremendous skills as a copyeditor and in the process gave up more tears and sweat than our meager recompense could justify. Without this dynamic duo, the volumes might never have seen publication.

Several institutions provided crucial support at points. The Ethics and Public Policy Center (EPPC) offered me and the project an extremely happy and hospitable base of operations from the moment The Pew Charitable Trusts decided to fund our research in June 1999 until I left the Center in July 2004. Elliott Abrams took a personal interest in the project and saw to it that I received all the help the EPPC could muster. Markus Österlund was an unexpected and enormously delightful and stimulating intellectual companion. Above all, EPPC vice president Michael Cromartie gave me the warmest possible welcome and made himself an instant and continuing friend of this project with his characteristic combination of sharp advice and strong encouragement. Fieldstead and Company gave valuable financial support, enabling us to considerably expand our June 2002 conference, thus helping to make it a great success.

In his new capacity as director of the Pew Forum on Religion and Public Life, Luis Lugo offered me and the project generous support when I joined the Forum in August 2004. Thanks to his remarkable generosity and consistent belief in the importance of the subject matter, I enjoyed tremendous freedom to work on the project as well as outstanding assistance from Forum staff. Among Forum staff, the most notable assistance came from Julia Kirby, who worked closely with Rachel Mumford in the summer of 2005 to prepare the manuscripts for their original review by Oxford University Press. Most recently, Boston University's Institute on Culture, Religion, and World Affairs (CURA) and the Council on Foreign Relations have provided the perfect institutional settings for thinking through the long-term significance and geopolitical consequences of evangelical expansion in the global South. My friends at these institutions, Peter Berger at CURA and Walter Mead at the Council, are the most perceptive, encouraging, and stimulating interlocutors on the issues addressed by this project that one could possibly hope for.

Numerous other individuals offered incisive commentary and valuable guidance at various stages of the project: Philip Jenkins, David Martin, Samuel Huntington, Mark Noll, Robert Woodberry, Paul Gifford, Daniel Levine, Susanne Rudolph, Christian Smith, Christopher Sugden, Haddon Willmer, Richard John Neuhaus, Virginia Garrard-Burnett, Jeffrey Klaiber, David Maxwell, Lamin Sanneh, Daniel Philpott, Ken Woodward, Paul Marshall, Ron Sider, Jim Skillen, Keith Pavlischek, Oliver O'Donovan, Joan Lockwood O'Donovan, N. J. Demerath, José Míguez Bonino, Paul Sigmund, Timothy Steigenga, Hannah Stewart-Gambino, John Green, Dennis Hoover, Ruth Melkonian-Hoover, Hillel Fradkin, Daniel Bays, Marc Plattner, Carol Hamrin, David Aikman, Rosalind Hackett, John Wolffe, Matthews Ojo, Uwe Siemon-Netto, John Wilson, and Phil Costopoulos.

At Oxford University Press, Cynthia Read has been marvelously encouraging and unfailingly patient at every stage, despite the fact that the process of seeing the volumes to publication proved much more time-consuming and difficult than she ever dreamed possible. Christine Dahlin handled the volumes in the final stages with extraordinary efficiency and professionalism. We are also grateful for Theodore Calderara's and Julia TerMaat's assistance.

There would of course be no project and no volumes without our dedicated team of scholars. It has been a particular honor to work with our abundantly talented regional research directors: Terence Ranger, director of the

African research; Vikram Chand, the first director of the Asian research, who had to give up his responsibilities with the project when he assumed a senior position with the World Bank in New Delhi in 2000; David Lumsdaine, who succeeded Dr. Chand as the director of the Asian research; and, as I have already noted, Paul Freston, director of the Latin American research. Each of these outstanding scholars contributed immeasurably to the project as a whole and not merely to his own piece of it. Above all, however, the chapter authors have been the heart and soul of this project. They have all produced rich and insightful case studies, and many braved considerable danger and difficulty in conducting their fieldwork. Along with the Latin America scholars already mentioned, our Asia scholars were Sushil Aaron, Sujatha Fernandes, Kim-Kwong Chan, Young-gi Hong, David Lim, and Bambang Budijanto; and our Africa scholars were Cyril Imo, John Karanja, Anthony Balcomb, Isabel Phiri, Isabel Mukonyora, and Teresa Cruz e Silva.

This project has had its highs and lows, with many of the lows falling thickly in the last two years prior to publication. Through it all, no one has proven a more constant and energetic encouragement than my wife, Becky. Though she has had every right to be exasperated by a project that I have been working on longer than we have been married, she has instead been consistently herself: ferociously loyal and supportive and adamantly uncomplaining about the additional psychic burdens this project placed on me and therefore on her. I am deeply grateful.

Finally, let me reiterate that this ambitious project began as an idea in the fertile and deeply evangelical mind of Vinay Samuel. Without his leadership, at once visionary and practical, no such project would have been organized, funded, or even imagined. On behalf of all those who have participated in the project, I therefore gratefully dedicate the project volumes to the Rev. Dr. Vinay Kumar Samuel and to the simultaneously struggling and thriving churches of the global South he intended the volumes to serve.

—Timothy Samuel Shah
Council on Foreign Relations
Boston University
August 15, 2007

NOTES

1. Philip Sampson, Vinay Samuel, and Chris Sugden, eds., *Faith and Modernity* (Oxford: Regnum, 1994); Herbert Schlossberg, Vinay Samuel, and Ronald J. Sider, eds., *Christianity and Economics in the Post–Cold War Era: The Oxford Declaration and Beyond* (Grand Rapids, Mich.: Eerdmans, 1994); and D. G. R. Belshaw, Robert Calderisi, and Chris Sugden, eds., *Faith in Development: Partnership between the World Bank and the Churches of Africa* (Oxford: Regnum, 2001). Major INFEMIT-sponsored analyses also appeared in the international evangelical journal *Transformation:*

An International Journal of Holistic Mission Studies, started in 1984, including a special 1998 issue on human disability edited by Rebecca Samuel Shah (October–December 1998; volume 15, number 4).

2. For an outstanding collection of sympathetic yet critical appraisals of the political activism of American evangelicals in recent years, see Michael Cromartie, ed., *A Public Faith: Evangelicals and Civic Engagement* (Lanham, Md.: Rowman & Littlefield, 2003). See also Christian Smith's powerful analysis in *American Evangelicalism: Embattled and Thriving* (1998).

3. Seventy-eight percent of white evangelical voters supported Bush in 2004, giving him 40 percent of his winning vote share, and in the 2006 congressional elections, 72 percent of white evangelicals voted Republican in races for the U.S. House nationwide. See John C. Green, Corwin E. Smidt, James L. Guth, and Lyman A. Kellstedt, "The American Religious Landscape and the 2004 Presidential Vote: Increased Polarization," available at http://pewforum.org/publications/surveys/postelection.pdf, last accessed on August 14, 2007; and the Pew Forum on Religion and Public Life, "Religion and the 2006 Elections," available at http://pewforum.org/docs/?DocID=174, last accessed on August 14, 2007.

4. Freston (2001).

5. Huntington (1991).

6. Arch Puddington, "Freedom in the World 2007: Freedom Stagnation amid Pushback against Democracy," January 2007, available at http://www.freedomhouse.org/template.cfm?page=130&year=2007, last accessed on August 9, 2007.

7. *The Economist*, "The Hogwash of Quiet Diplomacy," April 4, 2007.

8. See, for example, Michael Fleet and Brian Smith, *The Catholic Church and Democracy in Chile and Peru* (Notre Dame, Ind.: University of Notre Dame Press, 1997), and Jeffrey Klaiber, *The Church, Dictatorships, and Democracy in Latin America* (Maryknoll, N.Y.: Orbis, 1998), which, as their titles suggest, pay little attention to the politics of evangelicals and pentecostals in Latin America.

9. "As products of Evangelical enterprise, mainline churches in Africa uphold basic Evangelical doctrine with varying degrees of consciousness and conformity," notes Jehu J. Hanciles, in "Conversion and Social Change: A Review of the 'Unfinished Task' in West Africa," in Donald M. Lewis, ed., *Christianity Reborn: The Global Expansion of Evangelicalism in the Twentieth Century* (Grand Rapids, Mich.: Eerdmans, 2004), 171. On the evangelical and even fundamentalist tendencies of many mainline churches in other parts of the global South, see Lionel Caplan, *Class and Culture in Urban India: Fundamentalism in a Christian Community* (Oxford: Clarendon Press, 1987), and Philip Jenkins, *The New Faces of Christianity: Believing the Bible in the Global South* (Oxford: Oxford University Press, 2006).

10. K. M. Panikkar, *Asia and Western Dominance: A Survey of the Vasco Da Gama Epoch of Asian History, 1498–1945* (London: Allen & Unwin, 1959). Paul Gifford notes the predominance of this view among scholars of Africa during the era of decolonization in his introduction to Paul Gifford, ed., *The Christian Churches and the Democratisation of Africa* (Leiden: E. J. Brill, 1995), 2.

11. David B. Barrett and Todd M. Johnson, "Annual Statistical Table on Global Mission: 2004," *International Bulletin of Missionary Research* 28(January 2004):25. However, the figures in the text for 1900, 1970, and 2005 reflect revised and updated

statistics accessed from the World Christian Database, directed by Todd M. Johnson, as quoted in The Pew Forum on Religion and Public Life, "Overview: Pentecostalism in Africa," available at http://pewforum.org/surveys/pentecostal/africa, last accessed on August 9, 2007.

12. David B. Barrett, George T. Kurian, and Todd M. Johnson, *World Christian Encyclopedia*, 2nd ed. (New York: Oxford University Press, 2001), 4, 13–15; Robert Dudley Woodberry and Timothy Samuel Shah, "The Pioneering Protestants," *Journal of Democracy* 15(2):49.

13. The Pew Forum on Religion and Public Life, "Spirit and Power: A Ten-Country Survey of Pentecostals," October 2006, p. 3; available at http://pewforum.org/publications/surveys/pentecostals-06.pdf, last accessed on August 9, 2007.

14. Quoted in The Pew Forum on Religion and Public Life, "Overview: Pentecostalism in Latin America," available at http://pewforum.org/surveys/pentecostal/latinamerica, last accessed on August 14, 2007.

15. Tocqueville ([1835] 2000).

16. Martin (1990, 2001).

17. Cecília Mariz, *Coping with Poverty: Pentecostals and Christian Base Communities in Brazil* (Philadelphia: Temple University Press, 1994).

18. Peter L. Berger, "The Desecularization of the World: A Global Overview," in Peter L. Berger, ed., *The Desecularization of the World: Resurgent Religion and World Politics* (Washington, D.C.: Ethics and Public Policy Center, 1999), p. 16.

19. In the end, David Muñoz Condell did not produce a complete, publishable chapter.

20. Quoted in the Pew Forum, "Overview: Pentecostalism in Latin America." Pentecostals constitute as much as 70 percent of Latin American Protestants, the vast majority of whom are evangelicals (Freston 2001, 194).

21. Freston (2001), 212–213, 250–251, 263–265.

22. The Pew Forum on Religion and Public Life, "Historical Overview of Pentecostalism in Brazil," available at http://pewforum.org/surveys/pentecostal/countries/?CountryID=29, last accessed on August 14, 2007.

23. For a few recent examples, see Christopher Hitchens, *God Is Not Great: How Religion Has Poisoned Everything* (New York: Twelve, 2007); Sam Harris, *Letter to a Christian Nation* (New York: Knopf, 2006); and Randall Balmer, *Thy Kingdom Come: How the Religious Right Distorts the Faith and Threatens America, an Evangelical's Lament* (New York: Basic Books, 2006).

24. Rudyard Kipling, "The English Flag," 1891.

25. Berger, *Desecularization of the World*.

Acknowledgments

This book is the result of a three-year research project into Evangelical Christianity and Democracy in the Global South, funded by the Pew Charitable Trusts from 1999 to 2002. The project was the brainchild of Vinay Samuel, general secretary of the International Fellowship of Mission Theologians (INFEMIT), a network of evangelical thinkers that covers the three continents of the Third World. INFEMIT maintains the Oxford Centre for Mission Studies (OCMS), an institution through which many Third World Christian leaders have obtained doctorates via the Open University and the University of Wales.

The project envisaged an ambitious range of case studies into evangelicals and politics in Latin America, Africa, and Asia. A team of eighteen researchers was recruited, supervised by the three regional directors (Terence Ranger for Africa, myself for Latin America, and initially Vikram Chand for Asia, later replaced by David Lumsdaine after Chand had to withdraw). Vinay Samuel was the overall project director and attended one of the Latin American team meetings. Timothy Shah provided excellent direction to the three regional teams, attending all three meetings of the Latin American team (Campinas, Brazil, in October 1999; Miami in January 2001; and Chaclacayo, Peru, in September 2001). In addition, several guest scholars and evangelical political activists were invited to contribute to discussions of the first draft of the papers at Chaclacayo, as well as David Lumsdaine as regional director for Asia. (It was also my privilege, as regional director, to attend a meeting of the Africa team in Harare and of the Asia team in Bangkok.) Finally, all the papers were presented, together with those from Africa and Asia, at a conference in Washington, D.C., in June 2002, to which many leading scholars of religion and politics around the world were invited, including Daniel Levine, whose contribution to the Washington conference is included in this volume as a conclusion. (For publication, I translated the Vázquez, Zub, and López chapters from Spanish, and the Fonseca chapter from Portuguese.)

The editor's thanks (and that of the contributors to this volume) go therefore to the Pew Charitable Trusts for their generous funding of such a broad-ranging project; to Tim Shah and Vinay Samuel for their unflagging leadership of the project team, vital contributions to team discussions, and editorial supervision of the project volumes; and to my fellow regional directors Terry Ranger, Vikram Chand, and David Lumsdaine, for the enriching times of intellectual and personal camaraderie in meetings on five continents.

Contents

Contributors

Alexandre Brasil Fonseca is a Brazilian sociologist. He teaches and researches at the Federal University of Rio de Janeiro, Brazil, in the Laboratório de Estudos da Ciência (NUTES). His Ph.D. was from the University of São Paulo. He is the author of the book *Evangélicos e mídia no Brasil* (2003).

Paul Freston is Byker Chair in Sociology at Calvin College, Michigan, and professor of sociology in the post-graduate program in social sciences at the Universidade Federal de São Carlos, Brazil. He is British and Brazilian, and he has authored several books, including *Evangelicals and Politics in Asia, Africa, and Latin America* (2001) and *Protestant Political Parties: A Global Survey* (2004).

Daniel H. Levine is James Orin Murfin Professor of Political Science at the University of Michigan. He has published widely on issues of religion, society, and politics, including *Religion and Politics in Latin America* (1980), *Religion and Political Conflict in Latin America* (1986), *Popular Voices in Latin American Catholicism* (1992), and *Constructing Culture and Power in Latin America* (1993), along with numerous articles and chapters in books.

Felipe Vázquez Palacios is a Mexican anthropologist who teaches at the Centro de Investigación y Estudios Superiores en Antropología Social (CIESAS Golfo) in Jalapa. He received his Ph.D. from the Universidad Iberoamericana. He has published *La gran comisión: "Id y predicad el evangelio": Un estudio de interacción social y difusión religiosa* (1999).

Darío López Rodríguez is Peruvian and obtained a Ph.D. from the Oxford Centre for Mission Studies/Open University in 1997. He is the author of several books, including *Los evangélicos y los derechos humanos* (1998). He teaches in various theological institutions in Latin America. He has been president of the National Evangelical Council of Peru and a member of several civil rights commissions.

C. Mathews Samson is an anthropologist and lecturer in the Department of Anthropology at the University of Oklahoma. His Ph.D. at the State University of New York was on "Re-enchanting the World: Maya Identity and Protestantism in the Western Highlands of Guatemala." He is the author of *The Martyrdom of Manuel Saquic: Constructing Maya Protestantism in the Face of War in Contemporary Guatemala* (2003).

Timothy Samuel Shah is senior research scholar at the Institute on Culture, Religion, and World Affairs at Boston University; adjunct senior fellow for religion and foreign policy at the Council on Foreign Relations; and formerly senior fellow in religion and world affairs at the Pew Forum on Religion and Public Life. He also serves as a principal researcher for the Religion in Global Politics research project at Harvard University. Shah's work on religion and politics has appeared in the *Journal of Democracy, SAIS Review of International Affairs, Political Quarterly*, and *Foreign Policy*.

Roberto Zub is a Paraguayan who resided for many years in Nicaragua. He teaches sociology at the Catholic University and UniNorte in Encarnación, Paraguay, and at the Universidad Americana in Posadas, Argentina. His Ph.D. is from the Methodist University of São Paulo, Brazil. He has published several books, including *Protestantismo y participación política en Nicaragua* (2002).

Abbreviations

Chapter 1 (Mexico)

CRIACH	Consejo de Representantes Indígenas de los Altos de Chiapas (Coordinating Committee of Indigenous Representatives of Altos de Chiapas)
EZLN	Ejército Zapatista de Liberación Nacional (Zapatista Army of National Liberation)
MIEPI	Movimiento Iglesia Evangélica Pentecostés Independiente (Movement of Independent Pentecostal Evangelical Churches)
NAFTA	North American Free Trade Association
PAN	Partido de Acción Nacional (National Action Party)
PAR	Partido de Acción Republicana (Republican Action Party)
PES	Partido Encuentro Social (Social Encounter Party)
PRD	Partido de la Revolución Democrática (Democratic Revolution Party)
PRI	Partido Revolucionario Institucional (Institutional Revolutionary Party)

Chapter 2 (Guatemala)

AE	Alizana Evangélica (Evangelical Alliance)
ANN	Alianza Nueva Nación (New Nation Alliance)
ARDE	Acción Reconciliadora Democrática (Democratic Reconciling Action)
CEBs	Comunidades Eclesiales de Base (Ecclesial Base Communities)

CEG   Conferencia Episcopal de Guatemala (Episcopal Conference of Guatemala)

CEH   Comisión para el Esclaramiento Histórico (Commission for Historical Clarification)

CIEDEG   Conferencia de Iglesias Evangélicas de Guatemala (Conference of Evangelical Churches of Guatemala)

CLAI   Consejo Latinoamericano de Iglesias (Latin American Council of Churches)

COCIPE   Comisión Cívico Permanente (Permanent Civic Commission)

FDNG   Frente Democrático Nueva Guatemala (New Guatemala Democratic Front)

FRG   Frente Republicano Guatemalteco (Guatemalan Republican Front)

IENPG   Iglesia Evangélica Nacional Presbiteriana de Guatemala (National Evangelical Presbyterian Church of Guatemala)

MAS   Movimiento de Acción Solidaria (Movement of Solidary Action)

MINUGUA   United Nations Verification Mission in Guatemala

MPV   Movimiento de Principios y Valores (Movement of Principles and Values)

NGOs   Nongovernmental organizations

PAN   Partido Avanzado Nacional (National Advancement Party)

UNE   Unión Nacional de la Esperanza (National Union of Hope)

UNICEF   United Nations Children's Fund

Chapter 3 (Nicaragua)

CCN   Camino Cristiano Nicaragüense (Nicaraguan Christian Way)

CEPAD   Consejo Evangélico Pro Ayuda a los Damnificados (Evangelical Committee For Helping the Victims)

CEPRES   Comisión Evangélica para la Promoción de la Responsabilidad Social (Evangelical Commission for Social Responsibility)

CIEETS   Centro Intereclesial de Estudios Teológicos y Sociales (Inter-Ecclesial Center of Theological and Social Studies)

CLADE   Congreso Latinoamericano de Evangelización (Latin-American Congress on Evangelization)

FSLN   Frente Sandinista de Liberación Nacional (Sandinista Front for National Liberation)

MEP   Movimiento Evangélico Popular

MRS   Movimiento Renovador Sandinista (Sandinista Renewal Movement)

MUC   Movimiento de Unidad Cristiana (Christian Unity Movement)

PC   Partido Conservador (Conservative Party)

PDN   Partido por la Dignidad Nacional (Party for
       National Dignity)
PJN   Partido de Justicia Nacional (National Justice Party)
PL   Partido Liberal (Liberal Party)
PLC   Partido Liberal Constitucionalista (Liberal
       Constitutionalist Party)
PROVADENIC   Project of Vaccination and Communal Development
UNICA   Universidad Católica (Catholic University)
UNO   Unión Nacional Opositora (National Opposition Union)

Chapter 4 (Peru)

AGEUP   Asociación de Grupos Evangélicos Universitarios del Perú
       (Association of Evangelical Student Groups of Peru)
AMAR   Asociación Movimiento de Acción Renovadora (Association
       Movement for Renewing Action)
APRA   Alianza Popular Revolucionaria Americana (American
       Revolutionary Popular Alliance)
CEPS   Centro Cristiano de Promoción y Servicios (Christian
       Center for Promotion and Services)
CONEP   Concilio Nacional Evangélico del Perú (National Evangelical
       Council of Peru)
FIPAC   Fraternidad Internacional de Pastores Cristianos
       (International Fraternity of Christian Pastors)
IEP   Iglesia Evangélica Peruana (Peruvian Evangelical Church)
MED   Evangelicals for Democracy Movement
MRN   Movimiento de Restauración Nacional (Movement for
       National Restoration)
OAS   Organization of American States
SODE   Solidaridad y Democracia (Solidarity and Democracy)
UREP   Unión Renovadora del Perú (Renewal Union of Peru)

Chapter 5 (Brazil)

CEB   Comunidad Eclesial de Base (Ecclesial Base Community)
MEP   Movimiento Evangélico Progressista (Evangelical Progressive
       Movement)
PCdoB   Partido Comunista do Brasil (Communist Party of Brazil)
PDT   Partido Democrático Trabalhista (Democratic Labor Party)
PFL   Partido da Frente Liberal (Party of the Liberal Front)
PL   Partido Liberal (Liberal Party)
PMDB   Partido do Movimento Democrático Brasileiro (Party of the
       Brazilian Democratic Movement)

PPB   Partido Progressista Brasileiro (Brazilian Progressive Party)
PPS   Partido Popular Socialista (Popular Socialist Party)
PSB   Partido Socialista Brasileiro (Brazilian Socialist Party)
PSDB   Partido da Social Democracia Brasileira (Party of Brazilian Social Democracy)
PSL   Partido Social Liberal (Social Liberal Party)
PST   Partido Social Trabalhista (Social Labor Party)
PT   Partido dos Trabalhadores (Workers Party)
PTB   Partido Trabalhista Brasileiro (Brazilian Labor Party)
PV   Partido Verde (Green Party)
UCKG   Universal Church of the Kingdom of God (Igreja Universal do Reino de Deus)

Evangelical Christianity and Democracy in Latin America

Introduction: The Many Faces of Evangelical Politics in Latin America

Paul Freston

The Research Project on Evangelical Christianity and Democracy in the Global South that gave birth to this book and its companion volumes on Africa (edited by Terence O. Ranger) and Asia (edited by David H. Lumsdaine) rested on two assumptions and one main question. The two assumptions were, first, that evangelical Christianity has grown rapidly in many parts of the global South and has become a mass phenomenon, and second, that democracy has also expanded in parts of the global South in recent decades, although the high hopes of the early 1990s have now given way either to the hard slog of democratic consolidation or to rear-guard stands to salvage whatever is possible from the jaws of antidemocratic reaction. The question was: what is the connection between evangelical Christianity and democracy in Latin America, Africa, and Asia?

In the case of Latin America, at least, the question is clearly important, but the answer is not immediately clear. Evangelical Protestantism grew so much in the region in the second half of the twentieth century that some scholars have asked (in David Stoll's words [1990]) "Is Latin America turning Protestant?" In the same time period, Latin America went through a wave of military dictatorships followed by a wave of democratization, but even now its democratic regimes are not beyond the reach of antidemocratic reaction, and the depth of its democracy is challenged by economic inequality and stagnation. In this context, evangelicals have become significant new political actors in many countries. Sometimes portrayed as a new religious right and even as given to undemocratic dreams of theocracy, and at other times as a force for democracy, economic development, and a strong civil society, in fact Latin American evangelicals have been extraordinarily diverse in their first two decades of public prominence since the early 1980s. There has been, for example, a democratically elected evangelical president (Jorge Serrano, of Guatemala) as well as a military evangelical president installed by a coup d'état (Efrain Ríos Montt, also of Guatemala). The latter is even accused of genocide against sympathizers of left-wing guerrillas; but elsewhere in the region there have been evangelical ministers in a left-wing government. In various countries, new political parties have been founded on specifically "evangelical" grounds; but other evangelicals have rejected such parties and insisted on participating in existing secular parties. While in some places large denominations have presented official congressional candidates explicitly to defend their institutional interests, such concerns have been repudiated elsewhere in favor of political projects that contemplate the whole population.

But whether democratic or authoritarian, right-wing or left-wing, embracing existing parties or rejecting them, defending narrow corporatist projects or broader universalist ones, the political importance of this expanding religious movement increases daily. The studies in this book, all based on new empirical research, examine the interplay between contemporary religion and democracy at one of its key points: the relationship between the fast-growing grassroots Protestantism of the global South and the fragile democracies of one of its key regions, Latin America.

Protestantism and Democracy in Historical Perspective

Of all the major religions, Protestant Christianity has the longest historical links with processes of democratization. John Witte (1993) speaks of three waves of Christian democratizing impulses that accompanied, or even anticipated, Samuel Huntington's "three waves" of democratization (Huntington 1991). The first of Witte's waves was Protestant, in the northern Europe and North America of the seventeenth and eighteenth centuries. Of course, this first wave was largely an unintended result of the fracturing of the religious field and the experience of wars of religion, rather than the intended result of most Protestant leaders' convictions regarding democracy. Even so, "most of democracy's original exponents were deeply rooted in verities derived from Christian faith and ethics" (de Gruchy 1995, 49). In addition, "principled pluralism" was one of the early Protestant postures toward the state. This position, which first achieved political importance in the 1640s with the Levellers in England and the Baptist Roger Williams in Rhode Island, supplied the theological basis that allowed Protestant sectarian theology (intended for exclusive voluntary communities) to overflow into democratic politics by rejecting any division of the political world between the godly and the ungodly. The situation of Old Testament Israel was seen as entirely exceptional; today, the state should be nonconfessional.

Thus, whether through theological principle or the wisdom of experience, Protestantism became the first major religious current to give a positive answer to the fundamental question of its "compatibility" with political democracy. In consequence, today's Protestants, wherever they may be, are not usually required to allay fears regarding their religion's ultimate ability to coexist with democracy (as Muslims often are required to do). This is not just a question of having links with the developed West (which do not, in fact, always exist); it is a matter of theological resources and historical examples.

But that, of course, far from settles things. In reality there have always been *Protestantisms* in the plural. Not only was early Protestantism far from immediately or uniformly favorable to democracy, but some nondemocratic regimes in modern times have enjoyed Protestant support or at least acquiescence. This plurality of postures was likely to be reinforced, even amplified, if Protestantism managed to achieve a significant presence beyond its historic homeland in northern Europe and in areas of northern European immigration. By the late twentieth century, this had in fact happened. Protestantism is now a global religion (much more so than any other, with the possible exception of Catholicism); and it has become involved in politics in very diverse settings.

"Evangelicals"

The project's focus was on *evangelical* Protestantism, and in fact the vast majority of Protestants in Latin America come under this rubric. In comparison with the Protestantism of the developed West, the Third World version tends to be considerably more evangelical (and, indeed, largely pentecostal). As a working definition, "evangelicalism" was taken to refer to a subset of Protestant Christianity that is distinguished by both doctrinal and practical characteristics but not by denominational affiliation or even necessarily by self-labeling. Many studies in the past decade or so have borrowed a useful, ready-made, working definition from David Bebbington (1989). This consists of four constant characteristics: conversionism (emphasis on the need for change of life), activism (emphasis on evangelistic and missionary efforts), biblicism (a special importance attributed to the Bible, though not necessarily the fundamentalist concept of "inerrancy"), and crucicentrism (emphasis on the centrality of Christ's sacrifice on the cross). Evangelicals are not, therefore, a particular denomination, but are found in many different denominations. In Latin American Protestantism (especially its huge pentecostal wing), many home-grown denominations have sprung up with little or no contact with mainstream Western evangelicalism but nevertheless basically meeting the substantive criteria. And of course, in Latin America the definitional discussion has to take into account the fact that these Christians are not using the English language but Spanish or Portuguese or even one of the numerous indigenous languages of the region. In fact, the preferred self-definition of Latin American Protestants is as *evangélicos,* and the vast majority of those would fit Bebbington's characteristics.

They do not, however, fit very well into the category of "fundamentalism" as used in recent years by many authors who study religious actors in global (and especially Third World) politics. Evangelicalism and fundamentalism have a complex relationship. While there is overlap (some evangelicals can be considered fundamentalists), evangelicalism is an older and broader tendency within Protestantism, while the "fundamentalist" label has been extended in another direction to include phenomena from other religions.

Fundamentalism and evangelicalism relate differently to globalization, the former being more a reactive phenomenon of globalization, whereas the latter predates and possibly contributes to it. The Fundamentalism Project carried out in the 1990s through the University of Chicago illustrates this. The introduction to *Fundamentalisms and the State* defines *fundamentalism* as embracing "movements of religiously inspired reaction to aspects of global processes of modernization and secularization . . . the struggle to assert or reassert the norms and beliefs of 'traditional religion' in the public order" (Marty and Appleby 1993). But evangelicalism is far from traditional in most of the Third World. Little but Guatemalan neopentecostalism is contemplated in the fundamentalism project series, and even there the final volume admits how weakly it fits the project's schema. As generally a nontraditional religion (in local terms) spreading by conversion, evangelical Protestantism's interests are usually the opposite of those of a reactive fundamentalism. For evangelicalism, pluralism and cultural diffuseness would seem to be advantageous, whereas non-Christian fundamentalisms constitute one of its most serious barriers. The literature on worldwide fundamentalism is thus not a very safe guide for understanding evangelical politics in the Third World.

"Democracy"

Apart from the growth of evangelical Christianity, democracy has also expanded in Latin America in recent decades. In fact, the region has been one of the main sites of the "third wave" of democratization. But discussions regarding democratization have become more nuanced over the years, not only with respect to different degrees of democracy, and to the differences between "transition" and "consolidation" but also with regard to various "halfway houses" that were either implemented by canny autocrats or were defended as virtuous alternatives to "Western-style" democracy. The result is a terminological jungle, which does not concern us as such here, except insofar as it sheds light on the part of the world we are considering and on the role of religion in it.

Most of the qualified forms of "democracy" and of the hyphenated half-way houses between democracy and authoritarianism are located in the global South. The overall picture is that of a "third wave" that has not only lost its impetus but has even faced significant erosion in many countries. Continued advance, whether in the sense of new transitions to democracy or of the deepening and consolidation of democracy in countries where it already exists, is now rare.

Beyond a simple affirmation that democracy refers to more than the mere existence of a multiparty electoral system, there is little consensus among authors regarding definitions and typologies. Even Huntington's (1991) minimalist definition of democracy as a system in which "the most powerful collective decisionmakers are selected through fair, honest, and periodic elections in which candidates freely compete for votes" raises a host of criteria that various current multiparty systems worldwide clearly fail to meet. But such a narrowly procedural definition, while important, is often regarded as insufficient. Here we are referring not just to the demanding definitions of democracy that include socioeconomic participatory and egalitarian dimensions, or to Touraine's words quoted by Fonseca in the epigraph to chapter 5 ("we are no longer content with a democracy of deliberation; we need a democracy of liberation"), or even to Haynes's (1997) "substantive democracy," which involves lessening the unequal distribution of power, empowerment of subordinate classes through the vote, and increased citizens' participation. Even Diamond's (1997) distinction between electoral democracy and liberal democracy points in the same direction. The former is a minimal framework (regular, fair, and free elections), while the latter includes a deeper institutional structure of freedoms, civilian control over the military, accountability of office-holders, and the rule of law through an independent judiciary. Full liberal democracy presupposes high participation, authentic political choice, and extensive citizen rights; unlike the "virtual democracies" common to much of the Third World in which economic policies have been effectively insulated from popular involvement. While 61 percent of governments in the world met the definition of electoral democracy in 1996, only 41 percent met the definition of liberal democracy; in fact, the latter was losing ground outside the developed world. The same would be true if Dahl's (1971) classic concept of "polyarchy" were applied: not only free and fair competitive elections but also freedom of organization and expression, and access to alternative sources of information.

By 2002, Diamond was using a nuanced typology, in recognition of the passing (by the mid-1990s) of the crest of the third wave of democratization and the multiple hybrid forms being developed around the world to accommodate on the one hand the overwhelming ideological hegemony enjoyed by democracy and on the other the desire of regimes to retain authoritarian elements under the mask of democratic forms, producing regimes that authors variously label as "electoral authoritarian," "pseudodemocratic," "façade democracies," or "paternalistic Asian authoritarianism" (this last being Fukuyama's name for the economically successful Singaporean and Malaysian model, which he sees as liberal democracy's most serious competitor). In response to this, Diamond (2002) comes up with a sixfold typology to classify all the world's regimes. Seventy-three countries qualify as "liberal democracies," and another thirty-one as merely "electoral democracies"; seventeen are "ambiguous regimes"; twenty-one are "competitive authoritarian"; twenty-five are "hegemonic electoral authoritarian"; and another twenty-five are "politically closed authoritarian."

One thing that this sort of typology highlights is the importance of democratic consolidation, defined by Diamond and Plattner (1996a, xxviii) as the process by which democracy acquires deep and widespread legitimacy among all major elite groups and the citizenry at large, and becomes "the only game in town" (all other possible means of acquiring and maintaining power considered beyond the pale). Consolidation viewed as the evolution of a democratic culture may take generations, but other definitions would view a democracy as consolidated once power has changed hands, peacefully and through electoral means, from one party or bloc of parties to another. While the inauguration of democracy through a successful transition from authoritarianism is very important, consolidation is also vital if reversals in an authoritarian direction are to be avoided and progress is to be made beyond a merely electoral democracy. Consolidation is thus a distinct phase that may require distinct virtues from actors at the level of political society and civil society. These virtues may not be distributed equally among religious groups; in fact, characteristics of a particular church (e.g., a hierarchical and multiclass structure, and international links) that may be advantageous for facing down a dictatorial regime may be irrelevant or even disadvantageous for the long haul of democratic consolidation. Evaluations of the contributions of particular religious groups to democracy need to take these diverse moments into account.

Apart from diverse moments, diverse levels of contribution to political life can also lead to ambiguous findings. The third wave of global democratization and the end of the Cold War have caused renewed interest in "civil society," the realm of autonomous voluntary organizations that act in the public sphere as intermediaries between the state and private life (Diamond and Plattner 1996a, xxii). However, by the mid-1990s, with the "third wave" receding, civil society was being looked at in a more nuanced fashion. A strong civil society, it was now better realized, does not necessarily mean better chances for democracy. Civil society can also be uncivil; institutions may not promote pluralism and tolerance if they do not actually seek to do so. In fact, the same institution can play a mediating or a polarizing role in conflicts, the crucial variable being not its structure (e.g., whether it is a church) but the values inspiring it. "Actually existing" civil society, therefore, does not only contain elements favorable to democracy; it may contain some elements that are politically indifferent, and still others favorable to authoritarianism. Institutions in civil society can polarize conflicts and contribute to political instability. In addition, the civil society created by "religion from below" may lack connections to formal policy levels and thus fail to engage the state in consequential fashion.

If a thriving civil society is not necessarily positive for democracy, it is also important to differentiate between diverse types of associations, including religious ones. For some authors, voluntary associations promote pluralism and democracy, regardless of whether they are concerned explicitly with public affairs; for others, nonpolitical associations do not perform those tasks. The internal order of the association is also a bone of contention: does it matter whether associations are hierarchical or egalitarian?

Another blurred area in discussions of civil society is the definition of the ways in which it may contribute to democracy. Diamond (1996) enumerates nine possibilities: by limiting the power of the state; by stimulating political participation; by developing a democratic culture of tolerance and bargaining; by creating channels for the representation of interests; by generating crosscutting cleavages (to those of class, ethnicity, etc.); by training new political leaders; by helping democratic institutions to function better (through electoral monitoring, etc.); by widening the flow of information to citizens; and by supporting coalitions for economic reform.

By Third World standards, civil society is relatively strong in Latin America, says Haynes (1997); compared to Africa and Asia, Latin America's decolonization occurred much earlier, its ethnic and religious schisms are less profound, and its average indices of industrialization and urbanization are higher. However, institutionalized interest groups, such as the Catholic Church, have been very influential in Latin American civil society.

A key concept in discussions of civil society has been that of "social capital," defined by Coleman (1988) as "features of social organization, such as trust, norms, and networks, that can improve the efficiency of society by facilitating coordinated action." But the exact mechanisms by which religions create social capital are disputed. Putnam's (2000) distinction between "bonding capital" and "bridging capital" seems relevant, especially to many evangelical churches whose intense community involvement may create much of the former but neglect the latter. Data from Canada and the United States suggest that evangelical Christians are relatively untrusting socially yet active in civic volunteering (Smidt 1999). Third World data on such matters tend to be less solid, but there is considerable evidence of a "spillover" effect, with skills learned from religious activism being transferred to social and political militancy. In addition, "minorities" tend to be well represented in Third World evangelicalism, and this can open up new channels to political participation. Examples from Latin America include a black presidential candidate in Costa Rica, an evangelical Amerindian political party in Ecuador (Freston 2004), and black pentecostal members of congress in Brazil. And surprisingly, a recent poll in Rio de Janeiro showed that pentecostal women (despite being poorer than average) were more interested in voting in elections than women of any other religion or those "without religion" (Machado and Figueiredo 2002, 128–29).

In examining the relationship between evangelicals and democracy, therefore, it is necessary to keep in mind these diverse moments (transition, sustainability, and deepening) and diverse levels (direct political involvement through elections, parties, and governments, as well as indirect involvement through organs of civil society and the creation of social capital). In addition, one should look not only at intended but also unintended consequences of evangelical actions, since even an internally undemocratic church that enters politics with a theocratic project may, through the interplay of forces, end up strengthening democracy in spite of itself.

Latin America

Latin America falls in the medium range of Third World per capita income levels. It is "underdeveloped," but it is also, broadly speaking, "Western" and "Christian." It is the poor part of the Western world, an ambiguous position that is often cited as a reason for the emergence there of liberation theology. There is little chance (except in a few areas) of taking refuge in a premodern non-Western culture, an anti-Western reaction, or a return to precolonial roots. For most of the region, history is irredeemably linked to Western expansion, experienced largely as frustration.

The economic crisis, while less severe than in most of Africa, is marked by startling inequalities. The informal economy is often huge. A highly concentrated landholding structure in most countries is often given as a reason for inability to follow the Asian tigers; another is minimal public spending on education and health. Since the early 1980s, foreign debt has been a millstone around the region's neck. The eighties became known as the "Lost Decade" in which development hopes were shattered; and the trend to neoliberal policies in the 1990s accentuated social divisions and (with a few exceptions, such as Chile) produced hesitant macroeconomic results.

Nevertheless, civil society is fairly strong, and some countries have had considerable experience of multiparty democracy. The military regimes of the 1960s and 1970s, which were especially repressive in the Southern Cone, ceded to a wave of redemocratization from the mid-1980s, and there is currently formal democracy almost everywhere. However, one cannot take such trends for granted in Latin America; in the early 1960s, democratization seemed so invincible that a 1961 book was entitled *The Twilight of the Dictators*! Democracy is far from consolidated in many countries. Nevertheless, on Diamond's (2002, 30) classification of regimes based on the situation in 2001, the Spanish- and Portuguese-speaking countries of Latin America fell mostly within his two categories of democracies, being almost equally divided between full "liberal democracies" (Uruguay, Costa Rica, Panama, Bolivia, Peru, Chile, Dominican Republic) and merely "electoral democracies" (Argentina, El Salvador, Mexico, Brazil, Ecuador, Honduras, Nicaragua, Guatemala). Venezuela, Paraguay, and Colombia come in the next category of "ambiguous regimes," while Cuba is alone in the most undemocratic category of "politically closed authoritarian." This makes Latin America (together with the Pacific Islands) the most generally democratic region outside the developed West (ahead of the postcommunist world, Asia, Africa, and the Middle East–North Africa). But with regard to the five countries contemplated in this book, the classification (which is based largely on the Freedom House indicators) may raise some eyebrows. Peru alone ranks as a "liberal democracy" (in 2001 it had just emerged from Fujimori's authoritarian years). Mexico, Brazil, Nicaragua, and Guatemala are all classed as "electoral democracies." Putting Brazil and Guatemala, for example, in the same category would seem to obscure considerable differences in the degree of real political space, democratic deepening, and consolidation in those countries (highlighted by the presidential victory of the opposition left-wing Workers Party under Luís Inácio Lula da Silva in 2002 and the smooth transition that ensued).

Evangelicals in the Third World

According to the *Encyclopedia Britannica*, Christianity currently has the (at least nominal) adherence of about one-third of the world's population, of which Catholicism accounts for 19 percent and Protestantism about 11 percent. While Westerners tend to think Christianity is in decline, many in the global South perceive that it is growing. Globally, the percentage of Christians did not change much in the twentieth century, but their composition was greatly transformed. Christianity is now almost truly global. While Europeans and North Americans constituted 81 percent of Christians in 1900, they accounted for only 40 percent of Christians by the year 2000 (Barrett and Johnson 1999). On the one hand, this is due to lower birth rates, by which the Western percentage of world population fell dramatically from 30 percent to 13 percent, and to the decline of Christianity in the West. On the other hand, it reflects impressive Christian expansion outside the developed West, and the high birth rates of those regions. The result is that Christianity should no longer be thought of as par excellence the religion of the developed West.

This applies to Catholicism and perhaps even more to Protestantism, which has spread mostly "from below," through indigenous initiatives and in multiple institutional forms. Protestantism's lack of a Rome (organizational center) or even a Mecca (center of sentiment and pilgrimage) accentuates its institutional and cultural diversity. In absolute terms, the numerical heartland of Protestantism is now in the Third World (in countries such as Brazil, Nigeria, South Africa, China, and South Korea); and as a percentage of the population, some of the most Protestant countries in the world are now in the Pacific region.

The importance of global South Protestantism is accentuated by the fact that it is highly practicing (in both churchgoing and proselytism) and often fast-growing. In comparison with the Protestantism of the developed West, the younger Third World version tends to be considerably more pentecostal. Pentecostalism arose in the early twentieth century as a movement within Protestantism that stressed the contemporary nature of phenomena from the New Testament such as "speaking in tongues" (whether understood as an untaught ability to speak a foreign language or, more usually, as the ability to praise God in spontaneous and incomprehensible speech patterns), prophecy, divine healing, and expulsion of demons. This enthusiastic and highly supernaturalistic version of Protestantism has been adopted only by a minority of Protestants in the developed West, but in the Third World it has often become the predominant form. Four percent of the world's population may now be Protestant pentecostals (Martin 2002). Third World Protestantism is thus largely evangelical-pentecostal. It is also overwhelmingly an indigenous movement rather than one funded and run from the West. It is usually strongly practicing, rapidly expanding, bewilderingly fissiparous, decidedly nontraditional, and often overrepresented among the poor of what are already poor countries. As Jenkins (2002) points out, Christianity is once again deeply associated with poverty and migration, as well as impregnated with phenomena such as exorcism and healing, and in some places marked by experience of persecution and martyrdom. It is also mostly conservative in belief and morals; however, although Jenkins is probably right that it will be conservative on issues such as homosexuality and abortion, it may not always be so on women's rights.

The growth of Protestantism in the world's "South" has often led to political involvement. Protestantism may be as important for politics now in Fiji, South Korea, Zambia, Guatemala, and Brazil as it is in Holland or the United States. The fact that the politics of Third World Protestantism has taken many forms can partly be attributed to the social and organizational characteristics just mentioned. The institutional division into myriad denominations is functional for growth but not for concerted political action or for elaborating a normative "social doctrine." Protestantism's nontraditional status as a religion growing by conversion means it rarely enjoys any official or unofficial state patronage. Usually, it does not have strong institutions; often composed disproportionately of the poor in poor countries, its cultural and educational resources are limited. It operates a model of competitive pluralism, in competition for members and resources, which does not encourage reflection or costly stances on ethical principle. It often has no international contacts, cutting it off from the history of Christian reflection on politics. It may be an *arriviste* minority inexperienced in the public sphere and still lacking full political legitimacy, but it is nevertheless confident (even excessively so) about its future.

Evangelicals in Latin America

With exceptions such as secularized Uruguay, Latin America remains a profoundly religious continent. However, this religiosity is in flux. If Latin America was once regarded as a region that mirrored the religious structure of Latin Europe (traditional Catholic dominance and weak Protestant presence), it has now moved somewhat in the direction of the religious voluntarism typical of the United States. The Catholic monopoly of colonial and early postindependence times, and even the secure hegemony of the first half of the twentieth century, are under threat in most countries. The traditional Catholic claim of being an essential part of Latin American identity has lost plausibility as pluralism has increased and Protestantism become deep-rooted. Modernization and urbanization have not been favorable to Catholicism, whose institutional structure remains too tied to a rural Christendom mentality. The chronic shortage of priests in most countries highlights the gap between "official" churchly Catholicism and "popular" or "folk" Catholicism, often syncretic, which dominates the masses and has only a marginal relationship with ecclesiastical structures. Liberation theology and the Base Communities, important from the 1960s to 1980s but now on the wane, were in part attempts to revitalize the Church at the grassroots in the face of new challenges. The "Catholic charismatic renewal," now often larger than the Base Communities, is another example of this. Afro-Brazilian religions (far from limited to blacks and now exported) also compete for followers, while the main new religious phenomenon among the middle class is, as in Western Europe, esoterical and extrainstitutional.

Latin American Protestant identity was forged strongly in opposition to the dominant Catholicism. It had to fight its way up politically in a Catholic context, so the political operationalizing of specifically Protestant (rather than generically Christian) identity is generally more pronounced than in the rest of the world. However, to talk of a "Reformation," analogous with sixteenth-century Europe, is misleading. In contrast with northern Europe, Protestantism's penetration of Latin America owed nothing to national reformations under the aegis of the state; and in contrast with parts of Africa and Asia, it owed nothing to the support of colonial governments. Rather, the Protestant presence (initiated in the postcolonial period) had to be built painstakingly, at first by stretching the legal limitations on religious freedom. For a century or more, the Protestant presence in Latin America seemed doomed to remain almost as insignificant as it still is in Latin Europe. But from the 1950s in some countries, and from the 1970s and 1980s in other parts of the region, it achieved considerable numerical growth.

In colonial times, Protestantism (with temporary exceptions) was excluded from Spanish and Portuguese America. A permanent presence was only established around the time of independence in the early nineteenth century. The first tolerated Protestant communities were composed of foreigners linked to the commercial interests of Protestant countries. More important than these tiny trading communities were the Protestant immigrants who arrived in several countries from the 1820s. Immigration as a means of peopling territories, and Protestant immigration as a means of bringing progress and weakening Catholic political power, were defended by liberal anticlerical elites. Brazil, the Southern Cone, and Costa Rica received such immigrants. But churches for Latin Americans and using Spanish or Portuguese only appeared from the 1850s onward, as a late fruit of the worldwide Protestant missionary effort. The delay was partly due to the legally dubious status of such churches and to the feeling among some Protestant sectors that Latin America had already been Christianized. Most missions were not European but American, and were linked to the pietistic revivalism of "frontier" religion in the United States.

Thus, Protestantism entered Latin America as an effectively sectarian variant of the dominant religion, but in tandem with the political and economic liberalism brought by the Anglo-Saxon powers that spearheaded capitalist expansion. It thus effectively entered the region on the Anabaptist principle of separation of church and state and even of total rejection of politics as "worldly," and this inhibited the full flowering of the variety of political traditions that the denominations brought with them. Nevertheless, Protestant missions have often been regarded as carriers of a liberal critique of traditional Latin society, associated with Anglo-American economic interests and a civilizing pathos. But some missionaries defended the rights of Latin American countries, as in the Mexican Revolution (Freston 2001); and the belief that Protestantism meant education and progress was common to many liberals among the Latin American elites.

Historical Protestantism (as the first mission denominations such as the Presbyterians, Methodists, and Baptists are known) remained distant from the masses and achieved modest success only in Brazil. Protestantism only became truly "popular" (numerically successful among the lower classes) with the advent of pentecostalism from 1910. Latin American pentecostalism today is organized in a huge number of denominations, a few of which originated abroad while the majority are homegrown. A different phenomenon is that of middle-class pentecostalized groups (known in some countries as "neo-pentecostals" and in others as "charismatics"). Again, some are of foreign origin and others of local provenance. These have expanded in recent decades and been especially successful among the Guatemalan elite. In the last decades of the twentieth century, Protestantism (especially in pentecostal forms) made considerable headway among Amerindian peoples in southern Mexico, Central America, and the Andes.

By 2000, Protestantism was the religion of perhaps 12 percent of Latin Americans. In the largest country, Brazil, the 2000 census showed 15.5 percent Protestant; growth in the 1990s had been especially quick. But the highest percentage is probably in Guatemala (20 percent plus), although growth seems to have stagnated in the 1990s after being very rapid in the previous twenty years. The 2002 census in Chile showed 15.1 percent Protestant, up from 12.4 percent in 1992. At the other end of the scale, Uruguay is still below 5 percent. The middle range embraces the Andean countries such as Peru at the top end and Argentina, Mexico, and Colombia at the lower end. David Martin (1990) gives as a rule of thumb that Protestantism's chances of growth have been higher where the Catholic Church was politically weakened by liberalism in the nineteenth century but the culture remained unsecularized. Where secularization took hold, or where the Catholic Church retained great political power, growth has been slower.

With variations, one can say that Latin American Protestantism is characterized by being highly practicing and fast-growing, predominantly lower class, and organized in a plethora of nationally run and even nationally created denominations. Perhaps two-thirds of Latin America's fifty million or so Protestants are pentecostals (Brazilian Protestantism, a good bellwether for the region, was 68 percent pentecostal in the 2000 census), and this percentage is increasing. Protestantism is most pentecostalized in Chile (perhaps 80 percent) and least in the Andean countries (fewer than half).

Protestantism (and especially pentecostalism) is associated disproportionately with the poor, less educated, and darker skinned. This is true also of the founders of the major pentecostal denominations, most of whom were proletarians, independent artisans, or lower middle-class white collar workers. However, there is growing social diversification (greater presence among, for example, entrepreneurs, athletes, artists, and police officers). Membership is predominantly female, although leadership positions are largely male; but some pentecostal denominations were founded by women and accept female pastors. Some recent anthropological studies have spoken of pentecostalism's reconciliation of gender values as serving the interests of poor women, resocializing men away from machismo. Another recent focus of study has been the economic effects of conversion. Latin American pentecostalism does not have the classic Protestant work ethic, and operates in a different economic context. Evidence for mobility is scarce, and for a macro effect on economies even scarcer. But at the individual level, the transformative effect on the disorganized lives of many poor (and not so poor) people is evident.

In most of the region, therefore, there is fairly rapid numerical growth of evangelicalism in general and of pentecostal variants in particular, and it is this "dynamic profile as a private religion of salvation" (Casanova 1994, 224) that allows pentecostalism to assume more and more public roles, despite the lack of incentive from either its doctrine or its historical tradition. The pentecostal entry into politics in the last two decades has provided political mobility for some individuals who would normally stand very little chance of occupying such positions.

The regionwide picture we have painted should not, however, obscure the considerable diversity throughout the region. There is great variation in the degree to which evangelicals have achieved (or not) a secure niche in the national identity of each country (much more, for example, in Brazil than in Mexico). In some countries evangelical political legitimacy is much more precarious than elsewhere, and the invisible "ceiling" on evangelical pretensions in public life varies (being higher in some countries than in others, and having possibly disappeared altogether in a few). In a few places, freedom of religion itself is still not totally secure, while in others there is still a battle going on for legal equality; yet in other countries, these questions are long past and have been replaced by aspirations to equality in civil religion. In some countries, evangelical access to the media is very limited for legal or social reasons, whereas in others evangelicals have achieved a huge media presence. Different electoral systems combined with social prejudice have affected the chances of evangelical presence in parliaments: In the legislature elected in 2002, Brazil had over sixty evangelical members of congress, whereas Chile, with a similar percentage of evangelicals in the population, has none.

In some countries there is still effective discrimination at certain social levels against Protestants as individuals, as well as legal discrimination against their churches. Although official separation of church and state, effectuated in some countries in the nineteenth century and in others only in the 1990s, is now almost universal in the region (only Bolivia, Argentina, and Costa Rica still have an official religion), there are several countries where Protestant churches do not enjoy the same legal rights as the Catholic Church. Even where tolerance and complete freedom of worship are secure, there is often some way to go before the practice of full equality of all religions takes hold in public life and civil society. "Religious freedom" in this fuller sense (as not just freedom of action in the religious sphere but also equality of treatment in the public sphere) has been used as a rallying cry by some Protestants in politics in recent years.

Nevertheless, in many Latin American countries, Protestantism is now deeply embedded socially and is broadly legitimate politically. Sometimes, remaining limitations are due more to its disadvantaged social composition than to any religious prejudice. In the early twenty-first century, the multiple and highly fragmented Protestantisms of Latin America seem destined, in the foreseeable future, for continuing numerical growth and deeper penetration of their national societies. But it is debatable whether Latin America will eventually "become Protestant" in any significant sense. In Brazil and Chile, for which reliable data are available, only half of all those who cease regarding themselves as Catholics become Protestants. This suggests the region is becoming religiously pluralist rather than Protestant, and it seems unlikely that Protestants will become the majority in any Latin American country.

Political involvement by Protestants is not recent (they were disproportionately active in the Mexican Revolution, and the first Protestant member of congress in Brazil was elected in 1933), but since the 1980s this trend has increased, especially with the involvement of many previously apolitical pentecostal denominations. Two Protestant presidents have governed Guatemala, and there have been large Protestant congressional caucuses in several countries, notably Brazil. Over twenty political parties of Protestant inspiration have been founded in the Spanish-speaking republics, though none has achieved great success. Much Protestant political activity has been conservative and/or oriented to institutional aggrandizement, leading to a worsening of the public image of Protestants as a whole in some countries.

The context of the rise of Protestant politics has been redemocratization in a context of economic crisis and the discrediting of the established parties (which in some countries has been dramatic). Accentuated social disintegration in some countries has favored the idea of evangelical Christians as the only hope, an opinion that is not always limited to evangelicals themselves. Protestant electoral involvement is also related to the formal and effective extension of the suffrage, especially in view of the social composition of the *evangélicos*. Some countries in recent decades have seen the suffrage extended to illiterates, and migration to the cities has made its exercise less dependent on rural bosses.

Latin American Protestant politics is therefore a phenomenon *of* democratization, not just in the sense of regular ballots but also freer electorates and fairer elections. Whether it is also a phenomenon *for* democratization is the main query behind the case studies in this book; but it has certainly played a role in incorporating grassroots sectors into the democratic process and providing a significant route for individuals of lower social origin or marginalized communities to achieve political visibility.

Protestant politics is also related to transformations within the Protestant community. This is not just a question of sheer numerical growth but of what has accompanied it: growing self-confidence, overcoming the minority complex that has always dogged Protestantism in Latin America, and an increasing range of institutions (in social work and the media) that can undergird political action.

In a context lacking strong parties based on class identities, Protestants traditionally did not vote for Christian Democratic parties identified with Catholicism, but for an anticlerical party, providing the latter was not also antireligious in general. In recent decades, with the numerical growth of Protestantism, its penetration of new social levels and improved legal and social position (not to mention changes in Catholicism since Vatican II), the need to subordinate all other political objectives to support for anticlerical parties has diminished, with a consequent fragmenting of voting patterns, including (in several countries) attempts to form specifically Protestant parties.

The political implications of Protestantism (especially pentecostalism) in Latin America have been appraised in starkly varying ways. On the one side are authors (e.g., Christian Lalive D'Epinay [1968] and Jean-Pierre Bastian [1990]) who emphasize the repressive and corporatist nature of pentecostal churches and see them as reproducing traditional authoritarian political culture and social control. Other authors (e.g., Emilio Willems [1967] and David Martin [1990]) stress Protestantism's democratizing potential, citing its contributions to a vibrant civil society and drawing analogies with its historical effects in other countries. The churches offer a free social space, an experience of solidarity, and a new personal identity, as well as responsible participation in a community and, for some, the development of leadership gifts.

Theorists who favor the latter interpretation often reference Tocqueville's study of American democracy in the 1830s. The question for us is whether the evangelical Protestantism that grows in Latin America has the characteristics Tocqueville viewed as most beneficial to democracy. He did not regard just any voluntaristic Protestantism as beneficial to democracy, but emphasized characteristics such as clerical self-restraint in avoiding direct political involvement, and doctrines that moderate the people's taste for material well-being.

Evangelical Protestantism reached the Third World largely in the "principled pluralist" vein, often strengthened by the critique of Catholic or non-Christian "confusion" of religion and politics. However, the late twentieth century saw the numerical burgeoning of this evangelicalism and its rise to political influence. In this context, the political restraint shown even by most politically conservative Christians in the United States (in the sense of an acceptance of religious disestablishment and the democratic rules of the game) showed signs of being absent in some quarters.

However, time and place, which are all-important in considering the politics of any religious group, are even more important when analyzing the politics of a fast-growing religious community such as evangelicals in Latin America. There are, for example, three times as many evangelicals in

Brazil today as there were in 1980. This does not mean three times as much of the same thing, but rather a qualitative transformation in the nature of the religious community. Shifts in social composition, the rise of completely new institutional actors, and the enormously greater public awareness of the evangelical phenomenon can all profoundly affect its political implications from one decade to the next, as some of the studies in this volume illustrate.

On the whole, Third World evangelicalism is still poorly served (or totally neglected) in volumes relating religion to politics worldwide. There are, however, a growing number of in-depth country-level studies that treat wholly or principally evangelical Protestantism in relation to politics: examples for Latin America include Scott (1991) on Mexico; Grenfell (1995) on Guatemala; Zub (1993) on Nicaragua; Österlund (2001) on Peru; and Freston (1993a, 1993b, 1994, 1996) on Brazil. On Latin America as a whole, there are three edited volumes. Padilla (1991) is of very uneven value, but some chapters have useful information on the contemporary scene in several countries up to the time of its publication. Gutiérrez (1996) treats only Spanish-speaking countries; it is stronger on the historical side, but it adds little to our knowledge of the recent feverish political activity in many countries. Cleary and Stewart-Gambino (1997) limit themselves to pentecostals; Dodson's chapter in their volume has some useful theoretical reflections, and Wilson's chapter in the same volume adds to the growing understanding of the Guatemalan case. Three important books have treated Protestantism at the continental level: Stoll, Martin, and Bastian (all published in 1990), but they are not specifically on politics, and all except Martin are heavily biased toward the northern end of the region. Finally, Freston (2001) includes extensive material on Latin America.

This Book

The authors of this book set out from the premise that the question of the significance of evangelicals in Latin American politics was not a theoretical matter to be decided by an examination of theological or political dogmas but is instead an essentially empirical investigation belonging to the domains of history and the social sciences. Between religious doctrine and political practice there are many intervening factors. Size, social and ethnic composition, position relative to other confessions, internal church structures and conflicts, degree of legitimacy relative to national myths, and the presence or absence and nature of international connections—all these constrain political possibilities and affect behavior. It is not possible to decide only on the basis of evangelical doctrine whether the religion will be favorable or not to democracy.

Nevertheless, different religions are carriers of different historical heritages, varied organizational traditions, and diverse theological resources, all of which constrain their capacity to act in each new situation encountered. One of evangelicalism's defining characteristics is that it is conversionist. Successful proselytizing religions are often harder for researchers to relate to in a "neutral" way, if only because their interviewees sometimes regard them as potential converts! Some scholars tend to regard the evangelical expansionist impulse as inherently politically dangerous. Yet religious competition is not necessarily incompatible with democracy. It is not impossible for people to disagree strongly about matters they regard as of supreme importance (such as the need to convert others), and still be good democrats. In fact, they may regard democracy as an aid to genuine conversion, since it avoids the tendency to hypocrisy presented by alliances between religion and political power. Soares (1993) suggests this when analyzing what the media in the early 1990s called a "holy war" of some Brazilian pentecostals against the Afro-Brazilian religions. "In our holy war there is a dialogue, however abrasive, with the beliefs which are criticized," which is more than can be said for the "complacent and superior tolerance" of the older churches, which "do not feel their own superiority to be threatened. . . . Warring pentecostalism is carrying out our modernizing revolution, based on egalitarian principles" (1993, 48).

Another premise of these chapters is that the answer to the question of how evangelicals affect democracy would certainly be in the plural and probably in the paradoxical: that is, the investigation would uncover a variety of connections between evangelicalism and democracy, and what is more, some of these would be mutually contradictory. The authors did not set out with any expectation of unearthing a grand narrative of evangelical contribution to democratization or of evangelical collusion with antidemocratic forces.

The chapters in this book, therefore, seek to deepen empirical knowledge of evangelicals in Latin American politics through detailed case studies. Delving into the specificity of the religious and political fields in their particular countries, the authors concentrate heavily on the contemporary period: since 1990 in Peru and Nicaragua and since the late 1990s in the cases of Guatemala and Brazil. This is not just to complement earlier works but also because (given rapid numerical expansion) the relationship between evangelicals and politics in Latin America is a rapidly evolving one whose characteristics can change quite dramatically within a few years.

Apart from an emphasis on the empirical and the contemporary, most of the chapters concentrate on participation in electoral and party politics, while sometimes stressing (as in López's chapter on Peru) that the evangelical impact at the level of civil society can in fact be radically different from evangelicals' partisan and parliamentary performance.

The cases chosen include heavily evangelical and better studied countries such as Brazil and Guatemala, as well as less studied and less heavily evangelical nations like Mexico and Peru. Brazil and Guatemala are obvious choices: Brazil is the largest country in the region and has the largest evangelical community in absolute terms; it has also had extremely visible evangelical involvement in politics for many years, especially at the level of the national congress. Guatemala, meanwhile, is the most evangelical country in Latin America as a percentage of population and has had two evangelical presidents. The third country chosen for study is Peru: the Fujimori regime was perceived to have considerable evangelical support, having been initially elected with many evangelicals on its slate; but at the same time the National Evangelical Council was (by the standards of such councils in Latin America) remarkably outspoken in its criticism. The fourth country is Nicaragua, a counterpoint to most of the region in its experience of a Marxist-inspired revolution, under which pentecostalism grew rapidly, and which subsequently spawned a series of evangelical political parties. Finally, Mexico is included, not so much for any political prominence of its evangelical community, which is relatively small, but for Mexico's very different tradition of church-state relations and for its unique situation now as a member of a free trade bloc with its non-Latin neighbors. There were, obviously, other countries with good cases to be included (such as Chile, with its large Protestant population, or Colombia, with its ongoing violence); and countries whose subsequent political evolution might have made us choose them if we had had a crystal ball (such as Argentina and its economic and political dramas of 2001–2002). But the cases chosen illustrate many phenomena that are repeated in the relationship between evangelicals and politics throughout the region.

The great majority of the scholars participating in this project are people who live in the Third World and teach at Third World universities; in some of the cases, they even militate in their country's politics and/or in one of their country's evangelical churches. The research team of each continent not only met together on three occasions but also benefited from sharing an immense quantity of books and articles on processes of democratization, on religion and politics generally, and on the evangelical religious field in particular.

The researchers employed a range of methods, including surveys, interviews, participant observation, and archival and documentary research. They were encouraged, where possible, to let us hear the actual voices of the evangelical actors involved.

The Case Studies

Unlike all the other cases in this book, Mexican evangelicals have had little impact on partisan electoral politics. Thus, while looking at the changes in legislation in the 1990s regarding religion (through which Mexico toned down its tradition of secularism, which went far beyond the anticlericalism common to many Latin American countries) and examining the role of a few evangelical figures in public life (such as Pablo Salazar, the first evangelical to be elected governor of a Mexican state—and precisely in Chiapas, site of the Zapatista guerrilla rising!), most of Felipe Vázquez's chapter is about how ordinary evangelicals in diverse types of churches in different regions of the state of Veracruz view politics and how their worship practices may contribute to political awareness and the development of attitudes and skills potentially transferable into the political realm.

Vázquez says that "congregational prayers clarify the ways that political expectations are expressed before God and fellow believers" (44–45). He feels that the type of church (by which he means not just doctrine but also organizational and worship patterns) has a greater influence on political postures than the socioeconomic factors that differentiate evangelical churches from each other. With regard to the "neopentecostal" churches, Vázquez calls attention to the role of prayer seen as an essential political function and the greatest contribution these believers feel they can make to Mexico. The link between politics and supposedly essential ritual functions is extremely old, of course. What is new is the democratization of this, as a task open to anyone who has the vision to embrace it, regardless of social, economic, or educational standing, and even independent of clerical approval.

In his conclusion, Vázquez points to a series of ways in which evangelical church practices develop attitudes and abilities that are translatable into political life. He stresses that "eager to share their faith, they . . . build relationships that extend beyond the local community" and they learn to "structure coherent and convincing ideas and to communicate directly with individuals and with larger groups, as well as to participate in discussions . . . in the defense and dissemination of their faith." This reminds us that the evangelical concept of voluntarism and the right and duty to propagate the faith, to convince, and to publicize bears more than a resemblance to Habermas's concept of the public sphere and communicative action. The massive daily practice of grassroots persuasion inherent in evangelical proselytization may be vital for the quality of democracy and a robust public sphere, even when evangelical groups are not internally democratic. At the same time, Vázquez rightly warns us that these potentialities are often left without effect, because some believers, "enchanted with their religious identity and community, see no further than their own congregations" (58).

Vázquez's attempt to listen to ordinary members is a salutary reminder that merely looking at church leaders and their declarations is not enough. Too often, the declared positions of leaders are assumed to be all that one needs to know about evangelical, and especially pentecostal, politics. This point is especially important when the task of democratic transition gives way to the task of democratic deepening, as this usually implies a relative shift in focus from the leaders to the people.

In his section on the changes in government policy toward religion in the 1990s, Vázquez talks of the dilemma evangelical leaders believed themselves to be facing between the secularist tradition of the Revolution and the possible return to political influence of the Roman Catholic Church. But although they regarded themselves as "a strong and growing religious minority that demands to be respected and treated with dignity, both by society as a whole and by the authorities" (43), they remained unable to unite around a single organizational expression that could represent the evangelical position. This is a chronic problem in Latin American evangelicalism and one to which we shall return when commenting on other case studies.

The fact that the first elected evangelical governor in Mexico is from Chiapas is not coincidental. This southernmost state once belonged to the neighboring country of Guatemala, with which it still shares many characteristics, including that of a large percentage of evangelicals in the population. Guatemala is proportionally the most Protestant country in the region (sometimes claimed to be one-third, but probably just over 20 percent) and has had two charismatic evangelical presidents. In a very fragile and limited democracy, which was devastated by guerrilla warfare and brutal military governments for decades, charismatic evangelical churches have penetrated the elite. Historical Protestantism is weak, despite having arrived in the 1880s at the invitation of anticlerical governments anxious to weaken the political power of the Catholic Church. Recruiting among those disillusioned with Vatican II reforms, charismatic groups arrived from the United States, among them the Church of the Word, which soon recruited future president Efrain Ríos Montt. The model was copied by members of the Guatemalan elite, such as the founder of El Shaddai, from which was to spring another future president, Jorge Serrano. Both Ríos Montt and Serrano were politicians before conversion to charismatic churches. In Guatemala it was evangelicalism's extension upward in the class scale that brought it into politics, whereas in Brazil, the leading case in South America, it was the initiative of leading pastors of the mass popular churches.

C. Mathews Samson's chapter on Guatemala stresses the need to look beyond the two well-known cases of evangelical presidents and perceive the pluralism within the evangelical community. Too much attention has been paid, he says, to General Ríos Montt:

> The image of a self-professing Christian general presiding over a genocidal military in a poor Central American country victimized by military aid from the "colossus of the north" fed directly into stereotypical interpretations of a monolithically conservative Protestantism invading Latin America as an agent of cultural and political imperialism. (65)

Samson nuances the picture by examining evangelical candidates from opposite sides of the spectrum for president and vice president in 1999; by looking at the level of civil society and the variety of evangelical positions expressed regarding the heated debate over a new Children and Youth Code;

and by revealing the more localized concerns of evangelical Mayan Indian mayors far from the heat of national politics (Indians being 60 percent of the Guatemalan population). This rich weaving of different levels of analysis results, perhaps inevitably, in considerable ambiguity regarding evangelicals and democracy. It also reinforces the stress on plurality of evangelical political perspectives common to all our chapters; Samson shows that there is no evangelical consensus even on the political implications of an issue such as child-rearing, an issue so related to two key evangelical concerns (the family and the transmission of the faith) that one would expect to find a political consensus there if one were to be found anywhere. And Samson's section on the Mayan mayors also throws light on the increasing evangelical public role among Latin America's indigenous peoples, suggesting that it is far from being as destructive of indigenous unity as is sometimes claimed.

All of this has implications for fears that religio-political conflict might harm democracy in Latin America. Guatemala would be the place for any such conflict to manifest itself, yet it does not seem to. Religious discord seems to be less a limitation on the consolidation of liberal democracy than other structural and institutional constraints, concludes Samson. This is presumably, in part, due to the fact that conflict between religions presupposes unity within each religion, something which the evangelical world especially conspicuously lacks.

Not only the chapter on Guatemala but also those on Mexico and Peru draw attention to the ethnic dimension that is growing in importance in Latin American evangelicalism as it expands among indigenous peoples (see Freston 2001, 207–10; Martin 2002, 119–31; and Freston 2004 regarding Ecuador). Among them, politics has a different dynamic because the relationship between their faith and their ethnicity comes into play. Far from being a betrayal of their "Indianness," it usually seems to be a way of affirming ethnic differentiation and reinforcing political claims vis-à-vis the national societies dominated by whites or mestizos.

Moving slightly further south in Central America, Roberto Zub's chapter on Nicaragua concentrates on the period since the Marxist-inspired Sandinistas lost power in 1990, and on the process whereby pentecostals entered electoral politics through the founding of political parties of evangelical inspiration. He describes these parties as largely schemes for tapping into political power with the aim of creating a duopoly and sharing the privileges that the post-Sandinista state offers to the Catholic Church. The Sandinista regime helped create this situation in two ways. First, it had in fact offered unprecedented equality and importance to evangelicals, since its relations with the Catholic hierarchy had not been good, and second, the evangelical churches, and especially the pentecostal ones located in the poorer sectors, had grown enormously under Sandinismo. When the post-Sandinista government (close to the Catholic hierarchy) once again marginalized evangelicals, this lack of access was combined with a new awareness and numerical size and political potential. Zub thus concludes that in the 1990s important sectors of ecclesiastical leadership encouraged the creation of political parties to restore space for representation in the state.

All this, of course, did not happen in a vacuum, but rather in an electoral system that at the time allowed that option to be easily implemented, and in a social context of severe economic problems and widespread disillusionment with the existing parties. The limitations on this, as Zub points out, result from the fact that ecclesiastical fragmentation is transposed to the party political sphere; and from the fact that the preferred pentecostal solution was not a party that would be better at the art of politics, but rather a party that would bypass the art of politics and represent direct divine intervention. The most successful of these parties was grouped around a charismatic caudillo who preached that God had revealed he would be president. As Zub says, the emphasis on a transcendental calling frees him from party structures, assemblies, councillors or principles. When reaching decisions, as someone called by God through a revelation, he is self-sufficient and autonomous. This raises questions about the compatibility of a certain type of pentecostal political approach (not all types) and democratic participation. At the same time, one should note the democratic dimensions of all this; a political empowering of sectors whose educational and social level would normally preclude any chances of reaching congress (Zub notes that some of this party's deputies had previously been living on a minimum salary). And in his presidential campaign, this party's leader, a rabidly anti-Catholic preacher, felt obliged to call the cardinal of Managua a "great man of God." The political need for votes and allies can make one water down the firmest of principles; but it can also make one abandon the narrowest of prejudices. If political involvement can corrupt and make cynical the best of religious politicians, it can also civilize and educate the worst of them.

But the immediate results were disastrous. The election of deputies through an evangelical party created an expectation that they would encourage changes in the political culture. This hope was soon dashed. It was soon realized that being an evangelical was no antidote to corruption. A spiritual warfare mindset that attributes all a country's problems to the wrong people being in power, and imagines a manifest destiny for one's own group as incorruptible leaders, is bound to come to grief. "We who can govern from God have been isolated," complains one pentecostal leader; yet even before reaching government, while still scaling very low peaks of power, this new political class has shown itself all too susceptible to the worst (and most easily learned) aspects of the prevailing political culture. In this "spiritual warfare" concept, political programs and administrative experience pale into insignificance in the face of the all-important question of the religious identity of the rulers. As a result, there is no room for any concept of political apprenticeship, of constructing a movement painstakingly through years of voter education, party development, and internal democracy.

In the end, as Zub tells us, this rash of evangelical parties will probably be short-lived, since changes in the electoral laws have obliged new means of political survival. Looking at the 2001 elections, Zub notes how the original project of evangelical specificity based on principles and independent action had been eroded. Instead, the pentecostal search for mystical political solutions has alighted on a new object: the possibility of electing the Jewish mayor of Managua as the next president. If the understanding of the evangelicals as the "people of God" who inherit all the rights and privileges of the Israelites to govern over the nations does not seem to be working, then maybe the solution is to find a genuine "Israelite," whose government will necessarily be the object of divine blessing! The fact that he is also a Sandinista is not important to these pentecostals—one more indication of how risky it is to interpret the phenomenon of Third World evangelical politics in terms of North American religious ideologies.

The Nicaraguan case points to several elements that recur frequently in Latin American evangelical politics: the vulnerability to corruption; the desire for religious equality in the public sphere; the importance of electoral systems in determining modes and degree of evangelical political action. But the main relevance of the Nicaraguan case has to do with the question of evangelical political parties. While one or two examples have existed in Latin America since the 1970s, these have multiplied in the 1990s, and now exist in many countries. In some, there is more than one evangelical party.

Samson's chapter on Guatemala and Darío López's chapter on Peru also tell us about evangelical parties. According to López, they

> usually emerged without any previous reflection on political theology. In contrast, they were often motivated by a belief that "the moment had arrived" for evangelicals to have their own representatives in public life. One of their objectives was to demand equal treatment for all religious confessions, and they started with the premise that the only ones who could present the demands of the evangelical community were evangelicals themselves. (140)

They arose mostly at election times, seeing the churches as fields where votes could be harvested. They lacked long-term objectives, merely alleging the right to represent the evangelical community and the necessity of having Christians in power because of their superior spiritual discernment. As one such Peruvian party claimed, "only the Christians can discern the way in which the 'principalities and powers'...influence events....Only the Christians can perceive the curses which idolatrous and occult practices bring down on our people" (141). The claim to special knowledge of social ills, and the implied claim to special expertise in overcoming them, justify the political involvement of people who otherwise might be regarded as completely without political credentials. The question of how this esoteric knowledge might relate to the day-to-day life of a party in a democratic polity is not broached by the actors concerned.

Most evangelical parties in Latin America are based on the pentecostal/charismatic wing of evangelicalism (see Freston 2004). They do not manage to mobilize more than a fraction of the evangelical constituencies to which they appeal. They are usually not supported by most (or any) evangelical church leaders, since they compete with many other political strategies within the evangelical community. Founders have on the whole not been the leaders of large denominations, but rather lower level pastors or else leaders of new charismatic groups.

Protestant parties usually begin (either out of naïveté or cynicism) from the idea of a Protestant bloc vote, of which they are the proprietors. Neither of these assumptions are ever correct. Institutionally divided and theologically and socially diverse, the Protestant community is further divided electorally by the strength of nonreligious appeals and traditional party loyalties.

In Latin America, Protestant parties so far have been, most commonly, parties of "community representation" (whether denominational or trans-denominational) and/or parties of "spiritual warfare" (both of which are illustrated by our case studies). "Community representation" points to the supposed need to overcome the political marginalization of *evangélicos* and even milk the state for corporate privileges to underpin further numerical growth and institutional strengthening. "Spiritual warfare" goes beyond that, developing a doctrine of the "rule of the saints" based on superior insight into spiritual factors behind the problems of one's country. Yet all of these parties remain small. Other modes of political mobilization (such as official denominational candidates distributed throughout several existing parties) have been far more successful.

It is unlikely that any of the existing Protestant Latin American parties will evolve into cohesive and competitive political actors. They are too personalistic and/or naïve, being largely vehicles for personal ambitions or for theocratic projects, which in any case founder on the reality of evangelical division. The multiplication of parties should not be confused with strength; as we see in Nicaragua, they may rather be a sign of political weakness and exclusion. Throughout the region, their results have been poor, not only in terms of their own optimistic hopes but even as a reflection of evangelical percentages in the electorate. Other modes of political mobilization (such as official denominational candidates distributed throughout several existing parties, as in Brazil) have been far more successful. Even the Universal Church of the Kingdom of God, the powerful Brazilian church commented on later, did not for many years attempt a party. Under the Brazilian electoral system, as a separate party it would need more votes to elect the same number of candidates, and its influence in congress would diminish. Its partial take-over of the Liberal Party in Brazil since 1999, while keeping its other congress members spread over a variety of parties, represented a creative attempt at the best of both worlds, and as Fonseca says, created a larger political *locus* for the church without the need to found an evangelical party. However, after losing space in the Liberal Party, the Universal Church did in fact create a party in late 2005 (the Partido Municipalista Renovador [Municipal Renewal Party; the name later changed to the Brazilian Republican Party, or PRB]). As of this writing, however, in early 2006 it is not clear whether the party is merely an insurance policy for the church in case any of the proposals for radical reform of the party system are approved by Congress in the near future.

In Brazil, one does not find a plethora of evangelical parties, but rather evangelical involvement in a range of mainstream parties. As a general rule, where the party system is open to evangelicals, and especially where evan-gelicalism itself is not politically marginalized, there is little attraction for the option of forming evangelical parties. Brazil follows this pattern, mainly due to its electoral system of proportional representation with open party lists. This means that, for example, to elect a federal deputy, the voter can either vote for a party or (more usually) for a particular candidate. The number of places in congress the party wins will be decided by its overall vote, but the order of places within the party will depend on the individual ballots earned by each candidate. This has encouraged existing parties to diversify their social base. Aided by the fact that, although some political involvement (especially by pentecostals) has been controversial, there is very little prejudice against *evangélicos* as such; all the major parties are quite happy to have Protestant candidates on their lists. Where there is no exclusion of evangelicals from the party system, nor evangelical civil rights to secure, the disadvantages of such parties tend to prevail: they further divide the already divided evangelical community, and the variety in social composition makes it difficult to find a common platform (even on abortion there is no unanimity as to legislative policy, much less with regard to church-state relations, the role of the state, economic policy, etc). A party must have a position on a broad range of ques-tions, something that is usually beyond the evangelical community's limited educational resources.

López's chapter on Peru looks at the era of controversial president Alberto Fujimori (1990–2000). It examines the evangelical presence in the formal politics of this era (members of congress; voting patterns; attempts to found parties and movements) as well as at the level of civil society (in survival organizations run by women; in the peasant patrols in the areas affected by political violence; and the role of representative evangelical bodies at the cru-cial moments of the Fujimori regime, especially in its demise). López detects a gap between these two levels: while in formal politics the evangelical community might appear to have been a mainstay of the undemocratic regime, in civil society evangelical actors made useful contributions to democratic resistance. The pro-Fujimori evangelical members of congress, he says, "far from being the imagined 'moral reservoir' of the nation, contributed to the moral deterioration of public life by justifying the undemocratic actions of the regime" (139). On the other hand, López's examples of evangelicals' roles in organs of civil society point to "a growing awareness of civic responsibility in a religious community that was for many years regarded as a 'refuge of the masses' engaged in a "social strike." "Even so," he concludes, "most evangelicals still see democracy in terms of participation in periodic elections"; and "they have not yet understood the need to build a broad network of relationships, especially outside the limits of the evangelical world."

Two important themes for evangelical politics in Latin America are best illustrated by the Peruvian case. The first is the question of organizations of Protestant unity. Protestantism's fissiparous nature is often commented on, whether as an advantage or as a limitation. Dreams of influence founder on the reality of division. But there are also organizations that explicitly try to unite evangelicals across their divisions; and there is a close link between politics and unity. Political efficacy is often closely tied to evangelical unity, whether through the absolute dominance of one church within the evangelical field (not really the case in any Latin American context) or, more commonly, through effective transdenominational representative organizations (of which the National Evangelical Council of Peru [CONEP] is the outstanding example). What often happens is that, as the real possibility of political power beckons, preexisting entities become political footballs (e.g., the Brazilian Evangelical Confederation in 1987) and/or other supposed "unity" entities are founded as poorly disguised political trampolines (e.g., the Consejo de Pastores de Chile during the military regime). The Protestant world is institutionally divided and, in the growing churches of Latin America, institutionally underendowed. It has no doctrinal basis that obliges unity. It thus allows political interference in its internal structuring in a way that the Catholic world does not. But this political interference (whether from evangelicals or nonevangelicals) rarely achieves its aim, since at the very time that unity becomes concretely rewarding, its achievement becomes harder than ever. In such circumstances, unity would offer the chance of real power, but that serves merely to encourage the emergence of a plethora of would-be unifiers (as Vázquez shows for Mexico and as Zub hints at with regard to the role of the Evangelical Committee for Helping Development [CEPAD] in Nicaragua). This may throw some light on the trajectory of CONEP in Peru. In the Africa volume of this project, "third-termism" (the attempt of many African presidents to perpetuate their power through unconstitutional third terms) is said to have offered the only recent opportunity for the sort of prophetic challenge to authoritarian leadership that historic churches do best (Ranger 2008). In Latin America, the only example of third-termism is Peru; and for the role of the historic churches in Africa one can substitute the role of an organization of Protestant unity such as CONEP. In fact, as López tells us, more "prophetic" evangelical leaders were able to exercise considerable influence in CONEP at two moments: in the 1980s, when political violence and abuse of human rights threatened to engulf the country, and CONEP established its human rights arm, which has since carried out (in its own right and in collaboration with Catholic and secular organizations) a role so far unique among Latin American evangelical unity bodies; and precisely in 2000, during the crisis of Fujimori's "third-termism." CONEP called on Christians to prevent reelection, invoking a "moral obligation to disobey governments when they lack legitimacy." This was not just for legal reasons; Fujimori's rule was characterized by the absence of values such as truthfulness, justice, and solidarity. The state of law had been eroded, poverty and unemployment were up, corruption was rife. "The time has come to say No to the silence of complicity." On the other hand, CONEP's footing seems to have been much less sure in 1990, when Fujimori, a political outsider, was elected on a new slate that included a plethora of evangelical candidates and the head of CONEP as the candidate for second vice president. At that time, when politics appeared to be "normal" and the task of consolidating Peru's rickety democracy was the order of the day, the "prophetic" arm of Peruvian evangelicalism (which in fact comprises members of historical and pentecostal churches whose theological formation occurred basically through parachurch organizations) spoke with a very unclear voice. Ironically, its concern was largely to delegitimize any claim on the part of others to speak for the whole evangelical world—the very thing this group would be accused of doing in 2000 when it spoke out against Fujimori's reelection.

The other theme that emerges powerfully from the Peruvian case is that of evangelicals and violence. The theme is present in the Mexican, Nicaraguan, and Guatemalan cases, too, but is central in Peru. López paints a picture of small pentecostal churches, fast-growing largely because of the traumas of the violence and the withdrawal of Catholic pastoral agents, caught between a brutal Maoist insurgency and equally brutal military repression. Unlike in Guatemala, the main enemy of the indigenous peasants of the highlands seems to have been the guerrillas, in the form of the Shining Path movement. Where others fled or submitted, the evangelicals filled the peasant patrols. In their armed action, they saw themselves as fighting against the antichrist himself. As López concludes,

> While the fighters of Shining Path were ready to "offer themselves" without reservation for "the party" and for "President Gonzalo" [leader of Shining Path], the evangelicals were ready to die fearlessly for Jesus Christ and their faith. When Shining Path tried to control the personal and collective life of the peasants, including their

religious practices, it came up against a rival power that told it they could not "serve two masters." This rival power provided the strength needed both to resist Shining Path indoctrination and violence and to organize and fight against them. (153)

This was vital to saving some sort of democratic space in Peru. If evangelicals are not usually good at promoting democratic transitions in the Third World (though they may support such transitions once under way), they do appear to be good at resisting the claims of regimes or insurgents that make totalitarian (rather than simply authoritarian) claims.

In this book, Alexandre Fonseca gives us a fascinating account of the two major evangelical figures in Brazilian politics since 1998. The first of these is the governor of the state of Rio de Janeiro, Anthony Garotinho, a career politician who converted to the Presbyterian Church in 1994. The other is Bishop Carlos Rodrigues, federal deputy and political leader of the immensely powerful Universal Church of the Kingdom of God, a pentecostal church that was founded in Rio in 1977 and now has a large caucus in congress, owns the third largest television network in Brazil, and is present in about eighty countries. Both these figures are young (mid-forties), and both played important roles in Brazil's 2002 presidential election *on the left of the political spectrum*. Garotinho finished a close third in the election, as candidate of the Brazilian Socialist Party; and Rodrigues is deputy-leader of the Liberal Party, a small centrist party in which the Universal Church of the Kingdom of God has invested heavily, and which allied with the Workers Party in support of the main left-wing presidential candidate Luís Inácio Lula da Silva, the eventual winner. A poll showed that 35 percent of evangelical voters favored Garotinho (against a national average of 17 percent), and 31 percent favored Lula (against a national average of 41 percent). Thus, two-thirds of evangelical voters were favorable toward the candidates of the two major left-wing parties, being slightly more favorable to the left than the electorate as a whole.

As Fonseca reminds us, any significant shift to the left on the part of evangelicals may well be related to a shift to the right by the Catholic Church, leaving space on the "religious left" that evangelicals feel they can fill without embarrassment. This is not to say that an evangelical left did not exist before (Fonseca tells us about it); but for such positions to become common coin among evangelicals, it may be necessary for the Catholic Church to be perceived as no longer significantly associated with the left, as it certainly was in Brazil in the 1970s and 1980s.

Fonseca's chapter gives an in-depth, local-level study of the experience of one evangelical politician (Garotinho) who has already occupied an important executive post and may go even further. His detailed account illustrates the degree of complexity involved in understanding evangelical politics: the political fissures within the evangelical community (even among left-wing evangelicals) and the dynamics of operationalizing politically an explicitly evangelical identity at the level of majoritarian elections and administrative posts (in which an in-house discourse aimed purely at the evangelical electorate is counterproductive). It is at this level of fine-grained analysis that real political chances and motivations are unearthed. And the fact that this fine-grained analysis is necessary gives the lie to grand theories reflecting messianic hopes or apocalyptic fears regarding evangelical politics. Fonseca's study also challenges facile equations of evangelicalism with conservative stances. The distance of these actors—indeed, total independence of these actors—from the American evangelical right is also illustrative; after all, Brazil is one of the largest Third World democracies and has the largest practicing evangelical community outside the United States. The fact that the Universal Church of the Kingdom of God, via the Liberal Party, threw in its lot with Lula, and that the Assemblies of God declared support for the government's candidate, José Serra, shows how precarious are all claims to unite evangelicals politically, and how exaggerated are all fears of an evangelical political hegemony that would threaten democracy.

Fonseca's chapter recognizes limits to this leftward turn in Brazilian evangelical politics. This "new phase in relations between evangelicals and electoral politics" is based on the emergence of leaders "from above" who have adopted an oppositionist discourse, are in or allied with left-wing parties, and—through a discourse that values political means—criticize current powerholders and denounce the plight of large social sectors, contributing in their own ways to the politicization of impoverished segments of society. But Garotinho is often criticized for his populist style, hostile to genuine participation; and the Universal Church of the Kingdom of God makes no bones about not being a democratic church internally and not allowing ordinary church members to participate in the church's selection of candidates. The politics of the Universal Church is only a very limited space of democratic education for the mass of poor people affiliated with the church, Fonseca concludes.

Nevertheless, Fonseca talks of the growing trend to an "evangelical social discourse," with an emphasis on justice that would have been unthinkable a few years earlier. In the case of the Universal Church of the Kingdom of God, there may be all sorts of reasons for this change (Fonseca ventilates several), but the end result is the same. Rodrigues himself once attributed the change to the Universal Church's increasing contact with the social realities of Brazil (as the church spread and as it got heavily involved in social projects) and to the experience of being in parliament and dialoguing with colleagues on the left. "We started to dialogue [with the Workers Party]...and we saw that our truths were lies, that our fears were groundless," he declared in the Brazilian congress in 2000 (189). The Universal Church's commitment to the prosperity gospel does not seem to be an obstacle for this; on the contrary, it may even encourage it. Thus, the church's interest in the Lula campaign for president may be in part motivated by an understanding that the growth of the church is harmed by high levels of governmental corruption and by the stake's economic policies and the appalling income distribution resulting from them. Fonseca ends by asking whether Brazilian pentecostals can see the possibility of trust with other social actors who do not share the same faith, and even of taking part in networks with those who are currently demonized, something that the 2002 alliance between the Universal Church and Lula, the candidate it explicitly demonized during the 1989 and 1994 elections, would seem to suggest is perfectly possible.

Fonseca's text also illustrates the process by which leading politicians, including left-wing ones such as the Workers Party senator Marina Silva, convert to evangelicalism and continue their political militancy—a trend multiplied many times over by more anonymous figures in contemporary Brazil. Thus, whatever political profile evangelicalism may have had in the past, its continuing attraction as a religion of personal salvation brings in new types of people who end up changing that profile, showing it to have been merely contingent and not, as some analyses would have it, an essential part of evangelical identity. At the same time, the appearance of Garotinho as the first evangelical politician with a real chance of reaching the presidency of Brazil also brings into relief the messianism of some sectors of the evangelical ecclecsiastical leadership who dream—based on a theological fusion of Old and New Testaments—of an "evangelical president" who will channel the "blessings of God" onto the country.

In this regard, Fonseca mentions governor Garotinho's frequent trips outside his home state to preach in churches all over the country. On these occasions, what Garotinho did was basically an enthusiastic recounting of his evangelical testimony, but what he was aiming at was clear: to use his (genuine) connection with this nationwide religious community to make himself known outside his home state, as a basis for achieving a certain percentage in the opinion polls and launching a bid for the presidency. This prompted controversy in political circles and in the media and was even portrayed as an illegitimate reuniting of spheres that modernity had managed to separate at the cost of much shedding of blood. These two spheres are variously labeled on the one hand "church" or "religion" and on the other "state" or "politics." One suspects that, since a viable candidate for president who is not only evangelical but makes explicit electoral use of his religious identity is a novelty in Brazil, political rivals are tempted to attack him by trying to find out exactly where the "invisible social ceiling" on evangelical public aspirations is now situated in Brazil. But one suspects the ceiling is scarcely operative now for electoral purposes. In any case, Garotinho has insisted he is in favor of a secular state but also, rather confusingly, that he does not "mix religion and politics." In fact, as Fonseca points out, Garotinho's model is of a secular state with religious politics, a perfectly defensible position in comparative political terms (as Demerath [2001] shows).

On the other hand, the case of the Universal Church of the Kingdom of God also raises the specter of a powerful denominational force unprecedented in Latin American Protestantism, capable of fleshing out its corporatist dreams in ways that other evangelical groups can only dream about. How much power will the Universal Church in fact be able to accumulate, and how much will it be able (through one means or another) to subordinate other sectors of the evangelical world to its political leadership? And, above all, what use will it make of such power? Fonseca shows us a church in political flux and, it seems, undergoing political maturation. While its corporate interests (especially in the media) are still undoubtedly its political "bottom line," when these are not at stake, the church seems capable of developing a type of center-left populism based on a critique of globalization and neoliberalism. Its political success seems to owe much to what it has in common with the Catholic Church (hierarchical structure and the capacity for centralized political initiatives) rather than to its differences. As an interesting and evolving mix of *church* and *sect* (in sociological terms), it may be able to overcome some of the usual limitations on evangelical political action in Latin contexts, at the same time that it avoids some of the limitations faced by the Catholic hierarchy. What will result from this novel situation is uncertain.

Both the Universal Church and Garotinho point to another central theme in evangelical politics in Latin America: its connection with the media. Roberto Zub's chapter on Nicaragua also points heavily in this direction (the cases of Pastor Osorno, Pastor Duarte, and Miguel Angel Casco), the Peruvian and Guatemalan cases less so. Where evangelical access to radio and television is unproblematic and the evangelical community is sufficiently numerous, there is often a close relationship between media and politics. This is not just because it is often necessary to have political clout to own stations but also because the ownership or use of electronic media is a vital means of structuring an otherwise organizationally amorphous and institutionally underendowed community with few cultural resources.

Daniel Levine, of the University of Michigan and author of many works on the Catholic Church and politics in Latin America, took part in the final conference of our project and has contributed a concluding chapter, putting the case studies into the broader context of transformations in Latin American religion and in the expectations for political transformation. Indeed, by the early 1990s, after redemocratization and internal ecclesiastical shifts took their toll on Catholic liberationist movements, the evangelicals came onto the radar screens of many scholars of religion and politics in Latin America who had previously regarded them as irrelevant. The realization that evangelicals were here to stay in Latin American politics helped provoke a shift toward less polemical scholarship.

Levine speaks appropriately of the possible influences of politics on the evangelical community itself. A new dynamic is introduced, new temptations, new risks of becoming discredited. It is indeed true that in Brazil the public image of evangelicals has deteriorated in the last twenty years, largely because of its political performance. This may in time have a deleterious effect on the churches' ability to reproduce themselves, still more to maintain their head-long growth.

From the studies presented in this book it appears that the fragmentation of evangelicalism means that its direct political impact is always smaller than might be hoped or feared. No evangelical neo-Christendom potentially dangerous to democracy is feasible, however much numerical success the churches might still have. Just as modern democracy was helped more by the effects of the Reformation than by the politics of the Reformers, Third World democracy may end up owing more to evangelicalism than to evangelical church leaders and politicians. In any case, only a very small minority of evangelicals have political projects similar to those of militant Islamists. They are the fruit of advanced social differentiation and would not want to reinstitute organic unities.

Organizational fragmentation is supplemented by a plurality of political attitudes and behaviors, as illustrated by our case studies. Thus, it seems that Third World evangelicalism will not automatically line up with the First World Christian right on many issues.

The "fierce spirit of independence and free agency" (Shah 2003) that characterizes evangelicalism encompasses the individual's freedom to respond to the religious message, unite in worship, and separate to form other congregations. The result is an opting out of social "sacred canopies," the creation of autonomous social spaces, and an unending pluralism. The results for democracy are manifold and paradoxical. Totalitarian regimes or movements are resisted firmly (as are non-Christian religious nationalisms in Asia [Lumsdaine 2008]), but authoritarian regimes that do not impinge on the exercise of evangelical religion may not always be. The evangelical world is too fissured and independent to undergird national-level movements for major political change. While it can multiply individual actors to strengthen many social and political movements, its autonomous institutional strength will always disappoint. (There have been no national "Reformations" of Christendom or Protestant state churches in the Third World as there were in northern Europe.) Evangelicalism is thus of less "use" during phases of democratic transition than it is during the more extended periods of democratic consolidation (in which it helps to incorporate marginal social actors).

Although it is institutionally vulnerable to manipulation by political leaders (such as Fujimori in Peru), this manipulation is always partial and contested by other evangelical segments.

It is thus much easier to make negative ("they will not be able to do this or that, however much they want to") than positive predictions regarding evangelicals and democracy. Within the broad middle ground (between helping processes of democratic deepening and tolerating existing authoritarianisms), the prevailing tendencies have to be the subject of constant empirical examination. It seems that evangelicalism can be interpreted to require wildly varying political regimes. For some, it requires "spiritual warfare" against the cultural influence of other religions and an (unattainable) "rule of the saints." For many others, its emphasis on the cross of Christ (the death of its founder at the hands of the state), its traditional suspicion of "the world" and insistence on inward transformation of the heart as far more important than outward conformity, require freedom of conscience and expression.

Thus, while circumscribed by certain broad parameters, actual evangelical politics is very hard to predict, not only because evangelicalism is decentralized but also because it is now present in such a variety of contexts and often without international contacts. Of course, one implication of this localism is that imitation may prevail: local patterns of religion-state relations may be absorbed by evangelicalism as it grows and gains in political legitimacy. In Latin America, the now-fading heritage of a monolithic Catholic model may modify evangelical aspirations somewhat, but the more democratic and pluralist present will almost certainly keep it broadly within the democratic and nonconfessional track. Future growth curves, whatever they are, may well change the composition of the evangelical community and steer it toward more mainstream politics: in the case of numerical stagnation, by increasing the percentage of birth-members; or in the case of continued expansion, by incorporating other social sectors.

I

Democratic Activity and Religious Practices of Evangelicals in Mexico

Felipe Vázquez Palacios

In this chapter I analyze how evangelical faith relates to concrete political actions and how these affect democracy. Evangelical faith motivates (at the same time that it discourages) democratizing attitudes and actions, although with limited social impact due to its status as a dissident and fragmented minority, the social circumstances of each group, and the ecclesiastical organization and type of worship service believers experience. Using an anthropological approach, I offer an ethnography of the daily religious practices of the members of three types of evangelical churches (historical, pentecostal, and neopentecostal) in three distinct contexts (indigenous, rural, and urban). On this basis, I point to potential or actual influences of evangelicals on the process of democratization. The chapter is structured in three parts: (1) the context of evangelicals and politics in Mexico; (2) the data on the churches studied; and (3) an evaluation of evangelical participation in democratic processes.

Evangelicals and Politics in Mexico

The origins of Protestantism in Mexico are linked to a strong liberal reaction to the massive presence of the Catholic Church, which enjoyed great privileges and had immense landholdings. This reaction took the form of anticlerical measures such as the nationalization of church properties and freedom of worship, formulated in the so-called Reform Laws of the Juárez government in the 1850s. Protestantism, as an imported religion from the 1860s onward, perhaps not surprisingly stressed its nonpolitical nature, and found in the liberal governments a favorable environment for its development. Between those years and the outbreak of the Mexican Revolution (1910), Protestantism developed slowly, reaching perhaps 0.5 percent of the population, and was concentrated in the north, along the railway lines, and among the emerging lower middle class. Despite its small size, its role in the Revolution was disproportionate. The rural schoolmasters were important in interpreting the Revolution, and several Protestants held high posts in the Carranza government. A Presbyterian, Gregorio Velázquez, headed the office of strategic information and propaganda; the Methodist Andrés Osuna was secretary of public education. There were also three state governors and ten members of the 1917 Constituent Assembly who were Protestants. Osuna became governor of Tamaulipas, and the Presbyterian Aarón Sáenz governed the Federal District and later the state of Nuevo León, while his brother Moisés was the minister of education (Mondragón 1991, 71).

The period from 1910 to 1926 was the peak of the Protestant political presence, and in fact represented a high degree of political involvement by Protestants unprecedented in Latin America (Freston 2001, 202). But it was followed by the period of greatest repression of religion in Mexico (some states even prohibited all religious services), and the Protestant presence in public life diminished considerably. This was despite the fact that its presence in Mexican society was increasing and diversifying. Rural and indigenous communities began to be affected, as well as urban popular sectors and even small groups of better-off urbanites. Most of this expansion was not due to the growth of the historical denominations (such as the Presbyterians and Methodists), but to the rise of new churches, especially pentecostal ones. Labeled "sects" by the Catholic Church, these groups preached a sharp break with behavior such as alcoholism and participation in community *fiestas*. Being an evangelical began to be counterproductive for those who desired recognition in public life.

In the last third of the twentieth century, not only did the religious field diversify but the economic and political model implanted by the ruling party after the Revolution saw its prestige greatly eroded. The way to joining the North American Free Trade Association (NAFTA) in 1994 was smoothed by changes in Mexico's secularist policy, including the restoration of relations with the Vatican. In the early 1990s, questions of religious freedom were amply debated in meetings between the government and religious leaders, leading to a reform of article 130 of the 1917 Constitution, on which the strong anticlerical tradition was based. Churches were now allowed to own property, hold religious events outside church buildings, and participate in educational activities. The clergy gained the right to vote in political elections, and the state's right to restrict the number of clergy and worship services was repealed. While evangelicals also benefited from some of these measures, they began to fear that new forms of state control over religious life were being introduced, allied to an increase in Catholic influence over the state. The Vatican representative demanded preferential treatment for the Catholic Church in comparison with the evangelicals, saying: "Giving everybody the same is not true equality; rather, each one should get their part. An elephant does not eat in the same way as an ant" (in Blancarte 1993, 563). The reforms approved in 1992 included compulsory registration of religious groups, which made some evangelicals fear that Mexico would become closed to new religious movements and would develop a climate of intolerance. Political parties were forbidden to allude to religious creeds, and clergy were not allowed to express open support for any candidate or party. If a minister wished to be a candidate, he would have to renounce his ecclesiastical position and wait for five years. While the government now realizes it has to speak to a wide range of religious organizations, it has used one of the classical forms of state intervention in religion, creating departments of religious affairs in each state.

At the political level, the evangelicals have long supported anticlerical forces, including liberals and Freemasons, and have also tended to be favorable to the party in power. The new relations between the state and evangelicals since the reform of the laws on religion have led evangelicals to emphasize their religious identity at the church level, but not to develop a community identity that would permit a common front among diverse evangelical groups. Each denomination sought its own relationship with the state in order to obtain government recognition, but this weakened the possibilities of a unified identity that would allow Protestantism to rise above its marginal status.

Evangelicals are involved with all the three major parties in Mexico: the longtime governing party, the Partido Revolucionario Institucional (PRI, Institutional Revolutionary Party); the center-left Partido de la Revolución Democrática (PRD, Democratic Revolution Party); and even the right-wing party traditionally supported heavily by the Catholic Church, the Partido de Acción Nacional (PAN, National Action Party). There have also been initiatives in forming specifically evangelical parties or movements. One example is the Partido Encuentro Social (PES, Social Encounter Party), whose leading light is Hugo Flores, a member of an independent pentecostal church with a doctorate in international relations from Harvard and former advisor to President Zedillo. Another example is the Partido de Acción Republicana (PAR, Republican Action Party), more regionally based in the state of Veracruz and linked to a neopentecostal denomination called Amistad Cristiana (Christian Friendship). It admits only evangelicals as members. An example of a movement that aims at creating not an evangelical party but rather a more ethical civic culture is Convergencia Cristiana (Christian Convergence). This group played a key role in garnering evangelical support for the PAN candidate Vicente Fox in his successful presidential campaign in 2000. Besides supporting his economic proposals, Convergencia Cristiana emphasized the congruence between Reformed and Catholic social philosophy, as well as Fox's professed desire to collaborate more closely with all churches.

There are also evangelical city councillors, mayors, deputies, and senators. Additionally, Pablo Salazar, a member of the Nazarene Church, served as governor of the troubled southern state of Chiapas from 2000 to 2006. In 2000, Salazar became the first evangelical to be democratically elected as governor of a Mexican state. As governor, he attended the Nazarene church escorted by his security guards, and some members of his cabinet also joined the church. Salazar is of peasant origin and has a brother who is a pastor. He had been a deputy and senator with the PRI, the traditional governing party, and took part in the Agreement and Pacification Commission attempting to resolve the crisis with the Zapatista guerrillas. Due to tensions within the PRI over the candidacy for governor, he left the party and became the candidate for a coalition composed of the two other major parties, the PRD and the PAN. He did not campaign in the evangelical churches, although he never played down his evangelical affiliation. His adversaries attempted to politicize his religion. One of their leaflets warned electors that "the fiestas for the saints will be lost, and also the images that are celebrated in the churches such as the Virgin of Guadalupe, patron of all Mexicans . . . all because people want to vote for the PRD whose candidate is an evangelical who hates the saints of the Catholic Church."

Salazar replied that such mixing of religion and politics was explosive. In the end, he obtained 56 percent of the votes, although many analysts attribute his victory more to fatigue with the PRI than to Salazar's own charisma and achievements. In fact, he soon broke with the parties that had put him in power, and his administration ran into trouble. Abstention in the election was almost 50 percent, and many evangelicals seem to have been in this category. Salazar's government was not well regarded by many indigenous evangelicals, who did not see any advance on questions of intolerance toward them by local elites. (Protestantism is now proportionately larger among Indians than among the rest of the Mexican population, due mainly to endogenous initiatives rather than to missions undertaken by mestizos or foreigners.) Other evangelicals were unhappy about Salazar because he is seen as too favorable to the Zapatistas, who had expropriated the Presbyterian seminary in Ocotzingo. This is not to deny that there are evangelicals among the Zapatistas; their taking up of the cause of displaced indigenous evangelicals in the negotiations with the government in 1995 won them much evangelical sympathy. "The Confraternity of Christian Evangelical Churches (Confraternice) issued a pronouncement opposed to the Zapatista movement and critical of the politicization of the Catholic Church in the region, whereas at the local level many churches, whether Presbyterian, Adventist or pentecostal, express support for the Zapatistas" (Hernández 2000, 58). Still other evangelicals complain, as one did to me, that "we evangelicals are very disappointed in [Salazar]; we thought that because he was an evangelical we would have special treatment, but we don't."

Other prominent evangelicals in politics include Humberto Rice from the Congregational Church, who has had a long career in the PAN; Evangelina Corona, a Presbyterian of very humble origins who became leader of the seamstresses' union and a PRD deputy; and María de los Angeles Moreno, a Baptist parliamentarian with the PRI. All of these have been open about their evangelical affiliation but have participated politically as individuals, without involving their churches.

Thus we see that evangelicals in Mexico manifest their political ideals in various ways and with varying postures. Our study of the state of Verzacruz will illustrate more how they interact with local politics.

Evangelical Presence and Identity

Statistically, Mexican Protestantism is one of the weakest in Latin America. According to the 2000 census, only 5.2 percent of the population calls itself evangelical, out of the 12 percent who are non-Catholic. (It should be mentioned, however, that Adventists were classified outside the evangelical category, and that some neopentecostals may have been disqualified because their churches are not registered religions but are regarded as civil associations.) Veracruz is slightly above the national average, with a population that is 17 percent non-Catholic, including 6.9 percent evangelical. Of these, about 75 percent are pentecostal, especially strong in rural and indigenous areas; 19 percent are historical Protestants, mostly in urban and rural areas; and the remainder are neopentecostals, largely in the cities. For our research, we chose three contrasting areas of the state. The capital Xalapa, a medium-sized city with a population of 350,000, is 5 percent evangelical. The municipality of Alamo, in the north of the state, has 91,000 inhabitants and is 11.5 percent evangelical. The indigenous municipality of Mecayapan, 92 percent of whom speak Náhuatl, has experienced a dramatic religious transformation: in 1970, 97 percent of the population claimed to be Catholic, whereas in 2000 only 10 percent were Catholic and 75 percent were evangelical. This evolution is similar to what has taken place in many indigenous localities in the southern states of Chiapas and Tabasco. Since many people from Mecayapan are now migrants to the United States or to the *maquiladoras* (assembly plants) along the border, conversion may be linked to the search for new institutional references that are durable and useful in the transition to new and unfamiliar environments.

Evangelicals in Mexico are often divided into three main types: historical, pentecostal, and neopentecostal. The historical churches, such as the

Presbyterians, Methodists, Baptists, Nazarenes, and Lutherans, were the first to arrive in Mexico from the second half of the nineteenth century. The pentecostals, such as the Assemblies of God, the Movement of Independent Pentecostal Evangelical Churches (Movimiento Iglesia Evangélica Pentecostés Independiente; MIEPI), the Apostolic Faith Church, the Church of God, and others, began in the 1910s, but their rapid diffusion dates from the 1940s. The neopentecostals, a fusion of traditional pentecostalism with reformed and modern charismatic currents, consists of newer, usually middle-class churches that are often registered as civil associations rather than religious groups. Among the main ones are Christian Friendship, the Christian Center Cala-coaya, New Wine, and Castle of the King.

In northern Mexico, all three types are strong, but even the historical churches tend now to be heavily charismatic. In the center of the country, which is the bulwark of Catholicism, the influence of the historical churches is still strong, even though they no longer predominate numerically. In the south, which is now the heartland of Protestantism, ethnic evangelicalism is strong.

Beyond denominational frontiers, there is an evangelical macroidentity that allows common action on certain occasions. Examples of this include special events such as evangelistic crusades or artistic presentations. Another is the annual "march of faith" on March 21, the national holiday honoring the birth of President Benito Juárez (1806–1872), who introduced religious freedom. In the march, evangelicals parade through the main streets carrying banners with biblical texts, finishing in front of monuments to Juárez. Pastors of historical churches then make speeches emphasizing freedom of belief and praising Juárez. This is a way for evangelicals to have a link with one of the sources of Mexican nationalism; as to two other main sources, their relationship to the tradition stemming from the Revolution of the 1910s is ambiguous at best, and their relationship to the all-pervasive cult of the Virgin of Guadalupe is, of course, one of rejection and criticism.

There have been attempts to found associations broad enough to represent the evangelical position on public questions. But, as usually happens in Latin American Protestantism, this has merely led to a multiplication of such bodies, most of which suffer from a lack of support and resources and only meet and act sporadically. Examples would be the National Evangelical Defense Committee, the Evangelical Confraternity of Mexico (Conemex), the National Forum of Christian Evangelical Churches (Fonice), the Federation of Christian Evangelical Churches of Mexico (Ficemex) and the Confraternity of Christian Evangelical Churches (Confraternice). The latter has attracted the most media attention; it carried out a "march for peace" uniting thirty thousand evangelicals to summon the government and the Zapatista guerrillas to peace negotiations. Fonice was organized by two Assemblies of God pastors, Alberto Montalvo and Arturo Farela, and promoted many meetings on the theme of evangelical political participation and a judicial advisory committee for churches at the time of the constitutional changes on religion. A power struggle between them led Farela to break from Fonice and found Confraternice, using contacts with civil servants to gain space in the media. In the 2000 presidential elections, he supported the candidate of the then governing PRI.

Another important evangelical figure is Abner López, of peasant origins and from Chiapas, who has been moderator of the Presbyterian Church and rector of the Presbyterian seminary, in which role he promoted debates among the 1994 presidential candidates. He is currently director of the Bible Society, and has shown political sympathies with the left-leaning PRD. Esdras Alonso, a lawyer and Nazarene pastor, has for many years acted on behalf of the indigenous evangelicals expelled from their land in Chiapas. Previously aligned with governor Pablo Salazar, he has since broken with him. Another figure is Adolfo de la Sienra, leading light in the Convergencia Cristiana, which supported the Fox candidacy in 2000; strongly Reformed in theology, he has a doctorate in philosophy from Stanford University and is a researcher at the Veracruzana University. Domingo López Angel is a pentecostal pastor and leader of the Coordinating Committee of Indigenous Representatives of Altos de Chiapas (Consejo de Representantes Indígenas de los Altos de Chiapas; CRIACH). Carlos Martínez, a journalist with a national daily newspaper and an advisor to the governor of Chiapas, is the evangelical who has written and spoken most regarding religious intolerance and freedom of worship.

The aforementioned figures have made public pronouncements regarding diverse themes such as corruption, religious intolerance, economic policies, and unemployment. An example is the speech by the Presbyterian pastor Ricardo Aquino, president of the Association of Evangelical Ministers of Veracruz, on the occasion of the traditional March 21 parade in 2000.

> Today, we evangelicals are a strong and growing religious minority that demands to be respected and treated with dignity, both by society as a whole and by the authorities and the media. This minority is determined to make a contribution to the effort to forge a society with ethical values.... We speak out in favor of peace, in favor of respect for religious minorities. We denounce the harassment which evangelicals are subjected to in the indigenous communities.... We repudiate the silence of the civil authorities regarding these abuses.

Such speeches frequently denounce the businesses linked to money laundering, and call on civil society as a whole, regardless of creed, to join the battle against vice and corruption. The question of religious intolerance is usually present also, and according to evangelical leaders, Chiapas is just the tip of the iceberg, since similar problems exist in other states such as Oaxaca, Puebla, Guerrero, Veracruz, and Hidalgo. Clear respect for the secular nature of the state is sometimes demanded of the president. For evangelical leaders,

Mexico is being "Chiapanized," as illustrated by the 2001 case of Ixmiquilpan, in the state of Hidalgo, only one hundred kilometers from the national capital, where local authorities cut off the water supply to evangelicals, destroyed their plantations, and denied them the right to bury their dead in the local cemetery.

Beyond these common themes, it is difficult to talk of political trends; as a pentecostal pastor told me, "in my church we have all the political currents and you cannot say that my congregation favors this or that party."

Evangelical Attitudes in Veracruz

The fieldwork in Veracruz was carried out between March 2000 and May 2001. Of the churches selcted for study, the Presbyterians are the oldest established in the state, and currently have about eighty churches there, being composed largely of middle and lower middle strata in the cities but of more marginalized sectors in the rural areas. The Methodist Church began in Alamo in the early twentieth century with the arrival of foreign workers in the oil industry, but its presence in Xalapa, the state capital, dates from the 1950s with a schism from the Presbyterians. It has forty-five churches in the state, predominantly in rural areas, and its social composition is similar to that of the Presbyterians. The Baptists, active in the state since the 1930s, have 130 churches, mostly middle class in the towns but among marginalized sectors in rural and indigenous areas.

The pentecostals are represented in this study by the MIEPI, present in Veracruz since 1932 and now with 250 churches among the poor; and by the Assemblies of God, who only arrived in the state in 1964 but already have 250 churches. The neopentecostals are represented by three groups (Christian Friendship, Castle of the King, and Calacoaya Center), all established since 1990 in the cities and with mainly middle-class members and a few from higher social strata.

My approach to these churches began with attendance at worship services and attempts to speak to members afterward. I circulated a short questionnaire among these members, and also asked leaders or founders for a longer interview. I also selected some key informants, mostly believers of long standing and current or former office-holders in the church, to sound out their reactions to the results of the questionnaire. The questionnaire was divided into three sections: (1) a sociological description of the respondent (gender, age, occupation, and socioeconomic and educational levels); (2) religious beliefs and practices; and (3) participation in civil associations and in politics.

Observation of worship services and other meetings was important for corroborating information from the interviews, since congregational prayers clarify the ways that political expectations are expressed before God and fellow believers. This helped in perceiving how an electoral period is experienced by the congregation, for example, the fervent prayer asking that the national or municipal elections should take place without violence or fraud, that the candidates should not subject each other to personal attacks, and that corruption and social instability should be overcome. Some prayers asked that the victorious candidate should be an instrument of God to open up more space for believers to disseminate the message of salvation.

I had some difficulty in researching the Christian Friendship neopentecostal church, since they were worried about the type of questions being asked. The leaders tried to withhold permission for me to speak to any member except with their authorization, delegating someone to accompany me at all times. The leader in Xalapa told me that it was enough to know what he thought about these questions, since everyone else in the church had exactly the same opinion. In the end, I was able to obtain quite a lot of information in members' homes, away from surveillance by the leaders.

In the indigenous context, I had to change the research method somewhat, since the questionnaires elicited either silence or extremely enigmatic replies. I then opted for informal conversations, disguising the themes in which I was most interested.

All the churches researched were founded by Mexicans and had no links with foreigners (except for occasional help with building or special campaigns, in the case of some neopentecostal and historical churches). Due to the strong migratory process to the United States or to other parts of Mexico, it was common to find fragmented families and problems of marital stability. The worship services usually had a large majority of women. Of those interviewed (I make no claim to a representative sample), about half had been converted within the last eight years. About a quarter had religiously mixed families in which not all the family members were evangelicals; this was especially the case in the indigenous area. There were cases in which, for instance, the mother was pentecostal, her husband was Catholic, the grandmother was a Jehovah's Witness, the daughter was an Adventist, and the son had no religion. I also found cases in which a migrant joined, for example, a historical Protestant church in his distant place of work but when back in his place of origin reverted to Catholicism or became a pentecostal.

Evangelicals and the Construction of Democracy

My aim in this section is to explore how evangelical faith contributes to democracy in the three types of evangelical churches examined (historical, pentecostal, and neopentecostal) and in the three regions chosen (urban, rural, and indigenous). I do this by looking at the practices of believers in contexts of worship, letting these evangelical voices speak for themselves as much as possible. Worship services often constitute a defining moment in which believers conceive and mold their everyday attitudes and behavior.

The Pentecostals

In pentecostal services, a privileged place goes to testimonies given as a sort of voluntary public confession by believers who wish to give them. These testimonies usually have to do with diverse responses to personal or family problems for which divine help has been solicited. By means of these testimonies, believers share not only models of discourse regarding religious experience but also practices for ordering their priorities in everyday life according to the congregation's expectations.

An example of such a testimony comes from an urban pentecostal woman, a member of a congregation of about eighty people, mostly office workers in commercial establishments or the civil service. Concha has been an evangelical for about twelve years, is divorced, and works as a secretary, and she gave this testimony in a prayer meeting.

> We evangelicals should not lose a single opportunity for testifying to what God does in our lives. Yesterday, my neighbor complained that my son had broken a vase with his ball. I didn't like the way he spoke to me and I told him that wasn't the way to ask me to repay the damage. My neighbor got furious and asked what use it was for me to go to church if I was the same or worse as the rest. His words hurt me a lot. Feeling sad, I started praying for God to calm me down, and as I did it I remembered the experiences of faith that I have had and how I have felt God's presence in my life in difficult moments. As I did so, I recovered my confidence in the one I believe in. Glory to God! This raised my self-esteem and my commitment as an evangelical to honor God in each moment of my life, and show other people in whom I believe through my conduct and my actions, to be and do the best that I can everywhere I go. So I immediately repaired the damage caused and even bought a present for my neighbor and said I was sorry.

Bartolo, an Indian pentecostal man, founded a congregation that now has about thirty members, all of them very poor. The church uses the Náhuatl language. He describes his conversion thus:

> I couldn't say anything without swearing; there wasn't one phrase where I didn't use a bad word. I used to tell myself I would change my vocabulary, but everybody just laughed at me. But when Jesus came into my life, my way of speaking started to change in such a

way that now I am surprised myself at how correctly I speak. Now, I respect other people and they respect me. Wherever I go, people greet me and I reply with good words.

Another testimony is that of Lucila, a member of an indigenous pentecostal church with about 170 members. She studied only up to the third year of primary school. When she was converted to pentecostalism, she received the Holy Spirit and began exercising the gift of healing. This has given her the respect of her husband and also higher social status as her work has been recognized by many people. It has also allowed her to improve her financial situation somewhat with the presents she receives in exchange for her healings. She says:

> I married at fifteen and was converted when I was eighteen. About two years later I was in a service and the pastor baptized me, and I felt something falling on me.... My body was shaken by the Holy Spirit. The pastor took me by the hand and said: "Daughter, you have been anointed by the Spirit and have received the gift of healing. Take care of this gift at all costs, because you are going to suffer, but God will act through you." Since I received the power of the Holy Spirit, I began to fast and pray for the sick.... I try to be humble and not proud, and the Lord keeps me busy. One day in the church I prayed for some sick children and they got well, and from then on people believed in me. When someone has sin, the Lord tells me: "Tell so-and-so to repent." I do so, and they accept it, because they recognize that the Holy Spirit speaks to me, that I have the power of discernment and can explain dreams.... That is why some brothers love me and others hate me.... Even at church they criticize me and say my gift is not from God.... Previously, my husband used to beat me, but since God anointed me with his power everything has changed and my home has improved. When anyone is blessed, they eat better. I tell the Lord: "You can see what I need." Soon, some brother comes and brings me beans, rice, sugar...I never ask for money, but if someone wants to give me something, I don't refuse.

During the prayer times of rural and urban pentecostals, I detected religious attitudes that take an interest in political problems. Sometimes, God's intervention is requested to help the government find solutions to the problems of violence, insecurity, and poverty. I heard various urban pentecostal congregations interceding for successful negotiations with the Zapatista guerrillas of the Ejército Zapatista de Liberación Nacional (EZLN, Zapatista Army of National Liberation), whether or not those believers knew what the Zapatistas wanted. Generally those types of prayer occur in prayer meetings and only rarely (for example, at election times) in the Sunday services. An example of such a prayer follows. It was made by Luis, an Assemblies of God member living in the outskirts of a city. Luis is a stonelayer and has organized the building committee of the church. Since he listens to the radio all day while working, he knows about the main problems the country faces and how difficult it is for governments to solve most problems. He prayed thus:

> Lord, I ask for your intervention in the talks which the EZLN will be having with the government. May both sides be ruled by a spirit of peace and common feeling. I ask for the Indians who suffer hunger and lack of work. Especially, I ask for our brothers who are being forced off their lands for preaching your word. God, keep them firm. Your word says we are blessed when for your sake we are cursed and persecuted. Blessed be God! Praise him!

Another example of a prayer on political themes comes from Yolanda, a member of a pentecostal church in a rural area. She is a housewife and has been converted for about eight years. She was converted through her husband, and both of them speak in tongues. I present a few fragments of a prayer relating to corruption and social inequality.

> God, we know that we are living in the last times and that for
> that reason evil is multiplying. Lord, we feel very sad about the evils
> that are weighing on our society. So we ask you at this time, in the
> name of Jesus Christ, to change those hearts that harbor injustice, corruption, violence, hatred, and evil. Change them! You have
> the power to do it, Lord! You made us perfect, but through our own
> sin and capricious will, through our forgetfulness of your word, we
> suffer these consequences as human beings. Have mercy, Lord!
> Help us to preach your word and by doing so little by little to combat
> sin.

We note here her desire for a change in attitudes and ways of thinking that cause harm to society, and also her belief that the way she and the church can contribute to the desired change is through preaching the biblical message.

Returning to the organizational structure of pentecostal churches, we see that tithes and offerings are given not only in money but also in kind (in wood, bricks, sand, etc.) and in work (bricklaying, painting, cleaning). Nearly everything goes to building the church and very little to the pastor, who usually supports himself through his other work. The organization of these churches is usually through a governing body elected democratically by the members. This is illustrated by the case that one informant described to me of the dismissal of a pastor from an indigenous pentecostal church of some 170 members, in a very "politicized" atmosphere. The very same space in which the liturgy had taken place was transformed into a debating room.

That day, the pastor could not imagine that it would be the last Sunday service he would lead. Before the end of the service, a brother in the church got up and asked the leaders of the congregation to stay behind to look into a delicate matter. Almost nobody wanted to leave, and after the blessing the pastor sat down in the front pews. The brother who had asked people to stay started speaking and said: "Brothers, we have asked you to stay because we wanted to tell you that we have proof that pastor Juan Salas is living in adultery, and this is a great offense to our God and to our congregation." Some of the brothers already knew about this, but others were surprised and waited to see what attitude the pastor would take. He just bent down with his arms resting on his knees and let people speak. Another brother got up and told the place and the day he had seen the pastor committing adultery. The pastor's wife, crying, said it was all slander. The atmosphere got heavier and heavier, and some members started to shout out: "Hypocrite! How can you preach like that?!" Finally the pastor got up and said: "Only God is going to judge me, not all of you. I shall leave my ministry here and may God help you." Then the pastor left, with his wife and children, amid shouts of "Adulterer! Hypocrite!" Some of us kept silence, because the pastor had worked hard and helped many of us in difficult times. When he had gone, the brothers who had pressed for his dismissal began to plan what they were going to do. Some said they should tell the authorities in the city so they could send another pastor. Responsibilities were divided up so that the church activities should not stop.

Generally pentecostal churches lack an organizational manual or set of disciplinary regulations. Where they do exist, they have usually been brought in from other churches, which are generally situated in the cities. In their absence, the rules are decided upon by the pastor or the leaders, often in conjunction with the members. The spiritual leaders, without much theological elaboration or complex institutional schemes, organize the congregation in whatever seems the most logical way. Anyone can become a leader of a congregation just by being self-taught and willing to put himself or herself forward. Very few churches exclude women from pastoral leadership. A basic requirement of leaders is to have received a "call," "heard the voice of God," and been "baptized in the Holy Spirit," the proof of which is manifested in the exercise of spiritual gifts. The believers usually act within a radius based on physical proximity and ties of kinship or friendship. Their proselytism and their most effective social actions happen around the residences of the most dynamic members.

The interpretation of everyday action in light of the written word of the Bible is the most influential practice carried out in these churches. Members emphasize the importance of staying as close as possible to the Bible and Christian teachings recommended by the leaders who seek to maintain "doctrinal purity" and avoid involvement with social principles and values from outside the church. At the same time, obtaining and exercising spiritual gifts requires a strict discipline of prayer and fasting that leaves little time for other activities.

Pentecostals in rural and indigenous areas have meetings every day and all day on Sundays, leaving little time for social and political activity. They behave virtually as an extended family, with intense sociability.

With regard to opinions concerning social and political affairs, there is diversity within each of the three contexts. Some see the religious and the political as distinct spheres that should not be mixed. Don Emilio, a pentecostal from the MIEPI churches, explains the relationship thus: "Those of us who have God in our lives do not have to go about seeking anything at all from the government, nor wasting our time with politics. The word of God is one thing, and politics is something totally different."

However, a minority of pentecostals are in favor of involvement in political affairs, as long as these do not lessen one's interest in divine things. According to Esteban, an indigenous pentecostal peasant, "If we have God we shall respect our family, we shall respect the government, pay our taxes, respect everything. If we do not have God, we are enemies of our government. As long as we know how to give to God what is God's and to Caesar what is Caesar's, there is no problem." This expresses a tendency to behave as *believers* rather than as *believers and citizens*, in the sense that religious identity is seen as all-consuming and exclusive.

One interview illustrates such a concept of politics and political involvement. Cruz is the founder of an Assemblies of God congregation in a rural area, currently with about 150 members. Cruz maintains his family by citriculture and dedicates all his free time to the church.

> "*Do you believe that God chooses the authorities or that people choose them by election?*"
>
> "The Bible says that the authorities are designated by God. Those whom God has not chosen to govern will not win even if people vote for him. He who wins, wins because God has determined that he will. He owes his election to God, not to men."
>
> "*So God permitted the PRD to govern in this locality?*"
>
> "The one whom God determines has to win, whether he is PRI, PAN, or PRD."
>
> "*This time you voted for the PRD and the PRI won, isn't that right?*"
>
> "God decides on the authorities, and even though this time we voted for the PRD, that candidate was not destined by God, and so the PRI won. Now we have to accept it."

"Do you support Fox even though he is a Catholic?"

"We have entered a new phase. Now it is the turn of the PAN to govern with Fox, but their turn will not be like the PRI's turn that lasted seventy years. Now it will last about twelve years. God imposes limits, because we are already in the last times, and that is why the empires are crumbling; they can't last seventy years like they used to. As for support, of course we support him, because he is the winner, he is the father of the nation, and everyone has to obey his mandate, even though I have heard prophecies that he will try to unify the churches because that is what the Vatican wants. Didn't you see him when he went to the Basilica [of the Virgin of Guadalupe] before his inauguration? He went to pray to the statue. That is why we evangelicals are praying. God is powerful and for him nothing is impossible. We are confident that God will free us from the persecutions, and even though these have been prophesied, he will not allow them. We have to obey his word, remain in constant prayer, and expect his mercy so that this does not happen."

"As an evangelical what can you do to contribute to the common good?"

"As Christians, what we have to do is to do good, work, avoid sin. When we don't do that, people begin to criticize.... That is why many parties decay just like religions. We must seek justice, but not the justice of men but of God. Jesus did not open his mouth, he never defended himself against injustice. He won out, because he went to be with his Father. A Christian is not allowed to judge whether a government does good or does evil. In politics, there are lies; the politicians say: 'Look, don't believe in this for this or that reason'; and another says the same things about his adversary. They say they will help you, they make promises, and when they come to power they forget what they have promised; it is all lies. Liars will not enter the kingdom of God."

We can affirm that, in the case of the pentecostals, their otherworldly theology leads them to see politics as a matter of human community, a horizontal relationship that seeks to ensure that society goes on its way normally, while religion is a transcendental question that is above everything, whatever the context. That is why we can find a fairly homogeneous posture among pentecostals in all three contexts (urban, rural, and indigenous), which suggests that the theological type counts for much in evangelical political positions. In other words, among pentecostals, reflection on political participation is based on pentecostalism's own doctrines and theological convictions, and it is only where political space is too limited and they suffer direct political aggression that pentecostals get involved in social and political movements.

The Neopentecostals

Neopentecostal worship services often take place in nontraditional settings, such as restaurants, cinemas, hotels, or clubs. There are also meetings in homes, often called "prayer cells." Testimonies are important, as in pentecostal churches, but they often reflect the "prosperity theology" current in neopentecostalism, referring to the practical and effective answers to personal problems that believers have experienced. Neopentecostals tend to seek a practical Christianity that gives answers to the economic crisis and the crisis of values and meaning. An example is the testimony of a neopentecostal believer from the Christian Friendship church.

> I am a primary school teacher. Last week there was a women's congress where they gave us counsel about how to handle the situation when our husbands get irritated with us for going to church meetings. I used to be one of those who get rebellious when not allowed to come. There, they taught me that I shouldn't contradict my husband, because he is the head of the home, that I should be in subjection because I can get more by good ways than by bad. When my husband saw that I didn't contradict what he told me to do, I managed to get him to agree not only for me to come more frequently but even for him to come with me. Another thing they have taught me is that I should respect those who do not have the same faith as I have. Previously, when the Jehovah's Witnesses called at my door, I got angry and I told them I wasn't interested in listening or in getting their propaganda. Sometimes I didn't even open the door. Now, I politely tell them that I have a direct relationship with God and I thank them for their visit. They understand and respect me as well. I have also learned from the experience of others about better ways to administer a house, to resolve the common problems of the couple in the home. I have even learned some teaching techniques that I have applied with my pupils in primary school. In the congregation I get ideas about how to live in society, with my family and at my work. It makes me reflect and learn from my errors and my responsibilities and to seek and develop new ways of doing things with people who are my equals.

To the question of whether she would like the leaders of her church to take part in politics, she replied:

> Yes, as long as it is within God's plans, since politics can make God-fearing people get lost. When it is the will of God, everything has a purpose. Maybe through that politician we can have access to

television to preach and present the message to the multitudes. They would be honest people, not like the politicians who have no divine direction. They would have better opinions regarding our municipality; they would combat egotism and would motivate us to multiply our prayers to combat injustices. For us, the parties do not matter; it is the people who matter, although the best people are in the main parties, which is why many of us vote for the PRI, the PAN and the PRD.

When I asked this woman if the believers could do anything else besides pray, she answered: "Prayer is the only response of the congregation, and God is the one who solves everything through it. Of course, together with our prayer we need to evangelize and give testimony. God wants a prosperous country in economic and spiritual terms, full of love."

As can be seen, prayer has an essential function in this view. It is regarded as a form of political praxis, by means of which evangelical believers participate for the good of Mexico. Praying does not happen in a decontextualized way, nor is it purely ecclesiastical, but it reflects the believer's social awareness in interrelationship with his or her fellow human beings. It manifests the believer's social experiences, the desire to be not only spiritual but a basically social being. It is a task mandated by God, by which believers defend justice, peace, and democracy. And it is a task that is open to all who embrace it, regardless of their social status, and with or without the approval of church leaders. It would seem that, in comparison with other evangelical churches, prayer is given an even higher status. While it is important to "save souls," it is even more important to transform them into "prayer warriors."

The Historical Churches

In the historical churches, the services follow one of two broad types: traditional or charismatic. The former have a well-defined liturgy, while the latter (more and more frequent) are a mixture of elements from the traditional service and the spontaneity of the neopentecostals.

Due to their earlier arrival in the country and their generally more middle-class social composition, the historical churches see themselves as part of society and as pioneers of new relations between the evangelical churches and the Mexican state. In comparison with the pentecostals and neopentecostals, the historical churches are the most interested in new ways of relating to the state. In the 2000 presidential elections, it was leaders from the historical churches who were most often in contact with the candidates. Educational levels and theology both contribute to this: their theology tends to be less otherworldly than that of the pentecostals. In their meetings with candidates, the pastors were most concerned about questions of freedom of worship, religious intolerance, access to mass media, and changes in educational curricula.

According to Francisco, a longtime member of a Baptist church in a Náhuatl-speaking indigenous context, "each believer regards politics according to his own convictions, which may be that it is good or evil. Good, because it can influence the population; bad, because politics can lead the believer to give it more importance than he gives to God."

Jonás Flores, a PRI deputy for Nayarit, described his relationship with politics in the following way: "Politics has been the love of my life. Before I was converted, it was everything for me. But after my conversion, I had a new order of priorities: God first, my family next, and then politics. I am still full-time in politics, but thank God I manage to balance my duties to God and my public duties."

Some opinions of believers in historical churches in the three contexts studied show the way they conceive of their political participation.

> "We are immersed in the dynamics of this country and we can't withdraw."
>
> "God has allowed us to open wide the doors in the question of religious freedom and legal status of churches, so we should participate actively in all areas of development of the country."
>
> "We evangelicals have always applauded those in power. We applauded Salinas, Zedillo, and now Fox. We don't have any criterion. When the politicians fail, we evangelicals are silent; we are incapable of criticizing whoever is in power."
>
> "In my village, where the majority are evangelicals, the municipal presidents ask permission of the church to be absent because of the political commitment they have to fulfil, and after their three years they return and ask pardon for everything they have done. Which means that as evangelicals we are not giving a good testimony."

The Three Currents in the Three Contexts

Thus far, I have presented the typical characteristics of the three expressions of evangelicalism (historical, pentecostal, and neopentecostal) in the three contexts (urban, rural, and indigenous). Now I shall try to delineate the similarities and differences between them.

It is obviously impossible to speak of Mexican evangelicals as a homogeneous mass, despite a common tendency to reference the Bible. This constant practice of linking the Bible with one's everyday tasks is especially noticeable among the groups that have the greatest number of meetings and thus greater intensity of religious life. This is a factor both of context and theological type: frequent attendance at church meetings is greater among pentecostals than neopentecostals, and among the latter than among the historicals. But it is also, across the theological types, greater in indigenous areas than mestizo rural areas, and in the latter than in the urban areas.

Pentecostal groups focus their attention on biblical commands and on an apocalyptic vision. Political involvement is thus difficult to find, at least as an endogenous force, since for them politics means "being separated from the activities of the kingdom of God" and thus wasting one's time with "the things of this world." Nevertheless, political involvement can be triggered by exogenous forces, leading the believer to mix and adapt his or her biblical principles. Here, pentecostal faith moves in a tension between context and theological type, producing political action that sometimes relates more to the context and one's own needs, and at other times to the theology of the group. In other words, at times they act more as *believers* and at other times more as *citizens*. Perhaps the most significant contribution of pentecostals to democracy has been the dissemination and diversification of evangelical religion in rural and indigenous areas.

In neopentecostal groups, and in some historical groups with charismatic tendencies, attention is focused on a prosperity theology in which solving everyday problems and obtaining a new lifestyle are crucial components. In these cases, elements of importance to pentecostals, such as the mode of attire, are no longer important. Political involvement is conceived, in contrast to the conception of the pentecostals, as part of God's plan. Prayer is understood as more than asking for gifts and healing; it includes asking for wisdom and vision for extending Christian principles and values and asking God to raise up people of faith in the political field. Here, the theological type attempts to embrace everything and avoid the tensions pentecostalism suffers. Ritual means, such as forms of prayer, are used to control both private and public behavior. The public behavior of this neopentecostal faith can be described as that of a *citizenly believer*, seeing justice and democracy as divine mandates. Neopentecostal social location in cities has produced a greater pluralism among evangelicals, opening the door to a more diverse membership and drawing from the middle and upper strata of society.

Among the more traditional historical churches, we find an ordered, methodical religious life that requires biblical and doctrinal knowledge and inculcates a life of high ethical and moral values in believers. Here, political involvement is defined more by context than by the theological type. The public behavior of historicals can be defined as that of the *citizenly believer* in the case of those more influenced by charismatic tendencies, and as *believing citizen* in the case of the more traditional. The most significant contribution of the historical evangelicals to democracy is the capacity at times to generate a posture of critical commitment in the face of corruption, injustice, and fatalism.

Correlations and Connections

In this final section, I try to see how evangelical faith connects to political attitudes and actions, and to analyze its relevance in the construction of democracy. To this end, I observe how evangelical attitudes can be transformed into social capital and, subsequently, into political action.

Several studies (e.g., Burdick 1993; Freston 2001; C. Smith 1994; Woodberry 1999) suggest an important role for evangelicals in processes of democratization. At the same time, Coleman (1988) and Putnam (1993) suggest that religious associations can generate, in civil society, what they term "social capital," a set of moral resources or expectations that motivate greater cooperation between individuals, producing the trust, norms, and networks that make it feasible to carry out certain activities that would otherwise be impossible (Putnam 1993, 169). If we add to that the fact that urban popular sectors and peasants have traditionally been short of civil associations, we can see the importance of the role of religious associations in Mexican society. It is at this micro level that evangelicals are most contributing to democracy.

The religious practices that I have described, such as prayer, fasting, attendance at worship services, Bible reading, proselytism, and social work, are all opportunities for believers to internalize principles, values, and concepts and generate habits of behavior and models of collective action that can afterward be applied in other areas of their lives. Evangelicals who cannot read and write feel motivated to learn; they now dedicate considerable time to studying the Bible and taking courses in doctrine, evangelism, and Christian education. Participating almost daily in meetings, they become integrated into community life. Eager to share their faith, they walk long distances and build relationships that extend beyond the local community. When I asked a bilingual teacher from the Apostolic Faith church in an indigenous area whether he thought he participated more in social activities since his conversion, he replied:

> Yes, because in a dialogue such as I am having with you I can introduce the things of God. Before my conversion, I would get very anxious if I had to speak to people I didn't know. But now I can do it without fear, because I know I will present the word of God, and God will put words into my mouth and give me wisdom to answer difficult questions like the ones you are asking me. I only speak of the love of God, and that makes us have lots of friends who later become our brothers.

Practicing "life in the Spirit" means having an interest in obtaining spiritual gifts, a clear manifestation of the Holy Spirit in one's life, which leads to achieving a higher status among believers. In the case of women, it means obtaining greater self-esteem and recognition from the family, now not only as wife and mother but as spiritual guide. It provides a space in which believers construct and express a sense of personal and community dignity, and develop leadership skills such as speaking in public, organizing, negotiating, cooperating, planning, and evaluating. It also generates a sense of responsibility. Most of the evangelicals I interviewed were concerned to make me understand that before conversion their lives had either been chaotic or boring, but that since conversion they had quickly come to occupy important positions in their congregations, a fact that had radically transformed their lives. They had gone from being passive to being active, from lacking responsibilities to faithfully carrying out responsibilities. Conversion is lived as a process of finding a social place.

The importance of Bible reading, and of the discursive elaboration regarding the Bible that is developed to motivate the faithful, stimulates people not only to learn to read and write but also to structure coherent and convincing ideas and to communicate directly with individuals and with larger groups, as well as to participate in discussions with other people in the defense and dissemination of their faith. Similarly, degrees of authority are obtained as people make themselves responsible for certain activities and committees. Faithfulness and "consecration" helps build self-esteem in people who would be unlikely to attain it in society as a whole or in larger churches. The examples I have given of women in rural and indigenous congregations are typical of how these women manage to experience independence and power in a world full of ethnic, cultural, and sexist discrimination. The words of a rural Methodist woman illustrate this.

> As my husband is an alcoholic, I have to work to support my three children. I sell clothes that I bring from Mexico City; after the worship services, I discreetly offer my wares to the members. I also visit most members of the congregation regularly, since I sell them clothes on credit. During these visits, I get to know about their problems and I pray for them. Praying in their homes has made me feel their affection for me, which makes me very happy and encourages me to increase my own faithfulness and commitment to God and the church. The brothers who know about my economic situation help me, giving me things for my children. Recently, they elected me leader of the prayer meetings.

A female primary school teacher from the same church told me: "In the church I learned how to treat adolescent rebelliousness, to be responsible in my commitments, to write summaries, to lose the fear of speaking in public, to lead a service, to make an outline."

On the other hand, evangelicals can help generate a critical attitude in the face of corruption, injustice, lies, oppression, fatalism, and passivity, because in the act of conversion they "break" with their past and try to correct all that is evil in the eyes of God, putting on a new identity. However, there is the risk of a lack of interest in political participation because people do not wish to be accomplices to "sins." The testimony of a neopentecostal leader illustrates this; he gave up his career in law to dedicate himself to the ministry of music in his congregation: "I used to earn a lot of money by accompanying the politicians on their campaign tours . . . I learned how to cheat and to make dirty deals. Then one day, I got fed up and left all this dirty atmosphere and handed my time over to the Lord. Now I am calm, I am with my family and, most importantly, I am serving the Lord."

A Baptist peasant told me:

> We understand that we have to obey, but not in everything, because God does not make the laws. Rather, the laws are made in the cor- ridors of congress, behind the scenes. As long as there is peace and justice is sought, we shall obey; but if the government tries to change the laws and harm our religion, we shall defend ourselves. We want to be respected.

Most evangelicals interviewed agree that practicing the faith makes a cit- izen more aware of his or her responsibilities in society, since the gospel frees from "sin," promoting values and principles that are more related to the com- mon good. In fact, believers affirm the importance of political participation for the sake of greater religious freedom and the welfare of the community. As an urban Presbyterian put it:

> Politics, the parties, the state and the government may not be dirty, but just like the air and the water they get contaminated by sin. So we evangelicals need to decontaminate each one of these spheres. We must overcome the idea that we can transform Mexico by honesty, frugality, and hard work, because this clashes with the reality of poverty and inequality in this country. We need to seek social jus- tice, democracy, education, and fight against poverty.

Other evangelicals, however, enchanted with their religious identity and community, see no further than their own congregations.

The evangelical churches sometimes form a sort of alternative institutio- nal structure to the state, with a strong global orientation. As a Baptist be- liever told me:

> The services of the church are like a little window which allows me a view of the world around. I find out about what is going on in Af- ghanistan, Israel, the United States and Latin America, in Chiapas, in Ixmiquilpan, in my own society. Here we speak of scientific, political, social and cultural themes; we reason about the human, the practical, the moral, the divine, and we do it together, in a way that is accessible to all the members of the congregation. We seek solutions to our

problems, alternatives for our society. We almost always reach the conclusion that as long as there is no change in the human heart we shall have great difficulty in responding to individual and collective problems. That is why we evangelicals insist so much on presenting the message of salvation so that God may change people's hearts.

The attitudes generated inside the evangelical services have a moral dimension that empowers democracy with an ethic of the common good. They create a normative authority and a set of values that can put a break on the pathologies of modernization and guarantee responsible and other-oriented participation. This can help restore the control that has often been diminished by bureaucracy and the uncertainty of a state that does not really guarantee anything. As an urban Presbyterian said, "All my workmates know I am an evangelical, and that obliges me to improve in everything (to arrive on time for my commitments, carry out my work well, have a good character, be responsible, speak and think positively)." Or, in the words of a peasant man who is now a pentecostal lay preacher, "If God had not reached out to me, I would perhaps now be lying in the street drunk and my family would certainly have left me to my own fate. That is why, every time I see an alcoholic, I share my experience with him and help him to face up to his situation with his family, and I try to instill confidence in a better future, the hope that with God everything is possible."

The examination of evangelical attitudes and practices uncovers tendencies that are favorable to democracy, even though it also uncovers apolitical tendencies. But if it is possible to detect values favorable to democracy within the group, they are not always very obvious to the outside world, especially in the case of the more proselytizing groups. While the evangelical churches have been appropriate locales for learning and practicing the norms and behaviors that are indispensable to democracy (including debates, assemblies, agreements, voting, etc.), they have not yet created a widespread social impact or affected the functioning of the state. For nonevangelical Mexicans, it is not yet obvious that evangelical religion produces the associative experience that Tocqueville saw as so vital to American democracy in the 1830s.

Being evangelical and developing one's abilities can generate political involvement; it can also lead to a resigned attitude toward conditions of oppression and injustice, which is lethal to democracy. In the opinion of one rural pentecostal pastor,

> God put Vicente Fox there, and if one day he fails it is because God is allowing that. We recognize his authority and we hope that if God allowed him to become president it is because he is a good person. We shall never doubt the civil and military authorities because the Bible declares that they are appointed by God. We shall always pray for our authorities and obey the law of Mexico. In our religion

we have no time to get into trouble or into other people's problems, much less into politics and speaking badly of the government. We have to agree with the law of our authorities, because fulfilling that law we are fulfilling the law of God.... The way of politics is very dangerous and can make us fall into sin. So we prefer not to participate, except for voting in elections; but we don't judge, we are neutral.

None of the churches studied mandates a specific political orientation for its members. They leave it up to their members to act according to their convictions and consciences. Considering the confrontations that evangelicals still have with the Catholic Church in some areas of the country, and under Vicente Fox, a president who declared himself to be an active Catholic and raised a banner of the Virgin of Guadalupe in his campaign, it is perhaps not surprising that most churches should be cautious about expressing any political leanings.

Meanwhile, evangelicals attempt to overcome the pejorative epithets and inferior status that both the dominant religion and many social scientific studies have pinned on them. They no longer accept the idea of being catalogued as "sects," "dissidents," or even "Protestants," much less as the scandalous "alleluias." They want better social status and equal treatment in the public sphere. To this end, they have begun to convene press conferences just like the Catholic hierarchy, to express their opinions on certain measures and demands. They have also started to forge closer links with institutions and associations of civil society, with a view to achieving greater stature and freedom in both the religious and public spheres.

In conclusion, evangelicals in Mexico continue to be an increasingly fragmented minority, but with an intense community life that generates promising social capital, which at the micro level has a decisive influence but still has only a limited role in the political arena. They lack a clearly defined political project, oscillating according to the space the political system permits them (Fortuny 1994, 422).

Evangelical faith in Mexico operates with three models of political action. The first of these we can call *sectarian* (in the strict sociological sense) and operates with the logic of the *believer*, pure and simple. The second may be called *transformative* and operates with the logic of the *citizenly believer*, in which the evangelical aims to transform reality from the standpoint of the religious perspective. The third model is *adaptive*, in which the evangelical acts with the logic of the *believing citizen* and political, social, and economic reality determines the perspective to be adopted. The first two tendencies, as we have seen, are the predominant ones. Nevertheless, in all of them there is a desire to go beyond one's own interests and be socially and politically responsible in the search for peace and solidarity.

Evangelicals are opening up new spaces. They are getting involved in civil organizations such as human rights groups, in ecological organizations, in various political parties, in institutions entrusted with the welfare of the family, education, health, protection of abused children, and in guerrilla movements like the Zapatistas. In doing this, many denominational barriers begin to crumble. This may one day enable the reserves of social capital that Mexican evangelicals have accumulated to be brought more readily and widely into the country's political life.

2

From War to Reconciliation: Guatemalan Evangelicals and the Transition to Democracy, 1982–2001

C. Mathews Samson

The antidemocratic character of the Guatemalan political tradition has its roots in an economic structure characterized by the concentration of productive goods in a few hands. On that basis, a regime of multiple exclusions is established, to which were added the elements of a racist culture that is, in its turn, the most profound expression of a system of violent and dehumanizing social relations. The State slowly articulated itself as an instrument to safeguard this structure, guaranteeing the persistence of exclusion and injustice.
—Comisión para el Esclarecimiento Histórico,
Guatemala, memoria del silencio (1999, 17)

The past two decades have been a time of intense social and political turmoil in Guatemala. They encompass the most brutal part of a thirty-six-year internal war in which some two hundred thousand people lost their lives, a return to democratic civilian governance in 1986, a peace process culminating in the formal end to the civil war in December 1996, and the subsequent shaky process of institutionalizing aspects of the peace process in the past five years. Institutionalizing peace requires a process of democratization that, in turn, requires a broad range of participation from citizens. Participation includes space for pressing demands for social justice and for the formation of coalitions that can organize against the most pernicious forms of exclusion, such as those sketched in the epigraph, as described by the Commission for Historical Clarification (Comisión para el Esclarecimiento Histórico, CEH), established by the 1994 Oslo Accord between the Guatemalan government and the Unidad Revolucionaria Nacional Guatemalteca.

In this context, this chapter examines the contributions of evangelicals to the consolidation of democracy in that strife-torn nation. I argue that, despite the pluralism within the Protestant community of Guatemala, there is considerable ambiguity when considering whether or not evangelicals make a positive contribution to democratic consolidation. While the diversity of political perspectives within the evangelical community points toward a type of participation in civil society that leans in the direction of democratization, the meaning of Protestantism's ties to the country's power structure remains highly ambivalent.[1]

Given ongoing stereotypes of evangelicals and concern about the specter of religious fundamentalism in many parts of the world, it is difficult to find assessments of evangelicals and politics in Latin America that are not overly optimistic, excessively critical, or simply uninformed about evangelical pluralism.[2] This chapter's focus on the political context and the social location of evangelical political actors contributes a case study to the growing literature on the role evangelicals play in Latin American politics. The nexus examined is the relationship of evangelical faith to the political activities of the people interviewed. While the theory of democracy and the political context of Guatemala provide a frame for analysis, an intentional effort is made to hear the voices of Guatemalan evangelicals as they themselves make sense of their public roles.

The 1982 starting point for this examination is selected because the sixteen-month period from March 1982 to August 1983, coinciding with the presidency of General Efraín Ríos Montt, following a *coup d'état* by junior military officers, saw some of the most brutal violence during Guatemala's counterinsurgency campaign. Ríos Montt's presidency was remarkable not only because of its violence but also because he was an evangelical Christian. As a conservative evangelical with ties to the religious right in the United States during the early Reagan years, Ríos Montt became something of a poster boy for the perception on the part of progressives that Latin American Protestantism contributed to state authoritarianism in the midst of the political and social turmoil in Central America. In addition, 1982 marked the centennial year of Protestantism's formal entrance into Guatemala, with celebrations that culminated in an October rally in Guatemala City led by the prominent Argentine evangelist Luis Palau.[3]

In the larger context of the study of religion in Latin America, Ríos Montt's presidency drew attention to the issue of evangelicals and politics during a time of rapid evangelical growth throughout the region. It was also the heyday in the Catholic Church of liberation theology and *comunidades eclesiales de base* (CEBs; ecclesial base communities). The national security state was on the eve of being replaced throughout the region by democratic governments, part of the "third wave" of democracy throughout the world (Huntington 1996). The image of a self-professing Christian general presiding over a genocidal military in a poor Central American country victimized by military aid from the "colossus of the North" fed directly into stereotypical interpretations of a monolithically conservative Protestantism invading Latin America as an agent of cultural and political imperialism emanating from the United States.

Even more nuanced investigations into Protestant growth in Latin America began to employ the term "fundamentalist"as a catchall for the vast majority of evangelicals. The corollary has been the assumption that evangelicals were directly supportive of United States policy in the region or apolitical altogether. As will be demonstrated, too much attention to Ríos Montt as representative of evangelicals in Guatemala hinders understanding of the plurality of evangelical expression. Furthermore, Pilar Sanchíz Ochoa notes how Ríos Montt's use of discursive symbols and the meaning of such symbols varied through time so that, "according to the circumstances, [his] biblical images are presented in a different form" (1998, 24).

Guatemala is a special case by virtue of having the highest percentage of evangelicals in Latin America, and the highest percentage of indigenous people in its population. The Maya represent some twenty-one language groups and between 55 and 60 percent of the population. Despite this demographic dominance, the Maya have been excluded from political and social power since Guatemala obtained independence from Spain in 1821 after nearly three hundred years of colonialism. Inequitable social relations in a context of ethnic pluralism are exacerbated by huge disparities of wealth, which together cause the indigenous population to have one of the lowest standards of living in the Western Hemisphere. At the same time, a new activism has taken hold under the rubric of the Maya Movement that has at its core the demand for a national political culture that is "multiethnic, pluricultural, and multilingual" (Fischer and Brown 1996; Gálvez Borrell and Choy 1997).

Setting the Stage

My approach to evangelicals and democracy assumes that social actors bring a diversity of religious and other commitments to the political arena. In addition, it assumes a diversity of belief and practice among Guatemalan evangelicals. One cue for my analysis comes from Wuthnow's view of religion as "a codified set of concepts and categories that is evident in discourse, reinforced by practical commitments, and advanced in institutional settings" (1992, 129). Any analysis of religion's political consequences must examine both the discourse and the practical commitments of religious actors in the public arena. Also, my approach includes a definition of democracy that encompasses not only free and fair elections but also participation of the citizenry in political processes. Contrary to the image of evangelicals seeking a mandate from God and the people to impose their will on the populace, an alternative perspective views Latin American evangelical communities as providing space for voluntary associations to function as actors within civil society. As such, they certainly have the potential to help strengthen civil society and develop a more substantial democracy than is possible on the basis of elections alone. The implications of this are succinctly stated by Ireland:

> the Latin American religious "infrastructure" plays an important role in molding "popular subjects" imbued with "an ethic of public involvement" and the capacity to propose alternatives to authoritarianism and clientelism. The result is an increasingly textured and nonhierarchical associational life, an essential ingredient in the emergence of a civic community. (1999, 7)

It should be emphasized that the scope of Ireland's work is the more inclusive category of "popular religions." His case studies of what he calls "the Tocquevillian parallel" are drawn from Catholicism, pentecostalism, and Afro-Brazilian religions. It is true that, in these examples and in those of evangelicals in Guatemala, there remains evidence of authoritarianism and clientelism. However, the sheer diversity of evangelical political actors in Guatemala points to a vibrant and flourishing "civic community."

Situating evangelical political actors in the context of contemporary perspectives on democratization globally, Diamond's use of "liberal democracy" provides more space for consideration of political actors than what he terms "electoral democracy." He envisions a continuum beyond "a civilian, constitutional system in which the legislative and chief executive offices are filled through regular, competitive, multiparty elections with universal suffrage" (1999, 10). Liberal democracy has additional constraints upon the exercise of power such as "the absence of reserved domains of power for the military or other actors not accountable to the electorate" and a requirement that leaders in governmental branches be horizontally accountable to other office-holders. A third characteristic of liberal democracy is the most relevant for this chapter: "extensive provisions for political and civic pluralism as well as for individual and group freedoms, so that contending interests and values may be expressed and compete through ongoing processes of articulation and representation, beyond periodic elections" (1999, 10–11).

Despite some direct involvement in electoral politics by individuals and groups, the vast majority of political action by evangelicals in Guatemala falls in the realm of expressing "interests and values" in response to items on the national political agenda. Since the signing of the peace accord, this has included mobilization on issues such as constitutional reforms mandated by the accords and the Children and Youth Code, which will be discussed later. Individuals who participate directly in electoral politics might represent the concerns of their particular evangelical community, but they are also representing themselves. Likewise, evangelical groups organize for their own internal purposes in addition to participating in political activities. This is the space of "articulation and representation" that Diamond refers to; and it is something of a truism in democratic theory that one key reason to protect the rights of minorities is to ensure that they can express themselves and to act in accordance with their beliefs in ways that do not infringe upon the rights of others.

In three stages, this chapter demonstrates how Guatemalan evangelicals express themselves in the political arena in a manner consistent with Diamond's conceptualization of liberal democracy. Following a brief section contextualizing evangelicals within the Guatemalan political scene, my account begins with a review of the 1999 elections and interviews with two evangelical candidates for national office. The interviews demonstrate how some evangelicals understand their political involvement, speaking from different sides of the political spectrum. The discourse of both candidates disavows any effort to create an evangelical political party, while simultaneously articulating a vision of how and why evangelicals should be involved in politics at the national level.

Second, by examining a case of evangelical involvement in the ongoing debate over the United Nations' Children and Youth Code, I draw attention to the pluralism of Protestantisms and of Protestant relationships in regard to a specific political issue. This is a primary issue for understanding the evangelical presence throughout Latin America as well as its relationship to the state. While there was considerable opposition to the code from evangelical quarters, a group from the conservative Alianza Evangélica (AE; Evangelical Alliance) participated with Catholics and others in pushing a consensus document that has not been adopted. This openness to dialogue affirms the willingness of some segments of the evangelical community to seek common cause with other Christians in particular cases. More than an example of "religious" dialogue or action, this type of activity demonstrates evangelical pluralism within the political process itself in regard to an issue of national importance.

The final section links the more localized concerns of community-based evangelicals with national-level issues. It analyzes interviews with evangelicals who have held political office in largely Maya communities as illustrating the link between faith and practice in contexts far removed from the capital and national politics. By focusing on Maya evangelicals, some of the contradictions of the Guatemalan political context will be brought forward, revealing the issues involved in implementing the peace accords and consolidating democracy in the face of considerable inertia.

Guatemalan evangelical groups, then, are part of a broad spectrum of civil society organizations that are exerting pressure to change the status quo politics of the past two decades, including the transition to civilian rule since 1985 after more than thirty years of overt or implicit military rule, beginning with the overthrow of the democratically elected government of Jacobo Arbenz in 1954. Despite the peace process resulting in the formal end of the civil war in the 1990s, the transition itself has yet to be consolidated. Susanne Jonas, reflecting on the first civilian presidency, remarked: "the Cerezo period (1986–1990) turned out to be not so much a genuine 'transition to democracy' as a necessary adjustment for trying to deal with Guatemala's multiple crises and to reestablish minimal international credibility" (2000, 26). Difficulties in consolidating the peace process a decade later show the long-term tensions in any democratic transition in Guatemala. In this context, evangelical involvement, paradoxically, has been both consistent with the basic norms of liberal democracy as well as somewhat ambiguous in form and substance when viewed historically and in terms of aspirations for full-fledged democratic consolidation.

Contextualizing Evangelicals and Democracy in Guatemala

The history of Christianity (Catholic or Protestant) in Guatemala has long been politically charged in one way or another. Whether it was the Spanish invasion and imposition of Catholicism on native peoples or the more recent arrival of evangelicals as part of political projects to break Catholic power and bring the perceived benefits of modernization, the state has repeatedly been involved in politicizing religion for its own ends. Protestants were formally invited into the country in 1882 when president and dictator Justo Rufino Barrios brought the Presbyterian minister John Clark Hill to Guatemala as part of a liberal political agenda. This reflected earlier liberal policies of encouraging European immigration to "whiten" the population, and extended the scope of Barrios's proclamation of freedom of worship in 1873. As a rule, evangelicals have not often been openly at odds with the Guatemalan state, regardless of who has been in power. Following the liberal dictatorship of Jorge Ubico (1931–44), Protestants even expressed tacit support for the revolution of 1944, which ushered in a period of social and political reform, until the 1954 coup supported by the United States Central Intelligence Agency (CIA). With some notable exceptions, evangelicals since have tended to side with political stability as long as churches were allowed to conduct their business as they saw fit. This lends credence to the notion of evangelicals as apolitical.

As already indicated, Ríos Montt's ascension to the presidency via a *coup d'état* gave evangelicals high visibility, at the same time that his counterinsurgency policies and complicity with genocide made many on the left more suspicious of evangelical presence as an "opium" that kept the masses in their place and promoted order at the expense of justice. Protestant growth by the end of the 1980s had some predicting that there would be a Protestant majority by the end of the century. Although those projections were not borne out, Ríos Montt did hold office during a period of considerable Protestant growth, beginning in the 1960s and gaining momentum after the earthquake of 1976, when doors were opened to relief work by religious and other nongovernmental agencies. Growth in the 1980s and early 1990s has often been attributed to massive social dislocation caused by the war, a variation of the crisis-solace or deprivation theory of conversion (Annis 1987). Other interpretations argue that it was "safer" to belong to an evangelical than a Catholic congregation when many rural inhabitants were caught in a crossfire between guerrillas and governmental repression (Stoll 1993). It is certainly true that some evangelical pastors and congregations took the side of the army. Meanwhile, Catholics were targeted because of their social commitment as expressed in movements like Catholic Action and presumed connections with the liberation theology that had been a powerful ideological force during the Nicaraguan Revolution of 1979 (Berryman 1984; Falla 1994).

Examination of Protestantism during the 1990s has focused less on growth and more on the diversity within the Protestant movement. Much research has looked at pentecostals and neopentecostals, who together make up 65 to 70 percent of the evangelical population (Cleary and Stewart-Gambino 1997; D. Smith 1991; Wilson 1997). Historical Protestantism has been the subject of some analysis (Bogenschild 1992; Garrard-Burnett 1998a), and Maya Protestants have received increasing attention as well (Adams 1999; Chiappari 1999; Goldin and Metz 1997; Scotchmer 1986, 1993). Reference to evangelicals in the political arena and their relationship to political authority is frequent. More recently, concentrated work has been done on evangelical involvement in political processes from both ideological sides of the spectrum— the side represented by Ríos Montt and that associated with the peace accord and the reconstruction of civil society (Jeffrey 1998; Steigenga 1999). Yet another line of research places evangelicals as transnational actors with international connections linking concerns in the international community with local social and political agendas (Garrard-Burnett 1998b; Levine and Stoll 1997).

Two issues in the late 1990s brought the relationship of evangelicals to liberal democracy vividly to light. One was the murder of bishop Juan Gerardi in April 1998, two days after the Archbishop's Office for Human Rights released its report on human rights during the civil war, *Guatemala: Never Again!* (ODHAG 1999). Although this was largely perceived as a political assassination, the most visible Presbyterian congregation in the capital, symbolically located just off the central plaza behind the national palace, refused to give permission for an ecumenical memorial service in its sanctuary. The Gerardi case has been a true test of the Guatemalan judicial system;

three men with links to the military and an auxiliary priest were eventually convicted.

The second example has to do with the constitutional reforms voted upon in a national referendum in May 1999. The reforms were mandated in agreements between government and guerrillas before the final peace accord of 1996. In the midst of 80 percent absenteeism nationally, the Evangelical Alliance had urged its members to vote no to the reforms.[4] The victory of the no vote made the future of the peace process uncertain, and two and a half years later the naming of a retired general to the ministry dealing with national security contributed to the specter of Guatemala's remilitarization.

While the role of evangelicals in both these matters is complex, the examples lend support to the idea that evangelicals are by nature in league with forces little concerned with any broader participation by civil society, much less the consolidation of democracy. Furthermore, the cases appear to argue in favor of conceptualizations of a sort of evangelical "spiritual hegemony" of the type articulated in the early 1990s by Stoll:

> With evangelical growth, the spectacle of Ríos Montt, and the election of Jorge Serrano as a guide, born-again Protestants seemed to be establishing a precarious spiritual hegemony in Guatemala. While the Catholic Church will continue to be an important institution, evangelical assumptions are increasingly defining how Guatemalans understand themselves and their world. No matter how deeply Guatemala plunges into poverty and chaos, the personal discipline encouraged by evangelical churches will have survival value compared to traditional folk Catholicism. What remains doubtful is whether evangelicals will be able to deal with the underlying inequalities and institutionalized violence which have brought Guatemala to its present state. (1994, 119)

After more than ten years have passed, Stoll's concern with the ability of evangelicals to deal with social inequality and violence remains well placed.

However, evangelicals never achieved any "spiritual hegemony" in Guatemala, "precarious" or otherwise. Any such perception is further undercut by the fact that both Ríos Montt and Serrano left the presidency under clouds related to human rights violations and corruption. While Ríos Montt's continued presence on Guatemala's political stage dictates that he be considered the most prominent evangelical political actor in the last two decades, too much focus on him obscures the true shape of the country's religious pluralism. In addition, the resurgence of interest in Maya spirituality and diverse expressions of Catholicism complicate impressions of evangelical dominance in the religious field. Finally, there is the messy business of statistics regarding the evangelical percentage of the population. Although claims as high as one-third have been common in recent years, few would disagree that the rate of increase slowed drastically in the late 1990s. Studies earlier in the decade indicated that 20 to 25 percent of the population is more accurate. While the percentage of evangelicals varies tremendously from one municipality to the next, the lower overall percentages refute any claim of evangelical "spiritual hegemony."

The 1999 Elections and Politics, Guatemalan Style

This perspective is borne out by considering the political role of evangelicals in the 1999 elections, including those who stood for president and vice president. These two candidates come from vastly different segments of society. Francisco Bianchi is a businessman with ties to the elite, while Vitalino Similox is a Kaqchikel Maya from Chimaltenango, one hour west of the capital. Although Similox is well educated, has worked in the city, and has connections with the international religious community, he also maintains connections to his area of origin. The intent is to discern what political involvement means to evangelicals active in party politics. Even here, however, some attention has to be given to Ríos Montt at the outset, as well as to some of the dynamics of party politics in contemporary Guatemala. The presidential elections of 1999 provide a lens for this examination.

The first round results in November 1999 led to a runoff between the same parties that had vied for the presidency in 1995 (table 2.1). The second round in December gave the presidency to Alfonso Portillo, candidate of the Frente Republicano Guatemalteco (FRG; Guatemalan Republican Front), with 68 percent of the vote (table 2.2). The FRG's victory raised concerns inside and outside Guatemala because Ríos Montt was the party's executive secretary and president of the congress. Despite being constitutionally

TABLE 2.1. 1999 Guatemalan Presidential Elections First Round, November 7

Party	Presidential Candidate	Vice Presidential Candidate	Total Vote	Percentage
FRG	Alfonso Portillo	Francisco Reyes	1,045,820	47.72
PAN	Oscar Berger	Arabella Castro	664,417	30.32
ANN	Alvaro Colom	Vitalino Similox	270,891	12.36
PLP	Acisclo Valladares	Guillermo Salazar Santizo	67,924	3.10
ARDE	Francisco Bianchi	Manolo Bendfeldt	45,470	2.07
Six other candidates			96,985	4.42

Source: Tribunal Supremo de Guatemala (TSE).

TABLE 2.2. 1999 Guatemalan Presidential Elections Second Round, December 26

Party	Presidential Candidate	Vice Presidential Candidate	Total Vote	Percentage
FRG	Alfonso Portillo	Francisco Reyes	1,185,160	68.31
PAN	Oscar Berger	Arabella Castro	549,936	31.69

Source: Tribunal Supremo Electoral (TSE).

Note: Absenteeism was 59.61 percent.

prevented from acceding to the presidency for having earlier come to power in a coup, he is generally considered the power behind the FRG's throne and continues to be referred to simply as "the General."

Generally considered the first evangelical president in Latin America, sometimes referred to in the past as "Dios Montt" because of his television sermonizing while in the president's office, Ríos Montt's continued presence certainly raises the issue of the place of evangelicals in democratic processes. Impressions of a link between evangelicals and authoritarian politics received further impetus in the early 1990s when another evangelical, Serrano Elías, was elected president in 1990 and subsequently forced into exile following an aborted attempt in 1993 at a self-coup in the style of Peruvian president Alberto Fujimori. Although Ríos Montt has decreased his public religious rhetoric and Serrano Elías has been largely disowned by his evangelical brethren, together they represent an image of conservative evangelicals in the service of Christian and political interests emanating from the United States. No doubt there is a certain mystique (in several senses of the word) that accrues to Guatemala for having had two evangelical presidents, but this distorts the degree of financial and other material influence from the United States and American evangelicals on Guatemalan political and social processes, which was never as great as some of the more apocalyptic projections claimed it would be during the period covered in this essay. Furthermore, attention to the potential relationship of Guatemalan evangelicals to the United States glosses over the pluralism of Protestantisms within Guatemala, as well as the extent to which evangelical religion in its various guises has become indigenized.

Several other aspects of the Guatemalan political process are important for contextualizing evangelical participation. First, Guatemalan presidents are not allowed reelection, in accordance with a constitutional amendment of 1994. Second, in the four presidential elections between the return to democracy in 1985 and the 1999 election, no party retained office for more than one term, and each party exiting the presidency subsequently fractured. Even as other parties have grown more competitive, the FRG has remained a strong

TABLE 2.3. Guatemala Congress Deputies by Party (January 2000)

FRG	PAN	ANN	DCG	UD-LOV	PLP
63	37	9	2	1	1

Source: www.congreso.gob.gt.

political force, though it was unable to garner more than 19 percent of the vote under Ríos Montt in the 2003 presidential elections.

The fractious nature of Guatemalan politics can be seen in a comparison of party affiliations in congress in the wake of the presidential elections in January 2000 and at the end of 2001. Table 2.3 shows the makeup following the presidential elections. Notable was the dominance of the FRG, the power of the Partido Avanzado Nacional (PAN; National Advancement Party) as a second force, and the leftist Alianza Nueva Nación (ANN; New Nation Alliance) as a small but viable third force.

Although the same two parties vied for the presidency in the 1995 and 1999 elections, the PAN, which under the leadership of Alvaro Arzú pushed through the final peace accord in 1996, fragmented into three groups after losing the 1999 election. One group, the Unionistas, had thirteen deputies in 2001, while a second group formed the base for the Unión Nacional de la Esperanza (UNE; National Union of Hope). The fragmentation of the PAN occurred despite its having won the mayoralty of Guatemala City. As a political party, the UNE began its formation in March 2001 under the leadership of Alvaro Colom, a past presidential candidate of the ANN, a coalition including the political wing of the former guerrilla movement. The ANN got 12 percent of the presidential vote, and Colom's defection once again placed the left in disarray following fourth- and third-place finishes in the last two elections.

To further complicate the picture, one of the major voices of the FRG, in addition to Efrain Ríos Montt, is actually Ríos Montt's daughter, Zury Ríos Sosa. Ríos Sosa had actually taken over leadership in congress for several months before Ríos Montt himself was cleared of charges in the Guategate scandal involving the alteration of taxes on an alcoholic beverage law passed in June 2000.[5] Two other former elected presidents (Vinicio Cerezo and Ramiro León de Carpio) also had seats in congress. The party that elected Serrano in 1991, the Movimiento de Acción Solidaria (MAS; Movement of Solidary Action), is no longer functioning. In January 2000, congress was dominated by the FRG, with sixty-three deputies, the PAN was second with thirty-seven, and the ANN had nine. The left-wing Frente Democrático Nueva Guatemala (FDNG; New Guatemala Democratic Front) that had placed fourth in the 1996 elections was abolished under a law stipulating that parties in the presidential

TABLE 2.4. Guatemala Congress Deputies by Party (December 2001)

FRG	PAN	Bancada Unionista	ANN	DCG	UD-LOV	PLP	Independent
63	17	13	8	2	1	1	8

Source: www.congreso.gob.gt.

race must receive at least 4 percent of the popular vote to stay in existence. A perusal of party affiliations in December 2001 further demonstrates the unstable nature of Guatemalan politics (see table 2.4). While the FRG maintained the vast majority of its deputies, the PAN had lost half of its delegation and the ANN was now fourth.

Evangelicals and Political Parties

Another party that was abolished, after receiving only 2 percent of the vote in the first round of the presidential elections of 1999, was the Acción Reconciliadora Democrática (ARDE; Democratic Reconciling Action). Its presidential candidate, Francisco Bianchi, is a businessman who was until recently an elder in the El Verbo (Word) church, which Ríos Montt made famous.[6] References to El Verbo are typically understood as referring to a large neopentecostal church in Guatemala City that proclaims a version of prosperity theology. In fact, El Verbo functions as a denomination with churches throughout Guatemala and other countries, including Nicaragua, Canada, and the United States. Bianchi attended and Ríos Montt continues to attend "La 16," a large congregation now located on the outskirts of Guatemala City's zone 16, near an elite residential area. The church compound includes schools for all ages, including the new Panamerican University.

Bianchi has been involved in politics for a number of years, having served in the Ríos Montt administration as secretary of public relations for the presidency. In that capacity, he was one of two representatives El Verbo sent to the government ostensibly as counselors to the president (Anfuso and Sczepanski 1984; Stoll 1990, 208).[7] What is Bianchi's view regarding evangelicals and the political process? I asked him directly whether or not his intent was to found an evangelical political party. The ARDE was widely reported to have been an evangelical party, yet it consistently preferred to call itself a party of biblical principles. The distinction is important for Bianchi, and his response demonstrates a nuanced perspective on the relationship between evangelicals and politics.

> I don't believe it is a question of an evangelical party. One needs to
> be very careful with that because it creates divisions between
> Catholic and evangelical. I believe that Catholics and evangelicals

believe in the same God, the same Christ, and have the same Bible. All Guatemalans have to be [considered] and not evangelicals and nobody else.... If one realizes that Guatemala is 97 percent Christian, either evangelical or Catholic, and we go according to our principles that are given in the Word of God, well, it is the same Bible, the same God, the same Christ. So ... we also work with Catholics, not only with evangelicals. But with people of principle, one might say.

Worthy of note here are Bianchi's implicit ecumenism (within limits) and the sense that the political process (and the nation itself) could be transformed if the unity existing between Catholics and evangelicals as Christians were put into practice.[8] Even if the stated intent is not to form a political party in the narrow sense, the intent is to guide the nation into prosperity and civic virtue, and thereby transform society through political involvement. For Bianchi, those who belong to the church are to be an influence for the good of society. To accomplish this, it is imperative to look for the principles of God's Word, which are universal. At one point he cited Acts 3:21, drawing on the image of Christ being kept in the heavens until the restoration of all things. The implication is that even Christ is waiting for Christians to become involved in the active redemption of society. Bianchi also mentioned his work with Asociación LIDER,[9] which he described as a registered Christian political association, with no party affiliation, that sponsors seminars for people involved in business and for religious leaders to encourage their political involvement. The intent of the seminars is to "give them a vision that a nation can be transformed by biblical principles.... Christ said that he sent us to be the light of the world. If we take refuge in the four walls of the church, to whom are we giving light?"

Even at that, the results are dubious. Asociación LIDER and ARDE have the same ends, and the discourse is pitched at the same elite sector of society. It is telling that ARDE received only 2 percent of the vote in the presidential elections, due partly to the stubborn perception that the party was a party of evangelicals. But Bianchi's continuing public discourse is consistent with my interview with him. When he spoke at a meeting where the topic was the formation of a new political party in March 2001, Movimiento de Principios y Valores (MPV; Movement of Principles and Values), he said: "We want the evolution of our society, and we can only accomplish that by defending the immutable values and principles given by God" (Campos 2001).[10] Finally, the rhetoric and latest attempt to resurrect a party of biblical principles has to be situated in a more expansive frame. A Maya evangelical and former mayor I interviewed in the western highlands said ARDE "was born dead." And he observed that one of its problems was the past association of a number of ARDE leaders with the political party of Serrano Elías, the MAS.

Another evangelical seeking high office in the 1999 elections was Vitalino Similox, a Kaqchikel Maya and Presbyterian minister who ran for vice president on the leftist ANN's ticket. While he had to resign from his church ministry to stand for election, he was soon functioning again as executive director of the Conferencia de Iglesias Evangélicas de Guatemala (CIEDEG; Conference of Evangelical Churches of Guatemala), a loose confederation supported by congregations related to the indigenous peoples and focused very much on social concerns. Similox has been involved in social and political activities in the Chimaltenango area for nearly twenty years. As a leader in the Kaqchikel Presbytery of the National Evangelical Presbyterian Church, he has been involved in pressing for justice in several cases during the 1990s, such as the murder of elder Pascual Serech and minister Manuel Saquic, largely for their efforts in the human rights work of the presbytery. Interestingly, he campaigned in 1999 in a coalition party that included former guerrillas. I asked him what he could offer to Guatemala's political process as an evangelical. Similox replied:

> There is a need in this country, including a reality of exclusion, of sectarianism, of intolerance. There isn't an opening to dialogue, to pluriculturalism, to political and ideological pluralism. So, I feel my work is to overcome this situation so we can all participate openly in whatever activity. It should not be felt that economic activity corresponds only to one sector of Guatemalan society. Neither does political life correspond only to one group, to one people; instead it corresponds to all the peoples of Guatemala.... Insofar as we are human beings, we are political beings; so we have the right to participate in the decisions of whatever type in order to construct a different nation, a different country. This includes political participation ... without renouncing one's identity, without renouncing one's faith. Instead, inspired by those principles of our faith, we can make an effective contribution. Regarding the Bible, there are very clear passages in which we are told that light is not to be hidden.... That is to say, where there is necessity, there is the need to struggle.... Guatemalan politics urgently needs to be healed, to be transformed.

Although from the other side of the political spectrum, elements of Similox's reply are not so different from Bianchi's. The emphasis on transformation seems an essential part of evangelical discourse, although the desired outcomes are worlds apart. Ethnicity and the issue of democracy come subtly into play in the emphasis on exclusion from economic and political resources that lead one to seek changes through political involvement. This subtext of exclusion is not contemplated in Bianchi's discourse of Christian unity. Both perspectives do, however, favor broad participation of evangelicals in a man-ner consistent with broader political and social goals.

Evangelicals and the Codigo de la Niñez y la Juventud

The response of segments of Guatemala's evangelical community to the Children and Youth Code provides another lens for understanding the efforts of some evangelicals to participate in issues on the national political agenda. The code is essentially a human rights code for children that was unanimously adopted by congress in 1996 within the frame of Guatemala's signing of the Convention of Rights of the Child in 1990 and the need to replace the Código de Menores (Code of Minors) of 1979 currently in force. Among other con-cerns, the Code of Minors "does not clearly delimit the differences between youthful transgressors and children in situations of danger or abandonment." The 1996 Children and Youth Code was produced by a commission of gov-ernment and nongovernmental agencies with the collaboration of UNICEF and other international organizations, and was to have come into force in Sep-tember 1997. By 2002, the activation of the code had been postponed indefi-nitely by a legislative decree of February 24, 2000.

The code has become one of many contentious issues on the Guatemalan political scene in recent years. Much of the contention revolves around the sense in many quarters that representatives of the international community produced the code and that the same community has been actively involved in working for its passage. Similar to issues surrounding the peace process in general, the involvement of the international community in sensitive po-litical issues is often interpreted by the political and social elite in Guatemala as undue foreign influence in internal affairs. The intense nationalism manifested on such issues becomes particularly strident around questions the international community interprets as having human rights implications. While part of this is a typical reaction to guard national sovereignty, the nationalistic rhetoric sometimes betrays an ironic twist in that so much of the Guatemalan elite turns toward the United States for models of consumerism and even political structure and ideology. It is striking how much of the argumentative discourse in regard to the Code parallels political battles waged over "culture war" issues perceived to have religious implications in the United States.[11]

Central to discussion over whether or not the code should enter into force are debates over the *patria potestad*, parental authority, within the household. The Episcopal Conference of Guatemala (CEG; Conference Episcopal de Guatemala), representing the Catholic Church, together with many segments of the evangelical community, have protested what they perceive to be the danger of state interference in family affairs and parental authority under the Code. The CEG issued a press release criticizing the document for the lack of a "fundamental ethical principle" and indicating that the code could be reworked to give more emphasis to the integrity of the family (CEG 1998).[12] As former vice president of the Evangelical Alliance, Francisco Bianchi's perspective on the code is representative of the negative views held by many evangelicals.

> The government doesn't have to involve itself in what belongs to the family. Again, this is the typical case of the government taking on the attributes of God. What happened there is that a lot of parental authority was taken and given to the government. How can they go pitting children against parents? It all sounds really nice—the rights of children—and we are defending them. But it hasn't worked. It has created a tremendous rebellion in a lot of children. We all know that we have to educate children. God's Word clearly says that the child needs discipline. What the codes end up doing is pitting children and adolescents against their parents.... Those who are responsible before God for their children are the parents, not the government.

Bianchi echoes a concern in various sectors regarding the level of bureaucracy needed to monitor the code, as well as the possibility of manipulating that bureaucracy for political ends. In my interview with him, he said the AE had presented over fifty thousand signatures to congress in opposition to the code. He also said that some people from the AE who had worked on the consensus document had perspectives that were more political than biblical. This seems to point to some of the subsequent infighting within the AE over the code, as well as to the genuine challenge for evangelicals of balancing political realism with biblical principle.

This was the frame for a striking example of ecumenical cooperation in October 1999 when a broad group of representatives created a consensus document in favor of implementing a revised version of the code. The group included the AE, the CEG, the Office of the Defense of Children and Youth of the Attorney General for Human Rights, and the Latin American Council of Churches (CLAI; Consejo Latinoamericano de Iglesias). A second document outlining some budgetary implications of the enforcement of the code was also produced. Supposedly, the committee representing the AE had the freedom to participate as it desired. Eventually, the consensus document itself created controversy in the AE when one leader allegedly withdrew support for the consensus. Other representatives of the AE still felt progress had been made, as the locus of responsibility for children had shifted from the state back to the family. While other issues were probably involved, the issue of the code contributed to tension within the alliance, and to a shakeup in its

leadership. One observer of the process said that the entire scenario manifested the lack of political seriousness within the church and of qualified
interlocutors within the evangelical community. Certainly, it manifests the potential for internal tension whenever a segment of the evangelical community
reaches out into the political arena, even in regard to an issue as traditionally
dear to evangelicals as child-rearing.

Nevertheless, the participation of the AE in the process itself remains a
significant example of an attempt by the organization representing the largest
contingent of evangelicals to make a contribution to a political issue in Guatemala. That it was done in ecumenical fashion demonstrates the potential
role of evangelicals in strengthening civil society in a manner that creates
independent, yet inclusive, contributions to debate on social policy. At one
point in the interview in the offices of the AE, I was told that both the AE and
another group called the Liga Pro-Patria (a group with evangelical connections
described by a prior interviewee as nearly fascist) had worked against the code
at the beginning. The sense communicated was that the Liga Pro-Patria had
been uniformly negative in its criticism, while the AE had tried to be constructive. The contrasting evangelical positions represent a wide range, from
neopentecostal perspectives such as Bianchi's to other approaches such as that
embodied in the FRG's efforts to derail the code.

The postponing of the implementation of the code took place about a
month after Alfonso Portillo took office. The decree stated that

> the Congress of the Republic must listen to the diverse opinions that
> are expressed in the context of society regarding the theme of chil-
> dren and youth, in order to reach a code of consensus and legislate
> how this corresponds to social interests, adopting measures for at-
> taining the integral strengthening of the family.

This action not only seemed to take the code off the national legislative agenda,
but also not so subtly aligned itself with the emphasis on the integrity of the
family that is so important to various religious sectors, Catholic as well as
evangelical. The decree betrays some of the FRG's political emphasis on what
are called in North America "family values." As the circus-like atmosphere
surrounding the FRG administration continued into 2001, debate over the
code receded. The CEG did remind the government of the consensus document in January 2001 (*La semana en Guatemala*, January 22–29, 2001). The
United Nations Verification Mission in Guatemala (MINUGUA) also issued
a lengthy document on the status of children and adolescents in the peace
process (MINUGUA 2000b).

It is important to note that Similox's organization, CIEDEG, supported
the code from the beginning. This is not surprising, given CIEDEG's support
from international nongovernmental organizations (NGOs) and its rather
populist working agenda and left-wing political contacts. In many ways, the

stances of CIEDEG and the AE represent divergent political options within Guatemala's evangelical community. Still, neither Bianchi nor Similox can be considered spokespersons for evangelicals apart from the political and social perspectives of their constituencies. Bianchi's agenda represents his ties to the political, social, and economic elite in Guatemala as much as an overtly religious perspective, despite the religious language in which he couches his objections to the code. While his religious commitment and his discourse about what informs his political participation should not be discounted, there are many components to his social location and the manner in which even his ecumenism is in the service of upholding the extant political and social structure in Guatemala.

Similarly, Similox's stance is informed by his political contacts as an indigenous activist and by his religious involvement with the National Evangelical Presbyterian Church of Guatemala (IENPG; Iglesia Evangélica Nacional Presbiteriana de Guatemala). This denomination is not currently active in the AE and has historically not shied away from taking stances on public issues. Nevertheless, the IENPG's political involvement at the national level has rarely challenged the power structure of Guatemala. Moreover, the internal politics of the denomination since the 1980s has often mirrored politics at the national level. The Maya population within the church experienced great difficulties during the war, and often received little support from their Ladino brethren in the denomination (Schäfer 1991; Scotchmer 1989, 305–6).[13] Internally, fights for positions of power within the denomination took up much energy during national meetings throughout the 1990s, and a housecleaning of corrupt denominational leadership in May 2001 resulted in Ladinos occupying the three primary positions of executive secretary, president, and treasurer.

Using the exclusive lens of either politics or religion to understand the commitments of Bianchi and Similox is inadequate. While not discounting their religious commitments and the manner in which these inform their political perspectives, the relative stances of both men and their organizations toward the Código de la Niñez reflect their social location. Bianchi represents the conservative elite, and he not only upholds the notion of family values but also the principle of noninterference in Guatemalan affairs by outside organizations.[14] This would include the international organizations responsible for the code and for some of its oversight once implemented. Similox represents an activist stance supported by the more progressive elements of the international community. This stance is also indicative of his religious commitments to social justice and to human rights. Focusing on their social locations and their political commitments, it is difficult to say that either person is truly representative of any large segment of the Guatemalan evangelical community. The focus on the AE and the Código de la Niñez provides a more nuanced perspective shaped by the concert of evangelical voices and their interaction with Guatemalan political and social institutions.

Evangelicals and Political Involvement at the Community Level

Moving from the macro level, it is instructive to consider something of evangelical political practice in local communities. For the rural population, especially the indigenous population, of Mesoamerica, localism is the frame of reference for culture and identity. One study comparing political regimes in Costa Rica and Guatemala argues for more attention to rural areas in the analysis of the construction and maintenance of either democratic or authoritarian political systems. The reason is that the countryside is often the locus of forces that can be disruptive and destabilizing for democracy, while, simultaneously, the focus on institutional arrangements in the urban environment neglects the relationship between political participation and the control of resources in rural areas (Yashar 1997, 213–15). I have already pointed out the overwhelming, and seemingly contradictory, support of rural communities for the FRG during the 1999 presidential elections. In addition to the mystique surrounding the figure of Riós Montt, three decades ago Roland Ebel noted the tendency toward *oficialismo* (support for the government) among voters in the Mam Maya community of San Juan Ostuncalco from 1935 to 1944.[15] Defined then as support for the party in power at the national level (Ebel 1972, 164), perhaps the pattern can now be interpreted as the tendency to side with those who seem to have the power and are able to deliver resources. Community members are adept at reading some of the winds of change and adapting.

The brief analysis provided here summarizes the perspectives of two sitting and two former *alcaldes* (mayors) representing three municipios in the department of Quetzaltenango in the western highlands. Cajolá, San Juan Ostuncalco, and San Martín Chileverde are predominately inhabited by the Mam Maya ethnic group, the second largest Maya-speaking group in Guatemala. The communities are located in the southern zone of the larger Mam culture region in the *altiplano* at about eight thousand feet in altitude, although San Martín is slightly lower on the escarpment. The area remains largely agricultural, with potatoes and corn the primary crops, plus some coffee in the municipio of San Martín and in the lower reaches of canyons in the San Juan, which is also a furniture-making, transportation, and marketing center.

All four mayors or ex-mayors are Presbyterians; this was the first denomination to establish a presence in the area in 1911 (Bogenschild 1992, 160).[16] Both the former and current mayors reflected in interviews on the relationship between political activity and evangelical political involvement. At this local level, the examination of the diversity of Protestant involvement shifts to indigenous communities and historical denominations, which, at least in theory, are more predisposed than pentecostal organizations to political involvement. None of the current or former mayors belong to the dominant political parties at the national level in recent elections. One held office in association with the Christian Democrats, two with the Democratic Union, and another with a civic committee.

Very likely there are more evangelical mayors in the Mam region, and certainly throughout the Guatemalan countryside. There are also a number of ways to analyze the presence of these individuals in relation to Guatemalan politics. Two patterns stand out at the level of the mayors' discourse and the potential creation of social capital within evangelical communities, both of which might contribute to strengthening liberal democracy in Guatemala. First is the uniform notion that it is the role of the evangelical to be active in one's community. As one mayor remarked:

> Many people think that we evangelicals can't participate in politics, and this is false. If we look at it biblically, the Bible says that evangelicals are the salt of the earth. How is it possible that we can be salt of the earth and afraid of participating? How can we be the light of the world if we don't like to serve our neighbor? It isn't possible. Sometimes people pray, "Take from me the danger in my road"...[but] I say, "God help me to overcome the obstacles of today. Give me force and strength and I'll survive anything." But I don't ask God to...clear my road...My mentality is a little different and sometimes I've been in contradiction with other *hermanos*. I don't believe this business of going to worship service in the afternoon, in the morning, and the next day. For me, the *evangelio* is working with the people, living it out, giving counsel, providing projects.

In certain regards, the language of salt and light is foundational for evangelical thinking about how to engage with the world—a place of darkness from which some believe they should be set apart. This concept of separation is the basis for the church's requirement that elders or ministers among Mam Presbyterians leave posts in the local congregation when they hold political office. While some see this as a conservative stance on the part of the denomination, it also frees them for political action by removing some of the scrutiny that might be placed upon them in other circumstances. The stance of the *alcaldes* (mayors) themselves emphasizes action in the world, a type of action both requiring and being rooted in local political involvement. To use Sanchíz Ochoa's term, this attitude is a "concreción de ética política" ("realization of political ethics") within the lives of these individuals who are, in fact, tied to a more mundane discourse than those who, like the neopentecostals, see themselves in the same light as the kings and prophets of the

Hebrew Bible. The Presbyterians I interviewed tend to see themselves as called to work in the world for the sake of God, whereas much neopentecostal discourse claims believers are destined to rule the world in the name of God.

Second, the mayors express the sense of having been called to their political involvement. "El partido me buscó" ("the party sought me out") was the comment of one mayor. And another said, "Yo fui llamado" ("I was called"). This calling is reminiscent of Christian discourse regarding the call to follow Christ or to undertake some prophetic action. Often, the words were not even attached to overtly religious discourse, but the sense is not so different. Here again, the emphasis is on both the desire and the responsibility to serve one's community. The reflection is one of the indigenous community's sense of unity (which evangelicals are often accused of destroying), and this is one place were evangelical discourse and localism come together in communities very much in the throes of political, social, and cultural change, and yes, conflict. While these *alcaldes* do indeed interact with the state, the horizon of interest is the village and not the struggle for power and authority of political parties, national social agendas, or even the possibility of national political office.

A caution is in order here. To an extent these *alcaldes* are not representative, even of evangelicals. All have their roots in Presbyterian circles, and this surely has an impact on their apparently Calvinistic sense of vocation rooted in service to the local community. The Presbyterian presence in their area includes the establishment of a medical clinic and educational and training center as early as 1940 with a concomitant focus on the Mam language in education. A translation of the New Testament in Mam was produced in the same year. While others were involved through the years, the philosophy guiding this work was largely that of a missionary couple, Dudley and Dorothy Peck, who arrived in Guatemala in 1922 and remained until 1970 (IENPG 1982, 169–77). Dudley Peck even completed a doctoral dissertation, "Practices and Training of Guatemalan Mam Shamans," for the Hartford Seminary Foundation in 1970.

The sense of community solidarity the Presbyterian *alcaldes* communicated is an aspect of the unity of indigenous culture, of Mayan-ness. It certainly dovetails as well with the concerns emphasized by those in the Movimiento Maya who are struggling to recover indigenous values and place them in dialogue with political and religious values that have historically repressed indigenous culture and religion.[17] In the words of another Maya Presbyterian, Kaqchikel minister Antonio Otzoy:

> The cosmogony and religious life of the Maya are not isolated from the rest of their lives.... There are people in the world who find fulfilment only in church; others find it in politics, or in the exercise of their personal and civic rights and duties. Such people make a

clear-cut distinction between religious rights and privileges and everything else they do in life. In stark contrast, spirituality is the totality of life for us Maya. (1997, 266)

Beyond the sense of community in the *alcaldes'* perspective on political involvement is the notion of calling reflected in the Maya religious context—a calling whereby the shaman is destined to assume the role of leadership at birth in accordance with Maya day and number signs, and through dreams and illnesses wherein shamanic apprenticeship is the path to healing.[18] Arguably, Maya evangelicals come by their sense of calling from the depths of both their ethnic and religious identity. The confluence of ethnicity, religion, and the sense of authority invested in local-level political leaders also reflects what a Maya friend of mine has referred to as "the multiple identities of each person."

Returning to the issue of pluralism, this examination of evangelicals and politics at the communal level ignores some of the inroads pentecostalism has made into the historical Protestant community (and Catholicism) in Guatemala. While pentecostalism itself changes and creates change, there is surely tension between its apolitical expression and the kind of political involvement signaled in this research. The Mam mayors represent an ethic rooted in the local communities and congregations of the *alcaldes* themselves. It is some distance from the pentecostal ethic once articulated negatively to me as rejection of the five "p's," *pecados,* or sins. *Política* was at the top of the list that included *pelota, peinado, pintura, y pantalones* (ball playing, hairdressing, makeup, and wearing pants).[19]

Recapitulation

The intent in this chapter has been to present diverse perspectives on the manner in which evangelicals relate to democratic political processes in Guatemala. Guatemala continues to confound conventional wisdom regarding evangelicals and politics in the region in that there are no evangelical political parties, and indications are that no evangelical voting bloc has developed on the national level in spite of the large percentage of evangelicals in the general population and two evangelical presidents in the past twenty years (Grenfell 1995). Moreover, prominent players on the evangelical political stage oppose the idea of forming an evangelical political party. The observations here constitute neither a prediction about the viability of democracy in Guatemala nor the last word on the ongoing and dynamic relation of evangelicals to political power. With or without the FRG, indications are that the military continues to wield tremendous power in relation to the civilian government. This is part of the structure of Guatemala's limited democracy, what some have even called "guardian democracy" (McSherry 1998).

Meanwhile, the FRG experienced ongoing conflict between factions allied with Portillo and others allied with Ríos Montt. Despite ongoing rumors of Ríos Montt having terminal prostate cancer, and efforts to put him on trial in Spanish courts for human rights abuses, there were continued attempts at overturning the constitution to allow him to try for the presidency. In July 2003, the Constitutional Court finally decided that he was eligible to run in the presidential elections at the end of that year. That decision brought some fears for Guatemalan democracy, as FRG sympathizers were accused of tactics designed to intimidate voters, especially in the violent protests that nearly paralyzed the capital for two days in late July. In the end, Ríos finished third in the first round of the election, with 19.3 percent; his percentage in the capital was well below that. But the FRG remained the largest party in congress and won a third of the mayoralties, showing it still has strong support in rural areas. Ríos's evangelical identity played little part in his campaign discourse. His elimination in the first round triggered new concerns that the democratic process might be interrupted (especially as he might face genocide charges after his congressional term had finished and he had lost his parliamentary immunity), but in fact he accepted defeat calmly.

Although on paper the sheer number of evangelicals could have turned the election in Ríos Montt's favor, there were clearly other factors at play. Already in 1999, the vote for the FRG was consistent across ethnic boundaries, despite the fact that the Maya had suffered disproportionately during the war.

While evangelicals and evangelicalism may have the potential to skew aspects of Guatemala's political system, several years after the end of the war, the system as a whole might still best be described as "low-intensity democracy." This is characterized by its fragility in response to increasing social demands when "the new democratic order widens the space for popular mobilisation," and by the continuing presence of the military, "always suspicious of the lessening of social control and the consequent threat to established interests" (Gills, Rocamora, and Wilson 1993, 21). The rubric of low-intensity democracy is reflective of Diamond's insistence that liberal democracy cannot have reserved domains of power, but its strength as an analytical tool is the focus on the tension between the appropriation of political and social space by social actors on the one hand and the military as the ultimate arbiter of power on the other. The fragility of Guatemala's peace, even in the wake of several transfers of power through democratic processes, is rooted in the very real conflict between coalitions expecting greater levels of participation from all sectors of society and those who continue to resist opening the system to coalitions demanding access to power and some equality in the distribution of social and material resources. The seemingly deaf ear toward calls for justice for crimes committed during the war, such as the murder of anthropologist Myrna Mack, and Ríos Montt's position until early 2004 as president of the congress, alongside his military connections and his past history, did nothing to allay these fears. The coincidence of his military and his evangelical identities confuses interpretations of the relationship between democratic processes and evangelical faith at the present time. As both president of congress and "the General," he casts a shadow over democratic consolidation and the difficult work of implementing the peace accords.

Another telling example in this vein was the stated effort of Alfonso Portillo in 2000 to put into his cabinet a civilian minister of defense. Placing a civilian was not possible in the end, because the Constitution of 1985 requires that a person from the military hold the position. In this case a reserved domain of power is legally codified. In the context of Guatemala, such a requirement puts the civilian population (and the president) on notice that there is more to the chain of command than meets the eye. More positively, one must acknowledge that at least the issues are now being debated. Nevertheless, I remember vividly how sometimes in the course of research among the Maya in the western highlands a person would simply look at me when we discussed the apparent political opening following the peace accord and say, "Las cosas pueden cambiar" ("Things can change").

How, then, do evangelicals fit into the larger framework of contemporary politics in Guatemala? My first response is to restate what I affirmed at the beginning. I believe the presence of Protestants and the internal diversity of the Protestant community represent an extension of burgeoning manifestations of social, political, and cultural pluralism within the nation. As such, consideration of evangelical subjects is best done out of a theoretical frame viewing religion not only as a contested field of identity and influence within the context of the state but also as a sphere of transnational activity wherein people and resources, according to Susanne Rudolph, "reach across national boundaries, disregarding or contravening the principle of national sovereignty" (1997a, 256). In the same article, Rudolph responds to Samuel Huntington's focus on "civilizational identity" as an important variable in future conflicts throughout the world. First, she reminds the reader that "religion competes for primacy with alternative categories of interest and identification. It is as likely to be used instrumentally to justify other interests as it is to be the dominant interest" (243). And in a more direct critique of Huntington, she says: "totalizing explanations are likely to miss more fine-grained interests and motivations that lead to war and peace" (243).

These seem appropriate caveats in the consideration of evangelicals and democracy in Guatemala.[20] Contrary to stereotypes of authoritarian evangelicals establishing separatist kingdoms as bulwarks of political conservatism seeking to impose ethical and moral agendas on society, evangelicals emerge as participants on a larger political stage where they act in concert with and in opposition to other interest groups that seek influence in political processes. No doubt some evangelicals would impose their will on the populace if they could, but the Guatemalan context does not allow for a single interpretation of evangelical reality. Evangelicals do represent a multifaceted presence in politics, and there is no basis for claiming that they alone are responsible for trying to bring the kingdom of the FRG or any other political kingdom at the present time.

It is difficult to make projections about the direction of democratization or evangelicalism in Guatemala. Steigenga's (1996, 1999) survey research on Protestant and Catholic relations and the perspectives of various religious groups toward political activity from 1993 makes an important contribution to understanding evangelical diversity in regard to ecumenical relations and politics. Part of his survey found relatively high levels of "perceived religious discrimination" and "religious conflict" among Catholics and across the spectrum of evangelical, sectarian, and nonaffiliated Guatemalans. The danger that such tension might create difficulty for the consolidation of democracy after the peace (1999, 172–73) is real. Still, religious strife has not proven any greater a source of instability than the other forms of communal strife, such as those represented by a rash of lynchings that claimed the lives of some 185 people in mostly rural and indigenous communities between 1996 and the release of a report addressing the problem by MINUGUA in December 2000 (MINUGUA 2000a). Many of the killings are in response to crimes against persons or property in places where the justice system seems not to function in any substantial way. There is talk of a culture of violence and impunity within Guatemala as a whole that manifests itself in vigilante justice. In this context, religious discord seems to be less a limitation on the consolidation of liberal democracy than other structural and institutional constraints.

Steigenga offers a measure of caution in surveying Guatemala's religious panorama:

> It is not difficult to predict a future of continued religious pluralism in Guatemala. It is more difficult to discern the implications of this pluralism for Guatemala's democratic consolidation. Clearly, we should not assume that continuing religious pluralism represents some sort of inevitable step forward in a process leading toward political modernization or even secularization. (1999, 174)

Like an increasing number of analysts of evangelical diversity throughout Latin America, Steigenga argues that the mobilization of Protestantism in the political sphere fosters a widening and deepening of "communal participation" that, in turn, will lead to a strengthening of civil society. According to Steigenga, however, this hope depends on the overcoming of "the vertical and authoritarian tendencies within Guatemalan Protestantism."

No sensible observer of the Guatemalan case wants to claim much more than the potential for evangelicals to contribute to the construction of liberal democracy. The two evangelical presidents marred the image of evangelicals for significant segments of the public both within and outside of Guatemala for the better part of a generation. Incidents of evangelical complicity with the Guatemalan military on the local level have also fed into the negative stereotypes of the entire evangelical community. Even within the evangelical community itself, there is skepticism regarding the ability and preparation of evangelicals for political involvement. One minister and longtime observer of neopentecostal religion in Guatemala was adamant that evangelicals had lost much in their dealings with Serrano Elías. "Perdimos la viriginidad política" ("We lost [our] political virginity"), he said. "Perdimos por la violación" ("We lost it through rape"). The rape had occurred at the hands of party politics.

In the midst of this rape was a type of spiritualism, or even a hermeneutic, seeking to apply situations from the Old Testament directly to the Guatemalan political situation. This hermeneutic included a prophecy that circulated in the Elim church comparing Serrano Elías to King David and his predecessor Vinicio Cerezo to King Saul. David would rise from the ashes and replace Saul. The contrast between the hermeneutic and political reality simply reveals that "evangelicals are not prepared to be involved in politics." Those who do get involved wind up losing their prestige or becoming *manchados* (stained) because of their political naïveté.

This kind of naïveté is also evident in the relationship between evangelicals and civil society. When I asked the same person about the concept of civil society, the response revolved around violence and the lack of space for action when one thinks of opposing the military. Religion is seen as particularly divisive because of the way new evangelical churches appear whenever someone becomes disaffected and leaves to found a new congregation.[21] Raising the concern of whether this has to do with creating new space or a mentality of power returns us once again to the issue of whether or not evangelicals might actually contribute to strengthening democratic processes in Guatemala.

Beginning with the Ríos Montt–Serrano Elías trajectory in the presidency, which ends at the midpoint of the time period under consideration here, Manuela Cantón Delgado has labeled the neopentecostal hermeneutic just referred to as a "biblical-ideological discourse." She links the experience of personal salvation with the salvation of the nation in an epilogue bearing the title "Political Millenarianism and Moral Reform." Much of her discussion grows out of interaction with the neopentecostal movement, and her description is useful as an exclamation mark to the foregoing paragraphs:

> Those who trust that Guatemala's salvation is a part of God's plan,
> the ones who have the ability to intervene in the affairs of the country
> (or who are close to those who have this ability, or who consider

themselves close by reason of their social position), have an idea that what constitutes salvation for Guatemala is a link between prosperity and the maintenance of a strict morality. This morality is associated with the rejection of drug addiction, homosexuality and pornography, and, at a distance, corruption. But institutional violence or the violation of human rights, for example, are never considered. If the concept of salvation as applied to "the nation" is the patrimony of those who are able to perform acts related to the political destiny of Guatemala, the content given to such a concept is also their patrimony. And it is in this content that they formulate proposals that recreate the discourse over moral reform without entering in a single case into consideration of concrete political actions. (Cantón Delgado 1998, 265)

One remarkable aspect of evangelical political discourse is its apparent class base. While the neopentecostal presence necessarily deserves attention in terms of its past and present relation to Guatemalan politics, too much attention slants the results of the investigation. Steigenga is correct in remarking how neopentecostals are "a unique group of Protestants in Guatemala" (1999, 173). They stand out for their higher levels of education and for having "lower levels of perceived religious discrimination and religious conflict in their communities." Cynically, one suspects that the reason for the lack of conflict is the relative homogeneity of the community of neopentecostals. Here one might even think of an enclave mentality similar to that which seems to afflict political processes at the national level. Nevertheless, Steigenga is also correct in asserting that the unique position of the neopentecostals in terms of "background, resources, and motivation" helps position them to capitalize on openings within democratic politics in Guatemala (Steigenga 1999, 173–74).

The assessment is compelling precisely because so much written about Guatemalan evangelicals in the media, and even in some scholarly circles, focuses on the neopentecostal presidents and on neopentecostal connections to conservative political and social agendas that seem to mirror evangelical discourse in the United States. There can be no doubt that neopentecostal discourse draws attention to itself because of its radical edge, as well as its association with the recent dark past of Guatemala. It also commands attention because it sounds out of place in a nation that is still one of the poorest in the Western Hemisphere and human rights violations are so rarely addressed by those in power. Returning to the rubric of "low-intensity democracy," it is striking how much neopentecostal discourse refuses to deal with economic issues beyond decentralization of the economy. The shortcomings of neoliberal economics (evident in the widening gap between rich and poor throughout the world) and continuing violations of human rights are simply not on the agenda. A strong argument can be made that this is further evidence of the political (and social) naïveté of those who would run for office with an evangelical perspective. On the surface, Ríos Montt appears the exception in terms of naïveté, as his continued appeal in the political arena has to do with his strong response to violence and corruption. People as diverse as representatives of the AE and a resident of a largely Maya community who would be considered left-wing remarked to me in different contexts that it was striking how people could actually leave their homes and walk in the streets after Ríos Montt took power in 1982. This may also be one of the reasons why the FRG retains some of its electoral popularity. Whatever Ríos Montt's political realism and successes, however, they come at a high human cost.

A prominent theme in the literature on evangelicals and democracy in Guatemala is that the hope for a contribution by evangelicals to the strengthening of democracy begins with recognition of diversity within the evangelical community itself. The cases examined here show that diversity in practice. With the consensus running against the formation of an evangelical political party, the research suggests that the significance of evangelicalism in the political sphere is best addressed by continued research on the manner in which various evangelical actors engage political and social issues in very specific contexts. Examples of how evangelicals engage particular national issues such as the Código de la Niñez have as much to teach us as concentration on candidates for national office, or former presidents who represent limited currents within the evangelical stream. Dennis Smith and James Grenfell have reflected on the dearth of substantive involvement by evangelicals in public policy issues since the then Evangelical Synod of Guatemala supported a literacy campaign during the 1944–54 revolutionary period (1999, 27–28). Involvement in debate over the Código is the most recent example of such potentially constructive involvement.[22]

Likewise, Maya occupants of local political office have much to teach about the role evangelicals play in daily village life where people enjoy firsthand contact and where their religious commitments are worked out in proximity to opposing positions in local contexts. Moreover, as representatives of groups systematically excluded from power at the national level, their influence holds the potential to be even more significant in terms of national politics than might at first appear. This is a complex issue from the political and religious vantage points, as well as from any type of perspective emphasizing identity politics. From the vantage point of civil society, the latter issue has taken on new salience since Serrano Elías left the presidency in disgrace. The issue of indigenous rights is a poignant example. Although Rigoberta Menchú won the Nobel Peace Prize in 1992, there was little talk in 1993 of a national-level Maya movement that could advocate in a concerted way for cultural as well as political and economic equality in Guatemala.

Research on the nexus between ethnicity, evangelicalism, and national politics after the war is only now beginning. Two of the Maya office-holders interviewed for this project were in power during the time leading up to the negotiation of the peace. The implications remain to be fleshed out in the light of new examples. What is demonstrable is a transcending of narrow preoccupations with conversion and personal salvation that holds out the possibility of evangelical engagement in other political contexts.

Conclusion

The most hopeful perspectives regarding evangelicals and politics in Guatemala are those that view evangelicals as part of a burgeoning civil society that challenges the impunity of the state. This comment is made with clear knowledge of the near truism that "civil society can be uncivil"; the recent spate of lynchings is the proof in contemporary Guatemala. Yet it is the pluralism of perspectives among evangelical communities and the desire to offer something out of their diverse experiences to processes larger than the communities themselves that hold out hope for constructive political participation based on more than a naïveté that seeks to create direct parallels between contemporary politics and images drawn from the Bible and a culture literally three thousand years and half a world away.

Comparing Guatemala's politically engaged evangelicals with those in Brazil and Zambia, a few key generalizations hold.[23] One is that the political legitimacy of both Guatemalan presidents, like the legitimacy of key evangelical actors in Brazil and Zambia such as former president Chiluba, has been called into question. Serrano Elías dug his own political grave and is now commonly referred to as a thief. Ironically, Ríos Montt maintains the image for many of a good evangelical. When I was finally able to meet him, he was teaching Sunday School at "La 16" congregation of El Verbo, and he referred to himself as an *anciano viejo* ("old elder") when I asked what his position was in relation to the governance of the church. In June 2001, a group called the Asociación de Justicia y Reconciliación filed a complaint against Ríos Montt and four other former army officers for the crime of genocide (*Guatemala Hoy,* June 7, 2001). Rumors indicate that he no longer leaves the country for fear of a Pinochet-style arrest on foreign soil, and in July 2006, a Spanish judge issued an international warrant for his arrest. Yet Ríos Montt remains a formidable figure in Guatemalan politics, announcing in early 2007 that he would run for Congress later in the year.

To be sure, the concept of civil society itself is complex and fraught with ambiguities (Diamond 1999; Lively and Reeve 1997). Dodson (1997) argues for the potential of evangelicals to make a positive contribution to civil society. His perspective is that the participation of pentecostals in congregational life and the subsequent "finding of one's voice in the context of an association" might "lead to participation in the wider activities of civil society" (1997, 37). This is the kind of optimism leading Ireland (1999) to suggest that popular religion in Latin America in Catholic communities, pentecostalism, and Afro-Brazilian religions does indeed have something to offer for the creation of democratic societies in the region. Ireland emphasizes the role of the groups mentioned in creating and maintaining civil associations, reinforcing the "Tocquevillian parallel." In the specific case of Guatemala, this perspective on evangelicals has to be seen in light of Yashar's conclusion "that without a publicly expressed division within the traditional elites over authoritarian practices, in conjunction with a rise in popular organization, prospects for a democratizing coalition in Guatemala...appear dim" (1997, 230).

By taking some of the attention away from Guatemala's evangelical presidents, I have tried to bring a greater focus on the diversity of evangelical responses in the midst of efforts at the state level to consolidate peace and democracy in a society scarred by violence, poverty, and bitter ethnic strife. The Guatemalan case is unique in Latin America because of the demographic prominence of the evangelicals and the exclusion of the majority ethnic group from political and social power. The pluralism of the evangelical community forces the recognition that overconfident predictions about the influence of evangelicals on democratic consolidation are unwarranted. While the "biblical-ideological" discourse of some individuals and groups favors a perception of evangelicals as power mongers, it is difficult to see them taking the full reins of power without an effective political base such as a political party. Beyond all stereotypes, the evidence points to a new day in the relationship of evangelicals to their society. Even in the shadow of the fear that "things can change," the evidence points to a more diverse and more astute evangelical engagement with political issues than ever before.

In the end, the question is not so much whether or not evangelicals contribute to liberal democracy or to the consolidation of democracy; the question has to do with the role evangelicals play in the larger context of a democratic process, the "how" of political participation—including democratic movements in rural areas. There is an edge of ambiguity at the moment. As Levine and Stoll note: "Building social capital is a project for the long haul: Closing the gap between empowerment and power is less a matter of bringing the majority to power than of learning to live and survive as a minority, playing the political game day to day at all levels" (1997, 94). While Ríos Montt continues to embody the authoritarian past, some groups perceived to have links to that past, such as the AE, demonstrate a willingness to pursue dialogue on some issues, although their agenda seems limited. The Maya mayors interviewed would seem to lend support to a positive response when one thinks of the formation of coalitions and the representation of new voices in politics. There is evidence that some evangelicals are moving beyond naïveté and into sustained engagement with political processes, at least on the community level and in regard to some national-level issues.

Too often evangelicals have been examined as a group somehow distinct from society. Yet if Yashar is correct in saying that "certain conditions encourage or discourage coalitions that will build democracy...and sustain [it] in the face of opposition" (1997, 15), then evangelicals are in fact part of coalitions broader than the constituency of their own *hermanos* in the faith. This recalls my friend's notion of the multiple identities of each person. In the hoped-for movement from the repressive and authoritarian politics of the past to the progressive politics of peace, no understanding of evangelicals and their relationship to power is possible without attention to the pluralism of Protestant voices. The multiple identities of each person do indeed affect the issue of who contributes to democracy and how. In 1982 when Ríos Montt landed in the presidency, the specter of spiritual as well as actual war hung over Guatemala. More than twenty-five years later, consolidation of peace and democracy holds out the possibility for reconciliation in the heart of Guatemalan society and between the country's diverse peoples. In this hard and multifaceted task, evangelicals are surely playing a role.

ACKNOWLEDGMENTS

This essay could not have been written without significant support by a number of people. First, my colleagues working in Latin America for this project have been engaging and insightful in their own work. Their enthusiasm and commitment to the project have inspired me. Our times together in Campinas, Miami, and Chaclacayo have been all too brief but have provided community in the best sense of that word. Paul Freston and Timothy Shah have kept our eyes focused on the final outcome of the larger project.

Dennis Smith, communications specialist with the Centro Evangélico de Estudios Pastorales en América Central (CEDEPCA), shared insights and resources based on his long experience. He also gave me access to the CEDEPCA documentation center in Guatemala City. Dennis and Maribel Smith, Ken and Kennis Kim, and Robert and Linda Moore all made my sojourns in the field pleasant. Dr. Rudy and Shirley Nelson and my doctoral advisor, Dr. Robert Carmack, all made helpful suggestions along the way. Dr. Carmack also pointed me in the direction of valuable bibliographical references. Tim O'Toole helped me with scanning photographs.

I thank those in Guatemala who graciously granted me interviews and helped me make contacts. Particularly helpful in the latter category were Maya Cu and Rosario Cruz. Rev. Rafael Escobar shared his insight into the pentecostal and neopentecostal communities. Alvaro Velásquez of the Universidad Rafael Landivar attended our meeting in Chaclacayo and made provocative comments on the work. A number of people in the Mam Presbytery of the National Evangelical Presbyterian Church have taught me much about Maya perspectives on evangelicalism and about the evangelical community in general. The usual disclaimer applies in terms of responsibility for errors.

NOTES

1. I have not entered the discussion of the difference between pluralism and diversity in this article. Within the confines of democracy in Guatemala, evangelical diversity translates into pluralism in terms of attempts to influence political processes. See Riis (1999) for a useful discussion of religious pluralism and the introductory comments in Beckford (1999) for a distinction between diversity as a fact and pluralism as an ideological strategy.

2. I generally use "evangelical" as opposed to "Protestant" as the term for non-Catholic Christians who are variously labeled Protestants, evangelicals, pentecostals, neopentecostals, and even fundamentalists. *Evangelical* is the most common self-identification among these groups in Guatemala. While the word glosses over diversity within the evangelical community, it does retain the sense that all groups give a certain degree of authority to Christian scripture (the Evangel), while simultaneously signaling their religious identity as other than Catholic. Pentecostals constitute the majority of evangelicals in Guatemala and elsewhere in Latin America. When further descriptors are necessary to emphasize differences, e.g. between historical Protestants and pentecostals or neopentecostals, I provide that information.

3. In her documentation of the celebration, Garrard-Burnett (1998a, 157–58) says that five hundred thousand people were reported to have attended the rally, although she questions that number in a footnote. Her chapter entitled "The Protestant President" (138–61) provides an analysis of Ríos Montt's tenure in office and the ambiguities his presence created within the evangelical community.

4. See Jonas (2000, chap. 8), on the referendum.

5. This was one of a series of scandals that have dogged the FRG and given the party the image of impunity in light of its dominance of the executive and legislature. Although several were later cleared, some twenty-four FRG deputies, including Ríos Montt, were initially implicated and stripped of their immunity from prosecution.

6. Bianchi left El Verbo in early 2001 and joined El Shaddai, another large neopentecostal congregation in Guatemala City in which Serrano Elías had been a "prophet" at the time of his election to the presidency. Information about the ARDE before the elections says that he served as "the director general for El Verbo ministries" beginning in 1996. The piece also indicates that he was vice president of the Evangelical Alliance of Guatemala during 1998–99. El Verbo congregations are governed by a council of elders, one of whom has primary responsibilities at any given time.

7. The Anfuso and Sczepanski volume is a hagiographic work emphasizing Ríos Montt's path to the presidency and role of his religious beliefs and relationship to El Verbo during his time in office. According to this work, Bianchi and Alvaro Contreras were required to renounce their positions in the church when they went to work in the national palace. Stoll mentions the "shepherding-style doctrine or spiritual pact" at the center of El Verbo's theology, so that "when Ríos went to the national palace, he did so under the spiritual authority of the Word church."

8. The use of the term *cristiano* here clearly has a more ecumenical sense than in much evangelical discourse in Mesoamerica, where it is often used only for those who have converted from Catholicism. Sanchíz Ochoa indicates that this is common among elite pentecostals and reflects class interests (1998, 55).

9. The term means *leader* in Spanish and the acronym is for "the liberty, development, and renewal of Guatemala."

10. This article notes that a new party has to formulate bylaws (*estatutos*) and collect five thousand signatures in order to register. Interestingly, the article also mentions the possibility of creating a school to train future political leaders. Two universities are said to have been contacted in this regard: Mariano Gálvez University, which has historical ties to the Protestant community in Guatemala, and the Panamerican University founded by El Verbo.

11. I thank Thomas Offit for helping me think through issues regarding the Code.

12. A lengthier document outlining this principle as "THE FAMILY, understood as the basic and natural form of the community and human society," was later disseminated by the bishops.

13. *Ladino* is the term used in Guatemala and southern Mexico for the Spanish-speaking, usually mestizo, population. The term has cultural connotations in the sense that it represents those who are not indigenous. One of the aspects of contemporary identity politics in Guatemala is the issue of what it means to have a large population perceived as not having a culture, such as the Maya population. The *Journal of Latin American Anthropology*, vol. 6, no. 2 (2001), has a major section devoted to "Rethinking Polarized Ethnicities" in Guatemala.

14. One work examining Guatemala's relationship with the United States and, consequently, with the international community emphasizes that "even in the 1980s this Central American nation had forged diplomatic relations with fewer than fifty other countries" (Ebel, Taras, and Cochrane 1991, 157). The authors use the lens of *caudillaje* (strong personalized leadership) as the interpretive frame for their work. Regardless of whether one accepts that model, social criticism from inside or outside the country is more difficult in such a context.

15. The *"intendente* system" of this period involved the president appointing the senior governing official in towns and rural communities. *Intendentes* were community outsiders, Ladinos, and not answerable to the local communities (Ebel 1972, 162–63).

16. The Iglesia de Cristo congregation was organized in 1926 (IENPG 1982, 292). Most early missionary work in the country and in the western highlands was among urban Ladinos. Amid struggles over the appropriate language for evangelization and the relationship of language to acculturating the native population, Cameron Townsend began work in 1919 among Kaqchikel speakers in San Antonio Aguascalientes (Garrard-Burnett 1989, 130). At the time Townsend was working with the Central American Mission. He went on to found the Wycliffe Bible Translators, also known in the field as the Summer Institute of Linguistics (Stoll 1982, 19–61).

17. The word used in Spanish for recovery in this sense is *reivindicación*. It denotes recovery, but also the vindicating of Maya culture in the face of opposition. A basic source for the Maya Movement is Fischer and Brown (1996). See also Gálvez Borrell and Esquit Choy (1997).

18. I thank Dr. Robert Carmack for making the parallel. See the helpful discussion in Tedlock (1992, 53–58). Two useful sources for the Mam area are Greenberg (1984, 93–162) and Peck (1970).

19. The interview was in 1996. For evidence of burgeoning social consciousness among Latin American pentecostals, see Petersen (1996).

20. For another critique of Huntington and a proposal for dealing with religion in pluralistic contexts, see Stepan (2000). One of Stepan's essential arguments is that there is a reciprocal need for "twin tolerations" between religious individuals and groups on the one hand and political institutions on the other. Fulfilling this necessity for toleration would result in "minimal freedom of action" for the institution or group in question at a particular moment. I thank Ed Cleary for this reference.

21. Tillich's notion of the Protestant Principle is relevant here. The term seems to have been used in a couple of senses, including as "an expression of the conquest of religion by the Spiritual Presence and consequently an expression of the victory over the ambiguities of religion, its profanization, and its demonization" (Tillich 1967, 42). The relevance to religious discourse is the contrast between the spiritual realm and the present realities of a particular religious community. This contrast allows for the subjective interpretation of religious truth, or for the possession of authority by individuals who might be inclined to form a community more reflective of the spiritual truth they know (subjectively) to be true. In this way, the transcendent becomes a source of division. This diffuse sense of authority in evangelical religion is a useful corollary to observations of Catholic corporatism and its relation to the state in Latin America. The notion poses the issue of religious meaning as a contrast to interpretations of evangelical reality based on institutional analysis or the marketing and appropriation of symbolic goods.

22. It is important to note that the AE had some participation in the National Reconciliation Commission that grew out of the Esquipulas II meeting in 1987 and led to the Diálogo Nacional in 1989, which demonstrated that civil society would have to be taken into account in discussions between the URNG and the government. The AE also participated in dialogue between the URNG and the religious sector in 1990. These were early steps in what became the peace process that was formally initiated in March 1990. One of the primary brokers of this process was the Lutheran World Federation. One interpretation is that AE participation faded when another evangelical voice from the left became more prominent in commission meetings and the leadership of the AE felt their participation was diminished. Several years ago, the AE also established the Permanent Civic Commission (COCIPE; Comisión Cívico Permanente) to deal with political and social issues of a civic nature.

23. For Brazil, see Freston (1996, 2001) and Fonseca (chapter 5 here). Freston (2001) also summarizes the Zambian case in some detail.

3

The Evolution of Protestant Participation in Nicaraguan Politics and the Rise of Evangelical Parties

Roberto Zub

To speak of Protestantism and politics is to speak of almost all the central themes of Nicaraguan history in the twentieth century. The Protestant presence dates from the last decade of the nineteenth century, although significant political involvement began only in the 1970s and gathered pace thereafter. In the 1990s, with governments once again enjoying close relations with the Catholic Church, the by now numerically strong and socially representative evangelicals turned to political action via a series of parties of evangelical inspiration. In this chapter, I concentrate mainly on the 1990s and on these evangelical parties, and especially on an analysis of the first pentecostals who reached the Nicaraguan congress during this period. I have used diverse documentary sources (internal documents produced by churches and parties; books; journals), questionnaires, and interviews with political and ecclesiastical leaders, as well as many years of close observation of Nicaraguan churches and politics.

My hypothesis is that Nicaraguan Protestantism contains antagonistic ideologies and structures; that the churches and evangelical parties reflect the *caudillismo* (strong personalistic leadership) that predominates in society; and that evangelical parties are in large part schemes for tapping into political power with the aim of creating a duopoly and sharing the privileges that the state offers to the Catholic Church.

It is worth adding that this chapter scarcely mentions the Protestantism of the Atlantic Coast, a region that is predominantly Indian and black and where the Moravian Church has an important presence. This ethnic Protestantism would merit an entirely separate examination. While the Pacific coast was colonized by the Spanish and evangelized by the Roman Catholics from the sixteenth century, the Atlantic (Caribbean) coast was under English influence from the seventeenth century. Moravian missionaries arrived in 1849, followed later by Anglicans and Baptists, with the result that the (sparsely populated) region is today predominantly Protestant.

Nicaragua, with a population of just over five million, still depends heavily on the export of agricultural products. Its location within the geopolitical sphere of the United States has had a massive effect on political and economic life, and its Protestantism is largely of American origin.[1] The Central American Mission (since 1901) was followed by the establishment of other churches, whether of missionary or national origin: the Assemblies of God (1912), Baptists (1917), Apostolics (1918), Church of Christ (1928), Nazarenes (1943), Church of God (1951), United Pentecostal Evangelical Mission (1954), Four-Square (1955), Christian Mission (1959), and others. All adopted an evangelistic posture antagonistic to the Catholic Church, which they blamed for the mistreatment of the indigenous population and for the symbiosis between the cross and the sword, as well as for keeping the people in religious ignorance.

The Protestant population in 1980, just after the Sandinista revolution, was an estimated 3.2 percent. By 1998, it had grown to an estimated 12.2 percent. Besides rapid expansion, Nicaraguan Protestantism is also characterized by fragmentation into over two hundred denominations, representing considerable theological, political, and social diversity. Most Protestants today are pentecostal or neopentecostal, heavily influenced by beliefs in "spiritual warfare," the prosperity gospel, divine healing, and speaking in tongues. The evangelical community is disproportionately female (62 percent) and strong among the rural population of the north (INDEF 1998, 11–17).

Protestantism as Supporting Actor in the Transition to a Modern State

In 1893 José Santos Zelaya, inspired by the ideals of the French Revolution and English liberalism, led a military coup that put an end to the conservative government allied with the Catholic Church. This resulted in both socioeconomic transformation and new laws on religious freedom guaranteeing toleration for non-Catholic groups. The Concordat with the Vatican was abolished, including economic support for the clergy, seminaries, and church buildings. Civil registration was introduced, cemeteries were secularized, and lay state education was implanted.

As the Spanish colonial ideological and social model was left behind, Nicaragua was more and more integrated into a neocolonial relationship with the United States. British and especially American missionaries soon arrived to establish the first Protestant churches and schools.[2] "In the collective imaginary of the Nicaraguan ruling class...the secret of civilization and progress lay abroad. This attitude helped the entry of Protestant foreigners" (Madrigal 1999, 89).[3] Foreign capital developed the infrastructure for Nicaragua to become a large-scale exporter of coffee. As Míguez Bonino says of the region as a whole: "At a time when Latin America was slowly emerging from its colonial history and seeking integration into the modern world, Protestantism signified a call to change, to transformation, centred on the religious sphere and with repercussions in the whole of life and society" (1983, 21). The missionaries were sympathetic to liberal anticlericalism and shared its modernizing project based on economic liberalization, cultural democratization, and individual rights. They favored economic and religious free enterprise, political pluralism, and a secular state.[4] In their preaching, they called for sobriety, hard work, family responsibility, and a life free of vices (such as drinking and gambling). Apparently apolitical, Protestantism sought to develop the individual, guarantee his or her efficiency at work, and integrate him or her into the nation and the modern world through trade. Political hopes were expressed through the project of transforming the people who would govern the nation and by social service to the needy. They believed that "the spiritual and moral values of Protestantism would be the key to solving not only the religious problems of Latin America, but also the economic crises (poverty), political crises (authoritarianism and corruption) and cultural crises (ignorance and superstition)" (Rooy 1992, 245). That is why the first Protestant denominations invested heavily in schools (the Baptist College of Managua was founded in 1918).

First Political Incursions

In early Protestant history in Nicaragua, there is a curious mixing of pastoral and military leadership. The most important examples were José Manuel Arguello, a general who was also a pastor of the Central American Mission church; Captain José Santos Mendoza, who was pastor of the First Baptist Church; Colonel Ramiro Cortés, a Baptist layman and later a founder of the Church of Christ; and General Francisco Montoya de Navarrete, also a Baptist layman. These leading figures in the liberal army, who were probably also Freemasons, reveal a close relationship between Protestantism and the remnants of *zelayismo* after Zelaya's United States–provoked fall in 1909 (in opposition to his nationalist attempts to reduce economic dependence on the United States) (Pixley and Ruiz 1992, 29).

The new Conservative government restricted freedom of religion, and Protestants occasionally suffered at the hands of mobs instigated by Catholic priests. Manuel Bustamante, a Mexican Assemblies of God missionary, found a way around the authorities' tolerance of religious persecution: "I asked the authorities for protection, but as my situation only got worse I sought protection from the guerrilla leader Augusto César Sandino, since we had become friends when he was in Mexico. . . . The protection he gave me was a flag, and with it the Indians no longer molested me" (in Matamoros 1984, 34–35).

The first Baptists did not make any public statements regarding the civil war between liberals and conservatives that erupted in 1926, or the occupation of the country by U.S. marines in 1927 that led to the anti-imperialist guerrilla movement headed by Sandino. For Mondragón, this silence is due to Protestants having assimilated the pan-Americanist perspective that undergirded U.S. interventionism (1994, 15). After Sandino was betrayed and killed in 1934, the United States nationalized the conflict by training a new National Guard, whose commander became, in 1936, the first member of the Somoza family to govern Nicaragua. The dynasty (of father and two sons) was to remain in power until it was overthrown by the Sandinista revolution in 1979.

In this period we find the first Protestant to occupy a seat in the Nicaraguan congress, the Moravian Alfred Hooker from the Atlantic Coast, elected in 1911 by the Liberal Party.

Sociopolitical Participation of Protestants in the Somoza Period (1936–79)

From the mid-1930s, Nicaragua achieved a semblance of stability under a rising military caste led by General Anastacio Somoza. Around him and his sons Luis and Anastacio there grew a power nucleus based mainly on personal loyalty. The Somozas' power was based on the simultaneous control of the state and the National Guard, and they enriched themselves fabulously through corruption and land-grabbing.

Somoza was officially a liberal and as such inherited solid Protestant support. But Protestantism's relationship with him over the years was ambiguous. Many were not convinced he could bring the moral and material changes they desired, but felt unable to delegitimize him since he was protected by, and protector of, American interests. On his part, Somoza saw little reason to relate to the numerically insignificant Protestant community, and grew progressively closer to the Catholic Church.

Protestantism as a whole had no influence in government, although a few members held public and elective posts thanks to their class position and friendship with the Somozas. Such was the case of the Baptist deputies elected by the Liberal Party in 1940, Fernando Delgadillo and General Luciano Astorga.[5]

In the 1950s, Protestant political participation was even scarcer. In part, this was due to the influence of fundamentalist ideas regarding "dirty" politics and the Cold War context. The pentecostals, beginning to grow in number, preached an "otherworldly" theology that resulted in self-exclusion from politics. The Cold War context was reinforced by the arrival of American missionaries expelled (or redirected) from China, and later by exiled Cuban pastors, some of whom came to occupy key positions in churches and seminaries.

In the early 1960s, the Catholic Church pressed for the reintroduction of compulsory Catholic religious education in schools. Protestants organized the "Evangelical Committee in Defense of Laicism," which they said encouraged "fraternal national life and a plurality of political, social and religious ideas, and avoided an official state religion" (Cortés 1989, 173). The struggle lasted from 1960 to 1966, during which time the organization Evangelism in Depth made its appearance in Nicaragua with mass "evangelical saturation campaigns."

In the 1970s, the Somoza regime was more open to Protestant participation. Napoleón Tapia, a Baptist coffee-grower and friend of Somoza, was elected deputy and then senator. The Baptist Armando Guido, the financier Raul Sandoval from the Central American Mission, and Rooy Hooker, a teacher from the Moravian Church, were all elected deputies for the Nationalist Liberal Party.[6] None of them owed their election specifically to support from evangelical voters. All were laymen, and were elected for their professional activities, proximity to Somoza, and local political leadership. In addition, Rodolfo Mejía, who had been president of the Baptist Convention in 1956–57, was nominated deputy-manager of the National Bank and then director of the controversial Agrarian Institute of Nicaragua (responsible for resettling thousands of peasants from land desired by the large cotton-growers).

The year 1972 was a changing-point in Protestant political involvement. After the destruction of Managua by an earthquake, the Evangelical Committee for Helping the Victims (CEPAD; Consejo Evangélico Pro-Ayuda a los Damnificados) was formed.[7] This was to have a profound effect on the churches, in their organization, leadership, and social programs. The churches took on a more holistic concept of mission and a more active sociopolitical role. Significantly, CEPAD refused to join the national relief committee presided over by Somoza, fearing what was later shown to have happened, that Somoza would divert international funds for his own personal and political benefit.

In the 1970s, various nongovernmental organizations (NGOs) were created that increased the churches' contact with the illiterate and excluded sectors of the population. These NGOs also linked Nicaraguan Protantism closer to European and North American agencies and to the World Council of Churches, the main sources of their funding. Institutions such as Alfalit, which struggled against illiteracy, the Baptist Hospital, the Project of Vaccination and Communal Development (PROVADENIC), the Polytechnical University (1967), and the Ondas de Luz Radio station (1958) created a feeling of evangelical identity and were at times subversive of the political status quo.

At the same time, the pentecostal field, much of it still closely linked to American initiatives, was enjoying rapid expansion through crusades and the founding of new churches. Their emphasis was on personal conversion, and concern for social problems was minimal; many even interpreted the earthquake as divine intervention to punish an idolatrous people. In any case, the class situation of most pentecostals at the time provided them with little capital (material or intellectual) for social intervention; but their numerical growth would in the end turn them into political actors in the 1990s.

On the other hand, a sector of urban Protestant youth, above all in student circles, had become progressively politicized since the mid-1960s, especially through the Student Christian Movement and the writings of theologians Richard Shaull (an American missionary in Brazil) and Dietrich Bonhoeffer. Some of these young people joined clandestine opposition movements in the 1970s.

By 1977 the business sector and the Catholic hierarchy were moving steadily into opposition to the regime. Somoza replied by bombing civilian areas. As the crisis neared its peak, Protestants were sharply divided. On the one hand, there were people such as Gustavo Wilson, director of the Baptist College, and Norberto Herrera, director of the Polytechnic University, who traveled to Washington to testify in defense of the regime regarding accusations from the Carter administration of human rights violations. In the face of this attack from a Baptist and evangelical U.S. president, Somoza mobilized pliant figures in the Nicaraguan Baptist elite to try and save his international image. On the other hand, broad Protestant sectors led by CEPAD were favorable to the Sandinista guerrillas, demanded the removal of press censorship, the state of siege, and martial law, denounced the regime's corruption, and justified armed revolt. The 1978 annual assembly of the Baptist Convention declared: "We cannot and should not, as evangelical citizens, continue to be silent and remain at the margin of national affairs." Instead, throwing aside selfish considerations, evangelicals "should renounce everything that impedes the re-establishment of justice, peace and fraternity" (Convención Bautista de Nicarágua, XLII Asamblea Anual, Manágua, January 12–16, 1978).

The Baptist seminary became a bastion of opposition activity, the students declaring that "the critical situation of the country is the result of the structural, institutional and individual sin of all" (*La Prensa*, April 14, 1978). The target of their critique was not only the regime but also pro-Somoza sectors of the Baptist leadership, notably the Cubans Mario Casanella, rector of the seminary, and Juan Pablo Tamayo, pastor of the First Baptist Church of Managua.

Protestantism and the Sandinista Revolution (1979–90)

With the fall of Somoza, a National Reconstruction junta came to power. It included business elements, but the real power lay with the former guerrillas. They identified themselves as heirs of Sandino, the nationalist leader of the 1930s, but much of the Sandinista movement (which had been founded in 1961) was strongly influenced by Marxism and Leninist and Cuban political models in particular.

Evangelical political participation during these years varied widely. On the one hand, there was some involvement in governmental structures. At the other extreme, some preached armed resistance and were even involved with the *contras* (the American-armed counterrevolutionary movements). Most, however, opted for neutrality and distance from politics.

In October 1979, an interdenominational pastors' retreat produced the "Declaration of the 500," giving "thanks to God our Father for the victory of the Nicaraguan people and for the instrument of liberation, the Sandinista Front for National Liberation [FSLN; Frente Sandinista de Liberación Nacional]. . . . We recognize that the evangelical churches have had a political, military, moral and spiritual participation in the freedom struggle."[8]

As the Sandinistas kept a grip on political hegemony, the initial alliance with the business sectors did not last, despite the mixed economic model. An armed counterrevolutionary movement soon arose, encouraged and funded by the new Reagan administration in the United States, and the Catholic hierarchy's relationship with the Sandinista government became strained. This was to have an effect on the government's approach to evangelicals.

In the first years of the new government, more radical sectors of Sandinismo classified the evangelical churches as "sects" and portrayed their services and evangelistic campaigns as part of an ideological invasion. Their rapid growth was viewed through the lens of a conspiracy theory that saw evangelical expansion as part of Washington's strategy to destabilize the revolution.

The theory was not without some grounding. In the 1980s, a significant number of pastors and laypeople were involved in military activity against the Sandinista government, which they identified with "atheistic communism." Others were involved with counterrevolutionary centers in Miami or Costa Rica, or with the *contra* training camps in Honduras. In addition, the perception of an evangelical counterrevolutionary conspiracy was based on aspects of evangelical religious life within the country. High-profile foreign evangelists carried out crusades in the poorer suburbs with sophisticated sound equipment and indirect criticism of the Nicaraguan situation. During a government vaccination campaign, one American evangelist told his listeners not to get vaccinated, as "health comes only from God." Another, Morris Cerullo, declared as he was boarding the plane to fly to Nicaragua that he was on his way "to expel the demons from Nicaragua," the demons being understood to be the Sandinistas. The Salvadoran preacher Dina Santamaría prophesied that the Sandinistas would poison the water of Managua. In addition, local evangelicals painted slogans on walls that were interpreted by many Sandinistas as being counterrevolutionary. "Christ is coming" was understood as "the counterrevolution is coming"; and "Christ yesterday, Christ today, Christ forever" as a caricature of the Sandinista slogan "Sandino yesterday, Sandino today, Sandino forever." Less ambiguous was the slogan "With God and patriotism we shall defeat communism."

Pastors returning from the United States were sometimes held temporarily in custody and accused of receiving aid from "counterrevolutionary" groups, such as the Central Intelligence Agency, the Christian Emergency Relief Team, or the Institute for Religion and Democracy. Groups of Sandinista Youth were involved in physical takeovers of evangelical church buildings. But fears of Soviet-style intervention in religious activity did not materialize, and pentecostal growth continued apace.

In October 1980, the FSLN produced an "Official Communiqué of the National Directorate on Religion," which recognized the Christian participation in the revolution. "For the FSLN, freedom to profess a religious faith is an inalienable right. . . . No one may be discriminated against in the New Nicaragua for publicly professing or propagating their religious beliefs" (Nicaráuac 1981, 93).

In May 1980, when the government created the Council of State, an appointed colegislative body that included opposition parties and representatives of mass organizations, economic groups, and other categories, it approached the very pro-Sandinista group called Ecumenical Axis. Its leader, Baptist pastor José Miguel Torres, proposed, as Protestant representative on the Council of State, the veteran Baptist José María Ruiz, and as his alternate the Assemblies of God pastor Oscar Godoy (later expelled from the Assemblies of God). Ruiz, who had been a Catholic priest with a doctorate from the Gregorian University and then rector of the Baptist seminary of Managua, proclaimed as he took up his appointment: "No-one can deny the magnificent intentions with which this revolutionary process has begun, with the objective of putting our people on the road to progress . . . and of cleansing it from the contaminations of the Somoza government" (Amanecer, June 1981).

When relations between Sandinistas and the Catholic hierarchy deteriorated in 1982, there was a corresponding strengthening of ties between the former and the leaders of some Protestant sectors, transforming the latter into "privileged clients" of the state just as the Catholic base communities were. Links with the Baptists were emphasized, in an effort to gain added legitimacy in the eyes of the international community, especially in the United States. This allowed the Baptist leadership to have a prophetic role by means of pastoral letters, although many Baptists supported the FSLN rather uncritically. In any case, evangelical leaders were able to play key roles in promoting peace, and this meant unprecedented visibility for the evangelical churches in the Nicaraguan context. In a way no previous Nicaraguan rulers had done, President Ortega and other *comandantes* of the FSLN accepted invitations to make speeches at denominational assemblies or at the crusades conducted by evangelists such as the Puerto Rican Yiye Avila and the Argentinian Alberto Mottesi. Never before had television, radio, and the press given such space to the activities and declarations of evangelical organizations as during the 1980s. This "substitution" of the traditional Catholic role had to do with evangelical numerical growth, as well as with the financial strength of CEPAD, whose annual budget was over ten million dollars.

In 1984, the first elections for president and members of the National Assembly took place. Evangelical candidates were chosen by the FSLN without consulting the churches. The candidates were the octogenarian Baptist leader José María Ruiz, who was reelected, and Sixto Ulloa, even though neither actually belonged to the Sandinista Front.

Sixto Ulloa, a Baptist layman without higher education, had been an important figure in CEPAD. He came to play the role of negotiator between the churches and the FSLN during several conflicts, especially the takeover of church buildings, military service for pastors, and the imprisonment of some pastors for antigovernment activities. In an interview with the author he explained his invitation to run for deputy as showing that "there is political pluralism in the Sandinista Front and the desire to have candidates who are not party members" (interview, November 3, 1999). Other evangelicals were elected as mayors and town councillors.

The novelty in all this, according to Pixley, is "a break with the classical model of looking for favors" (interview, January 26, 2001). In another sense, Ruiz and Ulloa continued the liberal Protestant tradition of political participation through existing structures rather than by creating specifically Protestant ones.

Ulloa accompanied the Sandinista presidential candidate Daniel Ortega during the campaign. "I went to each denomination to ask for their votes and all of them gave me moral and spiritual support. I believe I had the support of the Assemblies of God, the Central American church, and the Baptist Convention" (interview, November 3, 1999). (The support of the Assemblies of God, however, is dubious: only a few pastors were close to the FSLN, while many others were reluctant to jeopardize their privileged standing in the United States.)

Ulloa claims he accepted the Sandinista invitation to be a candidate "as long as they respected my principles: human rights and freedom of worship . . . I was opposed when the Sandinista Defence Committees took over churches. I did not agree with the persecution of certain pastors, or with the army's position on military service" (interview). Ulloa generally negotiated the release of imprisoned pastors and laypeople, and the return of church buildings, directly with President Ortega.

In 1987, the regional peace accord of Esquipulas required the government to nominate a National Reconciliation Commission to be composed of a Catholic bishop, representatives of the government and opposition, and a "notable person" to be chosen by the FSLN. The notable person chosen was the pastor of the first Baptist Church of Managua, the medical doctor Gustavo Parajón, leader of CEPAD since its founding in 1972. The choice was a recognition not just of Parajón's public leadership but also of the international links of the Baptists, especially with the United States.

Many other evangelicals were prominent in reconciliation and peace committees in the war zones. Institutions such as CEPAD, the Inter-Ecclesial Center of Theological and Social Studies (CIEETS; Centro Inter-eclesial de Estudios Teológicos y Sociales), the Baptist Convention, and the Moravian Church channeled services and protested against the blockade imposed by the Reagan administration. While the more fundamentalist sectors combated the revolution by all available means, the progressives linked to liberation theology were uncritically accepting of the FSLN. The Evangelical Commission for Social Responsibility (CEPRES; Comisión Evangélica para la Promoción de la Responsabilia Social), for example, led by a pentecostal, identified the revolution as "the arrival of the Kingdom of God."

Most pentecostals, however, were antipolitical and apocalyptic, emphasizing the salvation of souls, and this may have helped their rapid growth during the 1980s. Thus, in various ways, Protestantism under the Sandinistas ceased to be the peripheral and marginal phenomenon it had always been in most of Nicaragua and achieved enhanced social status and political prominence.

From the Election of Violeta Chamorro to the Rise
of the Evangelical Parties (1990–96)

In the February 1990 elections, the National Opposition Union (UNO; Unión Nacional Opositora) triumphed with 54 percent of the vote while the government received only 40 percent, putting an end to over a decade of Sandinista rule. The opposition candidate was Violeta Chamorro, widow of a famous journalist assassinated under Somoza.

A survey (Zub 1993) shows that 24.2 percent of evangelicals attended an election meeting during the campaign, although there was considerable variation between Baptists (34.7 percent) and Assemblies of God members (only

7.1 percent). Most evangelicals who did go to a meeting went to a Sandinista one (18.5 percent). In Managua, UNO obtained 60 percent of the vote among Assemblies of God members and 69 percent among Four-Square members, but only 39 percent among Baptists. The FSLN, on the other hand, received 20 percent of the Assemblies of God votes and 16 percent of Four-Square votes, but 41 percent of Baptist votes. This contrasts with the general population of Managua, which voted 53 percent for UNO and 43 percent for the FSLN.

The most anti-Sandinista sector in the churches can be found by crosstabulating the data for voting and for "years in the church." Those who entered the evangelical churches through baptism between 1980 and 1985, the first years of the Sandinista revolution, were the most opposed to the FSLN. One explanation sometimes suggested for this is that the anti-Sandinista rich fled to Miami, while the poor found refuge in the pentecostal churches.

Even among the Baptists, the vote for the FSLN is slightly lower than the average in Managua, while the Assemblies of God vote for the UNO is significantly higher. Another significant difference is that the Liberal Party (PL; Partido Liberal), which ran separately in the election and received only 0.6 percent, nevertheless obtained 10.2 percent among evangelicals (although only 1.8 percent in the Assemblies of God), reflecting the persistence of the traditional anticlerical link between Protestantism and the liberals.

After the 1990 elections, the evangelicals' lack of access to the new centers of power, allied to a new perception of the importance of their now greatly expanded constituency, led to greater concern with politics. My hypothesis is that in the 1990s, important sectors of ecclesiastical leadership encouraged the creation of political parties to restore space for representation in the state, in order to make themselves heard and respected and even to conquer slivers of power.

At the same time, we should not overlook external influences on these changes in evangelicalism. At international conferences such as that at Lausanne in 1974 and the Grand Rapids consultation of 1982, reference is made not only to social responsibility but also to political action. And the "Los Angeles 88" conference encouraged the churches to use their numerical influence to affect political systems. (More than twenty Nicaraguan evangelical leaders attended "Los Angeles 88" and tried, without success, to get the conference to issue a pronouncement against the Sandinistas.) In addition, the Third Latin American Congress on Evangelization (CLADE III; Congreso Latinoamericano de Evangelización) in 1992 issued statements favorable to political participation.

The Chamorro government reestablished relations with the Catholic Church, granted land and buildings for the Catholic University (UNICA; Universidad Católica), assisted the construction of the cathedral of Managua, and favored Catholic Church programs with state lottery money. The visit of the pope was preceded by heavy state investment in infrastructure and publicity.

In addition, various events during the Chamorro period contributed to a sense of marginalization on the part of Protestants. In 1992, the Finance Ministry levied taxes on Protestant churches but not on the Catholic Church. In Nicaragua, Protestant churches have the same juridical status as private companies, and the government wanted them to pay value-added tax on their donations received. At the same time, the Catholic Church was being consulted by the government on various state initiatives, had its masses broadcast on state television, chaplaincies assigned in the armed forces, and Catholic images displayed in public squares. Protestants began to demand equality in the use of state media, since the latter are maintained by taxes paid by the population. Their demands were a defense of their right to cultural reproduction and a reaction to the socioeconomic changes that threatened their financial capacity. At this time, Protestant groups started Channel 21 television and various radio stations.

In 1993, the education minister, a member of the Catholic organization Opus Dei, introduced a bill in congress to reestablish obligatory Catholic religious education in schools, provoking large demonstrations on the part of Protestants (Zub 1996, 121–23).

In the 1980s, the pentecostals had questioned the Sandinistas' commitment to religious freedom when some church premises were invaded and a few foreign preachers were denied entry to the country. But now, in the 1990s, under a democratic regime, the same question of religious freedom was being raised; and this time, both pentecostals and historical Protestants were united in believing there was a conspiracy to weaken their institutions.

During the Chamorro government, there was no formal channel of communication between the Protestant community and the state. Rodolfo Mejía, a Baptist, was the only Protestant elected to parliament in 1990 (with UNO), but a year into his mandate he died. The fluid interaction that had obtained during the Sandinista period was now lost. In this context of lack of channels of communication, some of the more conservative sectors of Protestantism began to create their own channels. The opening up to politics began with a series of "revelations" to leaders that served to legitimate the change. With a lack of precedents or of established political channels, divine legitimation was necessary for actions that had previously been off limits.

Initiatives to create an evangelical party may well be linked to the perceived abyss between the growing Assemblies of God denomination and the Nicaraguan state.By the 1990s, the Assemblies of God had reached about six hundred churches, some 150 schools, started with the help of American missions, and ninety thousand members, and they felt unjustly excluded from power. Uniting feelings of social and religious exclusion, they took action in the religious sphere to overcome their marginalization.

The new geopolitical situation of the 1990s after the disintegration of the socialist bloc in Europe and the end of the Cold War also prompted action based on a changing sense of reality. The image of pentecostalism as an alienating movement that impedes the political struggles of oppressed peoples is paradoxically being transformed, as pentecostals take up a form of political activity based on the churches themselves.

Steps toward the Formation of Evangelical Parties

The atomization of Nicaraguan Protestantism makes it unwise to speak of a Protestant "community" or "people"; rather, one can refer to a multiplicity of associations, committees, alliances, and conventions. Fragmentation means Nicaraguan Protestantism is incapable of constituting a single voice to speak to the state or to other social sectors. As we shall see, this fragmentation also affects its attempts at party and electoral unity.

By the 1990s, Protestantism was not only a numerical but also a social force, thanks to its universities, its eight radio stations, its television channel, some thirty-five Bible institutes, hundreds of schools, the Baptist Hospital, and relief and development organizations such as World Vision Nicaragua and CEPAD. As a result, evangelicals "demand[ed] the right to be considered valid and indispensable interlocutors in the construction of a better future for Nicaragua" (Bautz, González, and Orozco 1994, 5). But this was also possible thanks to political redemocratization that allowed the freer expression of numerous political currents. The evangelical parties were thus a new way of protecting church members, many of whom are marginalized socially and religiously.

A survey we carried out in 1992 (Zub 1993) among the evangelical population detected a growing current of opinion favorable to the idea of such parties; 51 percent said that they would consider affiliating with a political party, and 71 percent said they would do so if there were evangelical parties. However, on this point there were significant differences between Baptists and Assemblies of god members. While 44 percent of Assemblies of God members and 63 percent of Baptists believed that an evangelical could be affiliated to any political party, the question whether one could be affiliated to an evangelical party produced a positive response among 86 percent of Assemblies of God members and only 45 percent of Baptists. Subsequent evangelical parties did, in fact, start among members of the Assemblies of God, while Baptists, with a long tradition of participation in the Liberal and Sandinista parties, have been more resistant to the idea of confessional parties.

To the question "Who can solve the economic problems of Nicaragua?" the answer given by 37 percent of Assemblies of God members and 10 percent of Baptists was "an evangelical government." In addition, 25 percent from the

Assemblies of God and 18 percent of Baptists answered that God was the solution to Nicaragua's economic problems. Only 3 percent thought the FSLN could solve the country's economic problems, and other parties' percentages were even lower. These answers show the distrust of the traditional parties and the hope deposited in a future evangelical party. The latter hope, rather messianic, is especially prevalent among evangelical sectors that place great confidence in divine intervention and distrust the art of politics. As one person interviewed replied: "When there is an evangelical government, Christ will reign through it and there will be a fairer distribution of wealth and justice, because an evangelical president will have faith in the Lord, who will help him, and he will govern with redoubled strength" (in Zub 1993, 101).

We see that, in the Nicaragua of the early 1990s, a sector of Protestantism was already imbued with the idea that politics is a privileged space for God to act and to express himself toward human beings. The hope of divine intervention by means of "Christ's politicians" would be used by those who presented themselves as the ones called by God to execute the task.

The Rise of the Evangelical Parties

The first evangelical party was the National Justice Party (PJN; Partido de Justicia Nacional), organized in 1992 by a group of lay middle-class professionals and young people, mostly from the Assemblies of God but led by Jorge Díaz, a doctor from the International Baptist Church. Wishing to distinguish themselves from left-wing evangelicals, they intended to be ideologically neutral and politically clean but they lacked political-religious capital and leadership.

As a counterpoint to the PJN, the Popular Evangelical Movement (MEP; Movimiento Evangélico Popular—not to be confused with the Brazilian movement with an identical acronym) was born. It included the evangelical left of poor social origin that had taken part in the coffee-harvesting brigades and Sandinista militias, as well as people linked to CEPRES. Most were not high-profile ecclesiastical leaders.

As the 1996 elections approached, the evangelical "third way" was born, adopting the name Nicaraguan Christian Way (CCN; Camino Cristiano Nicaragüense). The origins of the CCN involve evangelicals and Catholic charismatics, including the former president of the Central Bank, Francisco Mayorga, a figure close to Cardinal Obando of Managua. It seems that the element that united Catholic charismatics and members of the Assemblies of God was the theology of "spiritual warfare" and the vision that Christians should direct history by taking over political power. This mixed group convinced pastor Guillermo Osorno that he should lead the process.

The immediate context for this was the discontent felt by Assemblies of God leaders with the PJN. As the PJN was still uncertain whether it would obtain its official registration in time to contest the elections independently, it had started conversations with the "Convergencia" (Convergence) group of evangelicals close to the FSLN. When the Assemblies of God leadership discovered this, they felt betrayed and did their utmost to destroy the PJN's credibility as a "Christian party." This is ironic in view of the later trajectory of the CCN; by 2000, its leader, Pastor Osorno, accepted that the party should include people of diverse religious origins "because the electorate is not only composed of evangelicals, and we struggle for power not for the churches but for the whole of Nicaraguan society" (*Tiempos del Mundo*, March 16, 2000).

The CCN was born primarily as an instrument of the Assemblies of God, the evangelical radio station Ondas de Luz and its owner, Pastor Osorno. The discrediting of the PJN as a mere appendage of Sandinismo was a strategy to justify the creation of another evangelical party. The discourse of the CCN claimed to be "revealed by God" and urged electors to vote for "Christian candidates" and not for the traditional parties. In the 1996 campaign, the CCN also received explicit support from the Church of God, the Church of God of Prophecy, the Pentecost Mission, and others.

The leaders of the PJN and the CCN recognize that they represent a very inexperienced group, with little social involvement or political education. This new "political class" is composed of pentecostal leaders, going against the oligarchical tradition of most parties. It also reflects the weakening of trade unions and social movements, allowing the evangelicals to emerge as new political actors.

Political experience is the exception rather than the rule in this new political class. In a public letter in July 1996, Osorno said, "There is no superman or super-party that can change the destiny of this nation; only Christ can do that. Our acronym, CCN, is not by chance, but reflects our belief that 'Christ Changes Nicaragua.' " This explicit use of religion in political propaganda was aimed at attracting those who were disillusioned with the other parties and enticed by the possibilities of theocratic government.

A survey among 304 pastors (Zub 1996) that I carried out in May 1995 (before the founding of the CCN) shows the market for this vision. Over 42 percent of pastors agreed that they had changed their political views in the previous five years, and 9 percent confessed to being involved in political activities. To the question whether they wished to be candidates in the 1996 elections, 13 percent replied in the affirmative. As to political loyalties, 42 percent said they did not sympathize with any existing party; 21 percent sympathized with the FSLN, 13 percent with the governing Liberal Constitutionalist Party (PLC; Partido Liberal Constitucionalista), and only 4 percent with the evangelical PJN. Asked who they would vote for if the election were tomorrow, 14 percent mentioned the eventual winner, Arnoldo Alemán of the governing party, and 10 percent mentioned Daniel Ortega of the Sandinistas; but 30 percent said they would want to vote for the candidate of an evangelical party. Clearly, however, the existing evangelical party, the PJN, was not capitalizing on this potential vote.

The 1996 Election Campaign

The CCN's candidate for president was Pastor Osorno, and his running mate was the economist Roberto Rodríguez, also of the Assemblies of God. The PJN's candidate was the Baptist medical doctor Jorge Díaz.

Except in the capital, Managua, the evangelical parties did not have their own premises for meetings, generally holding their campaign rallies and distributing campaign material in and around church buildings. Their campaigns were poorly funded, in sharp contrast to the Liberal and Sandinista parties' access to the media.

Church support was by no means unanimous. The evangelical candidates found most of their support among the pentecostals, but little among the Baptists, Apostolics, Church of Christ, or other nonpentecostal denominations.

The campaign was financed partly by the monies distributed to all the parties by the Supreme Electoral Court; but certain entrepreneurs are also thought to have financed the CCN's campaign. The party's growth was due to the figure of Pastor Osorno, who in ten years of preaching on the radio had established links with ample sectors of the population in rural areas and in the urban peripheries. As a candidate, radio was still his main means of communication for explaining his mission to govern Nicaragua. In two months of campaigning, he managed to separate himself from the category of "other candidates" and appear in his own right in the public opinion polls. He soon began to be characterized by the media as the "electoral surprise."

The CCN devised various brief messages for its permitted television time. One said: "Nicaragua *does* have a way," showing Osorno's footprints as he walked along a sandy beach, holding a small boy by the hand. The most polemical one simulated a ray of light coming down from the sky and marking the CCN's box on the ballot paper (which happened to be number 2) while a voice sounded: "If you believe in God, mark box number two" ("Si Usted cree en Dios, marque la casilla dos"). The scene was reminiscent of the film *The Ten Commandments* and reflected Osorno's idea that his party was the result of a divine revelation.

In another televised message, Osorno, despite the anti-Catholic tendency in his preaching campaigns over the years, declared that "Cardinal Obando is a great man of God." It was strategic to recognize the status of the Catholic Church and neutralize possible attacks, as well as to attract possible Catholic voters.

In general, the evangelical candidates publicly maintained a respectful posture toward the Catholic Church. The latter kept its silence, perhaps because it realized these candidates' scant chances of success. The Catholic hierarchy openly supported the PLC candidate Arnoldo Alemán and attacked the Sandinistas.

Only a few months before the elections, Osorno was practically unknown, and his political education and experience only impressed people negatively. Nevertheless, his image as an exciting preacher worked in his favor, as did the feeling common among evangelicals that they had been excluded by the Chamorro government. Another trump for Osorno were his connections with the leadership of many churches, which gave him many speaking opportunities in which to present his political project. His campaign discourse was heavily laced with Bible quotations and accounts of the divine revelation that had impelled him into politics. His campaign climaxed with fasting and an all-night prayer vigil so that "God would give victory to his servant." Never before had the pentecostals prayed and fasted with such fervour for such a worldly cause, and never before had an election been such a familiar topic to them. For the first time, they felt that the right and duty to elect the country's political leaders was theirs.

The MEP did not campaign separately in the elections, since its leader Miguel Angel Casco was a candidate for deputy with the FSLN.

The 1996 Election Results

The PLC candidate Arnoldo Alemán won the presidency with 51 percent of the votes, followed by the Sandinista Daniel Ortega with 37 percent. In third place, albeit a distant third, came Guillermo Osorno of the CCN with 4.3 percent, a result that had been totally unexpected a few months before.

However, the seventy-two thousand votes for Osorno certainly do not mean that "pentecostals vote for pentecostals," that is, a religious corporatist vote. The evangelical vote would be about three or more times greater than that, showing that Osorno's attempt to mobilize the evangelical electorate was only partially successful.

The PJN received less then six thousand votes, only 0.3 percent. Its poor showing meant it had to return the money received for its electoral campaign, which led it to fuse with the Conservative Party (PC; Partido Conservador) in 1998. The failure of the PJN, as a more rational project than the CCN, shows how important it is to have the blessing of the leaders of large denominations. An evangelical party formed by laypeople does not have the same ability to speak "in the name of the evangelicals" as does a party containing leading pastors. It also reflects the preference of the average evangelical for *caudillo*-type social leadership and for supernatural solutions to social problems. However, it should be remembered that the great majority of evangelicals must have voted for the major parties, ignoring the appeal of both evangelical candidates.

Nine evangelicals were elected as deputies. Four of these were from the CCN. Two CCN deputies were members of the Assemblies of God: Osorno himself (since he had passed the threshold that allowed defeated presidential candidates a seat in congress) and Francisco Saravia. One CCN deputy was from the Church of God (an accountant elected in the department of León), and one was an Adventist (Orlando Mayorga, a pastor and teacher). Saravia was a radio announcer from Osorno's station, and even before congress convened he deserted the CCN and joined the governing party (in search of a majority in a hung parliament) in exchange for certain parliamentary posts. The CCN also obtained one seat in the Central American Parliament, occupied by a Baptist.

Three evangelical deputies were elected with the governing PLC, all of them from the Atlantic Coast and all from the Moravian Church. The best known is Steadman Fagoth, a leader of the *contra* forces on the Atlantic Coast from 1981 onward. The other two evangelical deputies were Miguel Angel Casco of the FSLN and Ismael Calero of the Church of God and the PC. Evangelicals thus represented 10 percent of the deputies in congress, came from five denominations, and were in four different parties. Three evangelical mayors were also elected by the FSLN, besides several municipal councillors.

When Pastor Osorno's third place in the presidential election was announced, he began an intensive campaign to have the results annulled. He was trapped by his own prediction that God had chosen him to govern Nicaragua, reinforced by the fact that, as he told me, three days before the election, "God had spoken to me again, and I was convinced that I was going to win the presidency." Now, as he said, "I recognize that I am a long way short of the presidency," but at the time the cry of fraud was the explanation for God's "mistake."

Profile of the Elected Deputies

The Moravians, with their ethnic characteristics from the Atlantic Coast, are not always counted among the evangelicals in congress. Many Moravians are only nominally affiliated to the church, and there is no involvement in evangelical parties. References made to an "evangelical caucus" typically refer only to the CCN deputies.

This means that there was no "evangelical bloc" of nine deputies in the legislature elected in 1996, and no articulation to define unified legislative action. In general, all the deputies had their own political stance and voted according to their own or their party's conscience or convenience, without reference to their religious identity. No law contemplating the specific "needs" of the evangelical population was approved (a bill to introduce a national holiday called the "Day of the Bible" was proposed but was not ratified).

The social and professional profile of these deputies differs from the evangelical deputies of the Somoza era. Even though higher education has spread more in recent years, only five of them have university degrees, whereas the deputies of the later Somoza period were all university graduates and economically well off. Of the 1996–2001 deputies, some were under-employed people who earned the minimum wage before being elected. Osorno later complained that "before being elected they were maintained by us. They promised they could survive on five hundred dollars and would give the rest to the party, but when they reached parliament they deserted us" (referring specifically to Saravia). Most of these parliamentarians had no previous political experience. Ideologically, some were center-left, but most were on the right.

Guillermo Osorno

In the case of Pastor Guillermo Osorno, to understand how a beginner in political terms could become the surprise package of the 1996 elections requires knowledge of the political moment through which Nicaragua was passing. The phenomenon of the evangelical parties reflected the frustration of evangelicals at their lack of representation and interlocutors in the Chamorro government, as well as the distrust and rejection of the established parties. In this context, Osorno's message and its propagation via pastoral committees and pulpits found an echo with many believers.

Although the idea of the CCN was not only Osorno's, his charisma and network of contacts have been influential on the party's trajectory. The party's political discourse has been a continuation of the mass evangelistic gatherings that have sought to change Nicaragua by means of conversion to the evangelical faith.

Osorno comes from an urban Catholic family in which, he claims, he "often went to sleep hungry" (interview with Guillermo Osorno, February 2, 2001). He began a course in administration, changed to law, and did one year of international relations. He joined the Communist Party–controlled union and defines himself today as a "former Communist, atheist, and blasphemer." He claims to have always had a flair for business and at eighteen years of age "earned up to five thousand dollars a month." It is, of course, difficult to understand how a young bookkeeper in the customs office at the Managua airport could have had such an income, and there is no independent confirmation of his life as a "businessman." His conversion began in 1978 when he was in Costa Rica as an exiled political militant. In August 1979, just after the Sandinista Revolution, he claims he had another religious experience in the Church of God in a district of Managua. On becoming a pentecostal, he devalued his union militancy and discontinued his political activity. "When I was converted, they taught me that no Christian should take part in politics because it is a sin."

Osorno soon began an independent ministry known as "La Senda" (The Way). As the Church of God was not happy with this independence, he switched to the Assemblies of God, where he rose quickly. He became director of the evangelical radio station Ondas de Luz (Waves of Light), as well as promoting the radio ministry of the famous Puerto Rican evangelist Yiye Avila. With his vehement appeals for fasting and prayer, Osorno achieved fame among evangelical and peasant radio audiences. He also occupied important institutional spaces in the evangelical world, such as president of the National Council of Pastors and of the Evangelical Alliance, as well as vice president of the Evangelical Confederation of Central America. He was also president of the evangelical television channel Canal 21, which at the time of his election campaign was run by the Baptist Enrique Villagra, a member of the Supreme Court.

After many years of preaching against evangelicals involved in politics, Osorno now sought the miracle that would enable him to "govern Nicaragua with the power of God." In a public letter of July 1996, he said: "Many of you know that I have spoken strongly against those brothers who are involved in politics, but for the past few years God has been speaking to me about this question.... In 1994 God began to change me and I discovered that politics is not evil and corrupt, but it is the men themselves who are corrupt" (interview, February 2, 2001).

On another occasion, before a nonevangelical audience, Osorno did not talk about a "revelation" or about "God speaking to me." He simply said: "I was moved by the desire to educate our people in the path of God and help them to administer their money, which is what I learnt through being a Christian" (*El Seminario*, July 22–28, 1999). Here, he does not link his political vocation to a transcendent event but to the necessary task of "educating" people in the use of money. The "educational" element has been historically important in rotestantism and has to do with the Protestant ethic. With this argument, Osorno values reason and earthly well-being, instead of surrounding his political activity with an aura of religious mysticism.

However, when he speaks to evangelical publics, the discourse is different. Taking into account his past as the most antipolitical of preachers, he knows that there is nothing as difficult to argue against as a claim to divine revelation. In addition, he knows that most evangelicals are still antipolitical. By presenting his story in this way, he legitimates his political participation for circles where it was previously forbidden.

> My decision to take part in politics was, above everything else, obedience to a revelation that God gave me.... After a pastors' congress

in San Salvador, God showed me the error I was in.... Later, I had
an experience in Israel at a prayer congress, where God spoke
to me directly through many revelations. (interview, February 2,
2001)

Osorno's "election" by the transcendental, without any participation by
citizens, would determine the characteristics of his political activity and style
of leadership. This "election" frees him from party structures, assemblies,
councillors, or principles. When reaching decisions, as someone called by God
through a revelation, he is self-sufficient and autonomous. As Freston says
with reference to Brazil, "pentecostal prophecies and visions in politics are the
equivalent of the claim of the National [Catholic] Bishops' Conference to speak
in the name of God and as tutor of the people." They are different ways of
acting politically without admitting that one is a political actor. "The 'disguise'
varies according to the type of religious and social capital which each con-
fesssion possesses" (1993a, 286). As Max Weber points out, the *caudillo*-type
leader legitimates himself through his charisma, his divine calling ([1922]
1996, 193). Thus, the most antipolitical of preachers comes to believe himself
to be invested with a calling to direct the political destiny of the nation.

Osorno mentions conferences he attended abroad as helping to change
his vision, in tandem with divine revelations. A lay leader of the Assemblies of
God and member of the rival PJN party charcaterizes Osorno's talk of revelations as "a strategy which he elaborated, because the people he is appealing
to are pentecostals and believe in these things" (interview, January 30, 2001).
At the same time, it should be remembered that, with the defeat of the
Sandinistas and the end of the Cold War, the socioreligious scene in Nicaragua in the early 1990s was fast-changing, with many foreign evangelists and
evangelical television programs coming into the country, some of whom were
politically active in their countries of origin.

In 1995, Osorno had been invited to be the PJN's candidate for mayor of
Managua. His refusal may have had to do with his doubt whether a party run
by laypeople could carry with it the support of ecclesiastical leaders. For some
CCN deputies, Osorno is "totalitarian." Of the three deputies elected in 1996
with Osorno, one left the party even before parliament had convened, and
another later transferred to a new evangelical party, the Christian Unity
Movement (MUC; Movimiento de Unidad Cristiana).

In congress, the CCN deputies regularly voted with the government, either for ideological affinity or in order to receive benefits for churches or for
themselves personally. It should be stressed that, in countries where the law is
not automatically applied to the majority of the population, an exchange of
favors may be the only way to obtain legal registration for churches or permission for radio and television stations.

Miguel Angel Casco

The third of five sons of a peasant family, Miguel Angel Casco is from the western department of León. At seventeen he migrated to Managua, where he entered the Assemblies of God Bible Institute. From 1976, he was a pastor and itinerant evangelist of the denomination. During the 1980s, he completed his secondary education and received a degree in theology from the Baptist Theological Seminary. But he refers to his poor childhood as the "school" that marked his life.

> When I was about nine years old, my father sent my brother for tortillas. He returned with only one, which my father cut into four pieces and gave to each one of us, and he himself only drank some coffee. So I asked him: "Father, why are we so miserably poor?" And he replied: "My son, it is God's will." From then I had conflicts, and couldn't even pray the Our Father.... Later in life, I discovered that my father was sincerely wrong. For me, my main school was having been poor, having experienced for myself that Somoza's system brought death. So in 1977 I joined the FSLN. (interview, November 2, 1999)

Religion, education, and politics were Casco's routes to upward social mobility. Politics, he says, "is the divine calling for my life." After the triumph of the Sandinistas, Casco's support for the FSLN put him on a collision course with his denomination, but opened up space in other sectors. In 1980 he helped found CEPRES, and from 1981 to 1987 he was codirector of the Antonio Valdivieso Ecumenical Center, a predominantly Catholic entity in which his lack of formal education was a disadvantage. In 1986, he was expelled from the Assemblies of God, and he later joined Misión Cristiana, a small denomination that had no objection to his political activities. In 1992, he founded the MEP.

Casco is very active in the mass media. He first appeared on television as a singer, and later had a weekly program on the Sandinista TV channel; from 1993 to 1996 he presented the program *A Moment with God.* "This program gave me religious and political projection. It had an impact on the FSLN and on the electorate" (interview). Not surprisingly, when Casco confronted the Sandinista leadership in internal party elections in 1996, they canceled his TV program. However, in 1998–99 Casco had an hour-long nightly program on a Sandinista radio station, as well as a program on a private station and a weekly news program on the CEPAD station. It is interesting that Casco has had little access to Osorno's Ondas de Luz station or to evangelical television; he has found space in Sandinista or in privately owned media.

Casco says that "in 1990, after the Sandinista election defeat and the murder of one of my brothers, I decided to continue supporting the revolution no longer just from the religious trench, but in the political struggle" (interview). By 1995, he had managed to gain a place on the FSLN National Directorate. When the Jesuit and former government minister Fernando Cardenal resigned, Casco became president of the FSLN's Commission for Juridical and Ethical Affairs. In the party primaries of 1996, he was a candidate for the vice presidential slot, winning by a huge margin (147,000 votes) over one of the famous *comandantes*, Tomás Borge (12,500 votes), and Benigna Mendiola, a legendary peasant leader.

As we shall see later, Casco was not in fact allowed to run for vice president, and he was finally elected to congress in 1996 on the FSLN ticket. In 1999, he was the FSLN spokesman in the negotiations with the government that resulted in the so-called Liberal-Sandinista pact that opened the way for the reform of the constitution and the electoral system. But in March 2000, Casco was fired from his post on the FSLN's Commission for Religious Affairs on the allegation that he was "using the post for his own personal projection" and "creating parallel structures" that favored the evangelicals (*Boletín Popol Na*, March 11, 2000). Casco was known to be organizing evangelical committees and encouraging the candidacies of pastors through the FSLN in the forthcoming elections. The Sandinista leader Daniel Ortega said that Casco's dismissal was "a clear signal to the evangelicals and to the Christians in general that the FSLN is not a confessional party" (*ALC*; *Agéncia Latinoamericana y Caribeña de Comunicación*, March 29, 2000).

It is, of course, difficult to believe anyone would mistake the FSLN for a confessional party. The commission from which Casco was dismissed was the party's interface with the religious sector, and his Catholic counterpart was the priest and former foreign minister Miguel D'Escoto. Casco's dismissal seems to have had to do with internal readjustments within the FSLN after the pact with the Liberals, which had implications for Sandinismo's relations with the Catholic Church. Casco's activities and standing clouded the new relationship with the Catholic hierarchy that the party desired. (In fact, in the 2001 presidential elections the hierarchy still openly opposed Daniel Ortega's candidacy.)

At the same time, Casco's fall was part of the revenge taken by those close to Tomás Borge, whom Casco, without the "blessing" of the Sandinista leadership, had defeated in the internal primary in 1996. After that election, Borge had demanded his resignation as vice presidential candidate in order to facilitate alliances with other sectors. In the party congress, Casco had abandoned his vice presidential aspirations in exchange for second place on the list of the party's candidates for deputy.

In 2000, after his renewed conflict with the party leadership, Casco resigned from the FSLN. The party, to show that its action against him was not motivated by an antievangelical animus, made an electoral alliance with the evangelical MUC and reverted to using the Baptist former deputy Sixto Ulloa as its means of restoring an amicable and stable relationship with the evangelical community.

Casco, on the other hand, founded a new party called the Party of National Dignity (PDN; Partido por la Dignidad Nacional) and, to guarantee political survival under the new electoral law, allied with the governing PLC, whose presidential candidate Enrique Bolaños promised to create an office for religious affairs and guarantee tax exemption for churches. According to Casco, "this is not an ideological or a merely electoral agreement, but a commitment to democracy and the future of our people." Among the reasons Casco gave to vote for Bolaños was the desire for Nicaragua to have "fraternal relations with Israel and the United States . . . and not to go back to being a platform for sending arms to other countries."

Casco thus gave his support to a party that until recently he had criticized vehemently. The proposed "office of religious affairs" would be a repeat of his role in the FSLN and part of the art of keeping himself close to power and able to mediate benefits to his religious community.

The Evangelical Caucus and Corruption

The term "evangelical caucus" does not please the CCN deputies, but as one of them said, "however much we clarify that we are not the party of the evangelicals, it is impossible to change this viewpoint," which is widely held in Nicaraguan society.

After the 1996 elections, the governing PLC was left with a minority in congress, and the small CCN was able to play a swing role. For a while, many of its votes coincided with those of the Sandinistas, but (according to CCN congressman Roberto Rodríguez) this provoked discontent among party members. Their voting pattern thereafter was aligned with the government, and on many occasions they have been accused of accepting bribes and favors. The image prevalent in Nicaraguan society is of a party that sells its favors to the governing party, and on one occasion Osorno himself admitted as much. Pastor Osorno then acquired the nickname of "Pastor Soborno" (Pastor Bribe). In Nicaragua, the "favor" is often official title (for oneself or others) to real estate acquired by dubious means and in an irregular legal situation. Osorno has built a mansion for himself since becoming a deputy, a situation the press has amply explored.

With reference to Brazil, Freston argues that we need to distinguish between corruption and what is known in Brazil as *fisiologismo*, opportunistic time-serving or "the art of keeping oneself close to power, independently of ideologies, with the objective of receiving benefits for oneself or one's clients."

Pentecostalism in Brazil, he says, produces a lot of politicians who are *fisio-lógicos*, because it is a poor community with an intense community life and a strong sense of mission but also a minority complex.

Fisiologismo reflects the sectarian concept of mission. To guarantee good working conditions, alliances with nonmembers in positions of "worldly" power are acceptable. This is not naïveté in the face of power but a pragmatism that is authorized by the sectarian vision. Negotiating one's vote in parliament in exchange for benefits for the church, for example, is not viewed as treason to the church's message. Rather, the benefit received is viewed as "a sort of tax which 'worldly' power pays to the truth" (Freston 1993a, 285–86).

In Nicaragua, where the political upheavals of the last quarter-century have played havoc not only with the socioeconomic situation but above all with the legal bases of society, the exchange of favors has become the most efficient way of gathering a few crumbs and distributing them among one's electorate.

The election of a somewhat larger number of evangelical deputies created an expectation that they would encourage changes in the political culture. This hope was soon dashed. The evangelicals began to be seen as merely one set of political actors among others, and it was realized that being an evangelical was no antidote to corruption and that their votes were being used to negotiate benefits and not to increase space for democracy.

Legislative Initiatives and Relations between Parties

The CCN deputies were a small and inexperienced minority with scant legislative possibilities. They managed to achieve the recognition of "juridical personality" for some churches; and among the bills they proposed were tax exemption for churches and observance of the National Day of the Bible, as well as larger concerns such as electoral reform and privatizations. In Osorno's opinion, the CCN is the only party of "constructive opposition."

The Conservative Party's evangelical deputy, Ismael Torres Calero, of the Church of God, says he feels united in faith with the CCN deputies, above ideological differences, and works with them "to stop any initiative of the feminist movements that want to legalize abortion" (*Buenas Nuevas*, October 1999). The CCN deputy Orlando Mayorga, together with Conservative Party deputies, led the "March for Life" to demand the closure of clinics and NGOs that promote or perform abortion. Mayorga is against abortion even in the case of risk to the mother's life and demanded a thirty-year prison sentence for those practicing it.

Miguel Angel Casco, at the time still in the FSLN, told of two moments in which he felt fully united with his fellow evangelicals in other parties: in defense of the secular state against government attempts to introduce religious education in schools; and in favor of the bill to introduce the National

Day of the Bible. For the rest of the time, "there is only a religious link, but different political positions" (interview, November 2, 1999).

The "Day of the Bible" proposal was in large part an attempt to compete with the Catholic Church; it would be the first Protestant mark on the national calendar, as well as a recognition of the social and political importance of Protestants and an attempt to overcome the prevailing Catholic view of many Protestant churches (especially the pentecostals) as "sects."

It is not the fact of being evangelical that determines parliamentary stances, but rather the way in which each deputy was elected, the party he or she belongs to, and the place he or she occupies in the social structure.

While one legislature is a short time, it seems the CCN's parliamentary caucus has fallen far short of the expectations of its voters, many of whom accuse it of corruption and incompetence. A survey carried out in 1999 by the Universidad Centroamericana in fourteen northern municipalities regarding political culture and citizens' perceptions of the electoral process found differences between evangelicals and Catholics. Whereas 70 percent of Catholics had "no confidence in the political parties," among evangelicals the figure rose to 87 percent. Evangelicals were less "proud of the Nicaraguan political system than Catholics" (27 percent versus 37 percent). Evangelicals are generally more negative about the parties and the political system as a whole.

Theological Justification for Political Participation

Was the abrupt change in evangelical politics in the 1990s, especially on the part of pentecostals, merely at the level of practice or was there an accompanying (or antecedent) change at the level of theological ideas? As we have seen, the new politics reflected not just a broader social discontent with the traditional politicians but also a discontent with traditional readings of the Bible and the adoption of interpretations that supported active participation. Many pentecostal leaders now consider political activity to be legitimate for "the people of God."

The Bible, which was once used to justify apoliticism, is now used to find orders from God for his people to enter politics and, as the Bible says, "subdue the earth." Many now find in the Bible a sort of manifest destiny that would justify their leadership in society. Some leaders imagine themselves to be incorruptible and, in a spiritual warfare mindset, blame the Catholic Church for Nicaragua's negative heritage. Uri Rojas Videa, an Assemblies of God leader who is also general secretary of the CCN, finds a basis for political participation in Genesis 1:28: "be fruitful and multiply and replenish the earth; and subdue it and have dominion" (*El Heraldo*, September 1998). "To subdue," in this context, is interpreted as "to govern." Rojas continues:

There is no justification for saying "I don't mess with politics.". . . Politics is not an option, it is an obligation imposed by God.
We have been called, ever since Genesis, to govern not only Nicaragua but the whole earth. The Christian people are called to great
things in our country, not to go on giving our vote to the lovers of
Bacchus and of the blood of the people.

Pastor Saturnino Serrato, superintendent of the Assemblies of God and a
fierce critic of political participation in the 1980s, says: "we are still rather
sceptical, because we were outside politics for a hundred years. It is difficult to
shrug that off. We have to begin to open up our minds to accept the possibility
that we can, in fact, be involved" (*El Nuevo Diario*, May 1, 1999).

Serrato goes on to say: "We have had 506 years of Catholic governments,
which have been a disaster. . . . We have let the devil govern as he wants, using
his instruments, and we who can govern from God have been isolated." This
idea of superiority, of being able to "govern from God," is a spiritual warfare
concept that sees Protestantism as having been used by the devil to support
Catholic governments. Nevertheless, both Serrato and other Assemblies of God
pastors have openly supported the election of Violeta Chamorro and Enrique
Bolaños.

For Pastor Osorno, the evangelicals should govern because they can put
into practice the words of the Psalmist, "Blessed is he who remembers the
poor, because in the evil day God will free him" (Psalms 41:1), and of the
biblical proverb "When the righteous govern the peoples rejoice" (Proverbs
29:2) (*Buenas Nuevas*, September 1999).

Yet it is striking that in all these justifications for political involvement on
the part of pentecostal leaders, there is little or no reflection on concepts such
as the state, government, politics, economics, justice, work, or ecology.

Evangelical Politics at the Year 2000: Broader Options

As the municipal elections of 2000 approached, evangelical options diversified. In general, the Protestant world in Nicaragua is characterized by division
and by a culture of intolerance toward those who are different. Conflicts
are usually ended by breakaways and the emergence of new denominations.
Since the 1990s, this divisive culture has been transplanted to the political
sphere.

Movement of Christian Unity

In November 2000, MUC arrived on the scene; its founder was Pastor Omar
Duarte. Duarte had been a prominent leader of the Puerto Rican–founded

Iglesia de Dios Pentecostal Misión Internacional, but after a financial scandal (in which he reputedly diverted funds sent by the Puerto Rican church to build himself a luxurious house) he transferred to the Huerto de Dios (Garden of God) church. For over ten years he was director of the "Rios de Agua Viva" (Rivers of Living Water) ministry, in which he projected his fame via television and radio. He also achieved a certain fame outside the evangelical world through the independent newspaper *El Nuevo Diario*. An evangelical reporter in the paper ran a series in which Duarte's opinions on the most varied themes were aired, and Duarte was presented as "the most charismatic of Nicaraguan preachers."

The MUC was founded by Duarte and two disaffected CCN deputies (Saravia and Castillo). At its launch, Duarte said: "We have made the decision to go into politics not because we want to, but because we are tired of seeing the injustices our people suffer.... The traditional parties have converted power into spoils for getting rich" (*ALC*, March 10, 2000; *Tiempos del Mundo*, March 16, 2000). Another leader of the MUC justified the new party on the basis that the evangelical churches have grown to around 34 percent of the population. This grossly inflated estimate is one of the tactics used by these new political actors to increase their own importance; and it also implies the idea of an evangelical bloc vote of which they are supposedly the proprietors—two highly questionable assumptions.

The MUC stressed that it was an antithesis to the CCN, whose leader was characterized by Duarte as "a man who sells himself to other parties and has no principles" (*La Prensa*, March 1, 2000). Despite the FSLN's help, the MUC was unable to get registered. It is thought this bureaucratic obstacle was due to opposition from the PLC and the CCN. The PLC supposedly supported an amnesty for the ex-Sandinista Carlos Guadamúz so that he could be the CCN's candidate for mayor of Managua and split the Sandinista vote. As the MUC might represent competition for the CCN, the PLC is said to have prevented its registration. Later, the FSLN offered the vice-mayoralty of Managua on its ticket to a MUC member who had been director of the Baptist Hospital, but this was refused. However, after the municipal elections, the MUC reached an agreement with the FSLN to run jointly in the presidential elections of 2001; it is thought Duarte had ambitions of being Daniel Ortega's vice presidential candidate. Notwithstanding Duarte's unrealistic ambitions, this alliance of a sector of pentecostalism with Sandinismo was significant.

Party for National Dignity

Miguel Casco, after leaving the FSLN in 2000, continued in politics by dissolving his MEP and founding the PDN. Casco himself is the president, and the honorary president is Edén Pastora, the legendary former Sandinista guerrilla leader who was known as Commander Zero but who had later broken with the Sandinista government and fought alongside the *contras*. Pastora was intended to be the link between the PDN and dissatisfied Sandinistas in general.

The PDN is not an evangelical project in the way the CCN and MUC are. The objective is not primarily to attract the evangelical electorate, and Casco's leadership is not influential in the large denominations. The nomination of Pastora and not an evangelical leader as the honorary president showed that the project was to capitalize on discontented Sandinista voters. Casco now claims that "it is not possible to have a party only of evangelicals.... We could add strength to a national alliance with the Conservative Party, which is the only alternative left for the small parties" (interview, January 31, 2001).

We thus see the dynamism of the religio-political field, as hybrid alliances develop between the evangelical parties and the larger parties. None of this emanates from the evangelical "people," but it is all done in their name, as the party leaders seek posts or other crumbs that fall from the tables where power is distributed.

The Municipal Elections of 2000

Municipal elections took place in November 2000. Countrywide, the CCN obtained sixty-eight thousand votes, 4.3 percent of the total. It did not win any mayoralties and lost the third place in overall votes to the Conservative Party.

The CCN's candidate for mayor of Managua was Carlos Guadamúz, who in 1996 had almost been elected to that post when running for the FSLN. Guadamúz is an irreverent and antireligious radio presenter, and as a Sandinista had been in prison together with Daniel Ortega during the Somoza era. In the late 1990s he had been accused of defaming the Sandinista leaders and was expelled from the FSLN. This was due to his opposition to the Liberal-Sandinista pact then under negotiation, and he had even been imprisoned for a time. But subsequently he was released through a government amnesty, and the Liberals imposed him on the CCN as their mayoral candidate in an attempt to prevent the FSLN from winning Managua.

That, of course, is not the official CCN version. According to Pastor Osorno, the mayoral candidacy "was offered to various evangelical leaders and they all refused. Then we offered it to Guadamúz to show that the CCN is not a confessional party" (interview, February 2, 2001). This confused explanation seems to be an attempt to give respectability to a desperate attempt to prolong the existence of the CCN among the large parties under the new electoral system.

In Managua, where the evangelicals are estimated at 14 percent of the population, the Guadamúz candidacy obtained only 1.3 percent of the votes. The CCN did not get the corporate support it expected, perhaps because media denunciations of its parliamentary behavior had penetrated the evangelical community, and perhaps also because, as Nicaragua and other countries have shown, a large-scale corporate evangelical vote rarely occurs even when church leaders invest heavily in it. It seems that ordinary pentecostal church members regard themselves as owing obedience to their pastor in moral and ethical questions but do not always accept the pastor's authority in political questions.

In fact, in the 2000 election, the CCN abandoned the idea that its electorate could only come from within the Protestant world, as well as the idea that its leading candidates should reflect evangelical convictions. Admitting the candidacy of someone like Guadamúz, while potentially an astute move politically, meant a deviation from the supposed specificity of its original 1996 political project. The acceptance of a Catholic candidate for mayor, and his imposition on the party by another party (the PLC) that was well known as being an unconditional ally of the Catholic Church, was difficult for many pentecostals to swallow. In addition, the case showed the extent to which the internal decisions of the CCN were being managed from outside.

In order not to disappear from the political scene, the CCN allied with the PLC for the presidential elections of 2001. This was an attempt to save its parliamentary presence, but it showed clearly how far the original project of evangelical specificity based on principles and independent action had been eroded.

In the municipal election in Managua in 2000, the candidate who in fact attracted the support of the most influential evangelical sectors was the Sandinista Herty Lewites. There were two main reasons for this. One was his promise to regularize the legal situation of some two hundred evangelical churches that had been built in Managua during the Sandinista government and had not been granted legal title by subsequent administrations. The other factor was Lewites' Jewish origin. He attracted a majority of evangelical votes not because he was a Sandinista but because he was "of the family of our Lord," a descendent of "the people blessed by God." The idea spread that God had put Lewites forward as a candidate to test the people, to see if they would vote for someone of Jesus' "blood and race." Such a vote would be rewarded by God pouring out his blessings, since God blesses those who bless his people. Lewites, therefore, was incorporated in "God's plan for Nicaragua." He was "anointed" by leading pastors in a service held in a theatre; the idea of having "anointed a Jew" resonated deeply in the self-image of the evangelical community.

Lewites is actually a Catholic, but for many evangelicals it was his Jewish ethnicity that counted. Transforming him into a "God-fearer" from "the family of Christ," it was even thought that such evangelical support could transform him into a viable Sandinista candidate for the presidency in 2006 (a hope that failed to materialize).

The Liberal-Sandinista Pact and the Future of Minorities in Politics

Reforms to the constitution and the electoral system have weakened the possibilities of democratic participation for emerging social actors such as environmentalists, women, and evangelicals. These reforms have also increased immunity and impunity for those in power. It has become more difficult to found new parties, since these now require directorates in every municipality in the country (the previous law demanded only 50 percent), and they must also show the signed support of 3 percent of voters in the country. These and other conditions would have impeded the ability of the CCN to register for the 1996 elections.

Existing small parties are also threatened by the new law. If a party does not contest elections, it loses its registration; but the same thing happens if it does run and obtains less than 4 percent of the votes. An alliance between two parties would demand a minimum of 8 percent of the votes. The only possibility of survival is thus an alliance with one of the large parties.

Conclusions

Thus far in Nicaragua, Protestantism's most significant contribution has not been in politics but in the social and educational fields. Not all Protestant denominations have had the same degree of political participation, due in part to variations in their social capital. In the 1990s, the sectors that had previously held political leadership within the Protestant community, and had been important interlocutors of the state, have lost these advantages. The pentecostals, largely "apolitical" during Somoza's time and resistant to the Sandinista revolution, have started controversial political parties. Instead of preaching about "isolation from the world," they began to preach about the need to transform the world. In general, one can see a struggle for the equality of the churches in the public square, in the use of the media, in the distribution of governmental largesse, and in access to the ear of government on sensitive political questions.

Some Protestants had an active sociopolitical role in the 1980s, and an important sector seemed to be located on the left or center-left. However, the 1990s have produced far more evangelical parliamentarians linked to the right of the political spectrum.

Although the existence of evangelical parties is still recent, they do seem to represent a repeat of many of the vices of the traditional parties, such as clientelism, demagogy, vengefulness, opportunism, and corruption. Evangelicals have adapted to prevailing norms of power in the search for the same sort of privileges as the Catholic Church: space in the media, influence over nomination of judges and teachers, and positions in the state.

The so-called evangelical parties have been based on the personal charisma of their leaders. These parties are led by a small elite that has capitalized on the symbolic power of its religious authority. They are carriers of a culture that revolves around the figure of the founder who, like the traditional landowner, disposes of the party as his private possession. These parties do not live up to their billing as the "moral reservoir of the nation" and are by no means exempt from the authoritarianism and verticalism of the other parties. The *caudillo* figure closes the way to political alternatives, feeds corruption, and slows down the creation of solid institutions. The failure of the first ever evangelical party, the PJN, a more rational and depersonalized project, shows that the evangelical electorate prefers the *caudillos* and/or a supernatural solution to political problems. The Moravians, on the other hand, without evangelical parties but acting through their ecclesiastical structures, which are well integrated into the society of the Atlantic Coast, are assured political space.

The evangelical community today is much more recognized and taken into account by the full range of political actors in Nicaraguan society than was the case a few years ago. Their electoral potential excites interest on all sides.

However, the state with which the evangelical parliamentarians have come to terms has been compatible with human rights violations, the negation of effective citizenship, and impunity. Like other Nicaraguan political actors, the evangelicals appeal to the citizens only at election times. And as the saying goes, "without democrats, there is no democracy."

Evangelical participation has been through many different parties and has been oriented basically to obtaining political or economic benefits rather than to strengthening democracy. The phenomenon of the evangelical parties may turn out to be ephemeral and has largely represented personal projects of little benefit to society.

In the November 2001 elections, the CCN (by means of its pact with the PLC) managed to repeat the 1996 results and elect four deputies to congress. But evangelicals began to hope that the next presidential elections, in 2006, would see the predominance of a new strategy: an alliance between Sandinistas and a significant section of the evangelical community, to elect a Jewish "descendant of Christ" to the Palace of Managua.[9]

NOTES

1. On Protestant origins in Nicaragua, see Bardeguez (1998). On the Moravians, see Schneider (1998) and Wilson (1975).

2. Before this, the presence of Protestantism had been limited to visits by *colporteurs* such as James Thompson (1817) and Francisco Penzotti (1892), without the establishment of churches.

3. Very little is left of this image of Protestantism. It has been obscured by the expansion of pentecostalism among theologically and culturally deprived sectors of the population, concerned with church growth rather than rounded development.

4. The secular state and religious freedom are advances Baptists like to attribute to themselves. See the discourse by Jorge Truet, "Los bautistas y la libertad religiosa," given in Washington, D.C., in 1920 and published by the Baptist magazine *La Antorcha* (vols. 10 [1923] and 17 [1924]).

5. Father of Nora Astorga, later deputy foreign minister in the Sandinista government.

6. Armando Guido was the father of Lea Guido, guerrilla fighter and later minister of social welfare and of health in the Sandinista government.

7. Retaining the same acronym, CEPAD later changed into a development agency (the Consejo Evangélico Pro-Ayuda al Desarallo) and, more recently, into a representative organization of the evangelical churches (the Consejo de Iglesias Evangélicas Pro-Alianza Denominacional).

8. "Reflexiones sobre la paz y la realidad nacional," CEPAD, July 1983 (leaflet). This declaration was signed by pastors of many denominations, including some who were soon to oppose the Sandinistas, such as the Assemblies of God. At this time a short-lived group of Assemblies pastors was formed, known as the Movement of Revolutionary Pastors.

9. As this chapter was going to press, some of Nicaraguan evangelicals' fondest political dreams continued to go unrealized. Osorno's CCN continued to follow the pattern set in the 2000 municipal elections and the 2001 national elections (i.e., it ran in alliance with the PLC in the 2004 municipal elections and the 2006 national elections, and in so doing it continued to disappoint many evangelicals by what they considered its brazen opportunism). Herty Lewites, on the other hand, challenged Daniel Ortega for the 2006 FSCN presidential nomination but was expelled from the party in February 2005. Lewites then joined the dissident Sandinista Renewal Movement (MRS; Movimiento Renovador Sandinista) and became its presidential candidate. But he died in July 2006, four months before the presidential elections, and was replaced by vice presidential candidate Edmundo Jarquín. In the end, the MRS polled a distant fourth place, with 6.29 percent, behind Daniel Ortega's FSLN (37.99 percent), Eduardo Montealegre's ALN (28.30 percent), and José Rizo's PLC (27.1 percent).

4

Evangelicals and Politics in Fujimori's Peru

Darío López Rodríguez

To explain the entry of evangelicals into formal politics and their varied roles in recent Peruvian political life and civil society, we need to understand the context of the Fujimori era, which lasted from 1990 to 2000. This chapter will look at the evangelical presence in formal politics via political parties and movements, as well as the evangelical presence in civil society through social movements. My sources are documentary and bibliographical analysis and interviews, as well as direct observation and participation in some of the events described.

The analysis is presented in a thematic rather than chronological fashion. Besides key individual actors such as the parliamentarian Gilberto Siura, I have looked at important institutional actors such as the National Evangelical Council (CONEP; Concilio Nacional Evangélico del Perú). I have also examined the role of evangelical women in urban social movements and of evangelicals in general in the peasant patrols, examples chosen because they relate to two central questions of Peruvian life in the 1990s, the economic crisis, and political violence. My study shows that the behavior of evangelical politicians—who went into public life in an improvised fashion, with little knowledge of the political game and lacking any autonomous program—was not so different from that of the established political class; but also that, impelled by their biblical faith, some evangelical citizens in organized sectors of civil society acted in what one might refer to as a prophetic manner, helping to strengthen democratic tendencies.

Historical Antecedents

The first Peruvian evangelical church was founded in 1889, and evangelicals participated in the struggle that culminated in the Freedom of Worship Law of 1915. In addition, there were evangelicals involved in the social movements of the early decades of the twentieth century (Fonseca 2000, 207–60; Inocencio 1998, 175–78); and even an English missionary, Thomas Payne, was elected mayor of Calca, in Cuzco province, in 1916 and 1930. But the evangelical community has only really had a social presence as a community since the 1950s. It was in that decade that evangelicals linked to one of the main mass parties, the American Revolutionary Popular Alliance (APRA; Alianza Popular Revolucionaria Americana), began to appear in political life (Cleary 1997, 11; Romero 1994, 6). The parliamentary career of José Ferreyra with the leftish APRA in the 1950s and 1960s can be considered the main foreshadowing of the many evangelical members of congress of the 1990s. Ferreyra was a deputy from 1958 to 1962 and a senator from 1963 to 1968, returning to the senate between 1985 and 1990. Another foreshadowing was the presence in the Constituent Assembly of 1978–79 of the leading Presbyterian pastor (and later president of the Peruvian Bible society) Pedro Arana. Arana was also a staffworker with the Association of Evangelical Student Groups of Peru (AGEUP; Asociación de Grupos Evangélicos Universitarios del Perú), the evangelical student movement, and a member of APRA.

The Constituent Assembly of 1978 was called to restore the country to democracy after a period of military rule, and it culminated in the calling of general elections for 1980. This prompted a group of evangelical pastors and leaders to found an evangelical front with the intention of presenting candidates, but political and theological tensions between church leaders prevented that. On the national committee of the movement there were leaders from the Baptists, the Peruvian Evangelical Church (IEP; Iglesia Evangélica Peruana), the Assemblies of God, and the Nazarenes. Two of them would become politically prominent after 1990: Victor Arroyo as senator and Carlos García as second vice president.

Before the 1985 elections, another evangelical movement was formed, the Association Movement for Renewing Action (AMAR), which allied with a conservative party coalition known as Democratic Convergence. Five evangelicals (four from the Assemblies of God and one from the Anglican Church) ran as candidates for this coalition, but none of them was elected.

These pre-1990 forays into public life point to a variety of attempted channels and to a growing interest on the part of evangelicals. The most efficient channel was involvement in a mass party such as APRA (the election of José Ferreyra and Pedro Arana). Another channel was the formation of independent groups whose existence was short; and a third route was the formation of an initially independent group (AMAR) that later made broader political alliances. But in most cases, evangelical interest in public life was restricted to the period of elections. The study of the evangelical presence in Fujimori's Peru will help to explain this characteristic.

Evangelicals in Formal Politics in the Fujimori Period

The Fujimori Decade

Alberto Fujimori rose to power through democratic elections in 1990. Two years later, he carried out a "self-coup," installing a civilian-military regime that incrementally dismantled Peru's democratic institutions. The undemocratic measures he adopted had the support of approximately 80 percent of public opinion, which agreed with his criticisms of the inefficiency of the politicians. When he was originally elected, the two great problems afflicting Peru were political violence and inflation. The political violence had begun in 1980 in the Andean region of Ayacucho, one of the poorest parts of the country, where the violent Maoist guerrilla group, the Shining Path (Sendero Luminoso), had arisen. Guerrilla activity combined with the military's anti-insurgency measures had led to extrajudicial killings, disappearances, and thousands of displaced families. In addition, inflation had gone from 60 percent in 1980 to 7,650 percent in 1990. These two problems made the country seem ungovernable.

Fujimori's rise to power can also be located in a regional context of worn-out political systems and the rise of political outsiders in several countries (Cotler 1994, 171). In 1990, Fujimori specifically presented himself as an outsider, not linked to the established parties but enjoying academic prestige (as a former university chancellor) and the image of a technocrat capable of solving the country's problems without making deals with the traditional political elites (Linch 1999, 40). Three years after the 1992 self-coup, Fujimori was reelected president with the support of 60 percent of the electorate. Until 1999, a substantial percentage of public opinion continued to show support for Fujimori. But when the regime's authoritarian tendencies sharpened, especially before and during the 2000 elections, a growing percentage of voters, including many evangelicals, abandoned "Fujimorismo."

The Pro-Fujimori Parliamentarians

The arrival of an outsider, Fujimori, altered the political map and favored the emergence of new collective actors on the public scene. Several analysts saw the participation of evangelicals, a growing religious minority, as one factor explaining the remarkable Fujimori "phenomenon" (Brooke 1990, E2; *Caretas*, May 28, 1990, 21–22; Gutiérrez 2000, 8, 58; Klaiber 1990, 133; Míguez

Bonino 1999, 9; Padilla 1991, 6, 13; Romero 1994, 6). Others talk of evangelical "prominent" participation and their "noisy campaign" for Fujimori's party, Cambio 90 (Cleary 1997, 11; Dodson 1997, 35). Exaggeration and confusion surround many accounts of evangelical participation in these elections. One author says the "surprising political rise" of the evangelicals occurred in 1991, using the "corporatist slate" of CONEP and the "cohesion and discipline of the evangelical vote" (Bastian 1997, 160–61).

In fact, Fujimori's triumph in 1990 did not use the networks of CONEP, and the evangelical electorate did not vote in a cohesive way for Cambio 90. Evangelicals were only about 5 percent of the population; and in any case, the evangelical congressional candidates with Cambio 90 only received a total of about one hundred thousand votes, far below the potential of the evangelical electorate. Thus, there are no grounds for saying the evangelical vote was massively for Fujimori and was decisive for his victory. A more nuanced verdict is that "the presence of evangelicals in Cambio 90 . . . caused a reaction when Fujimori gained an unexpected second place in the first round. Both the Democratic Front of Mario Vargas Llosa [the Nobel Prize–winning author and presidential candidate] and the Catholic Church began an antievangelical campaign before the second round of voting, generating the belief that the evangelicals had been key in Fujimori's election" (*Noticias Aliadas*, September 11, 2000, 10).

Four evangelicals from Cambio 90 were elected to the senate: the small industrialist Julian Bustamante and the sociologist Victor Arroyo from the Peruvian Evangelical Church; the lawyer Eulogio Cárdenas from the Pentecostal Missionary Church; and the accountant Daniel Bocanegra from the Wesleyan Church. In addition, fourteen candidates from Cambio 90 were elected as deputies: Guillermo Yoshikawa, a Methodist teacher; Gilberto Siura, a barber from the Peruvian Evangelical Church; Jacinto Landeo, a teacher from the Pentecostal Missionary Church; Cesar Vargas, a singer from the Pentecostal Church of Peru; the Baptist lawyer Moisés Miranda, the teacher Gamaliel Barreto, and journalist Oswaldo García from the Wesleyan Church; Ramiro Jimenez and Oscar Cruzado of the Independent Baptists; and Gabino Vargas, the teachers Juana Avellaneda, Enrique Chucaya, and José Hurtado, and the engineer Mario Soto of the Biblical Baptists. There was also one evangelical deputy elected through APRA, the Presbyterian economist Milton Guerrero. And on Fujimori's ticket, the Baptist pastor Carlos García was elected as second vice president of the republic.

The fact that eighteen evangelicals without previous political experience could reach congress and an equally inexperienced Baptist pastor could be elected second vice president were clear signs of the disintegration of Peruvian public life and of a crisis in the party system (Freston 2001, 237). Immediately afterward, pastors well known for their previous opposition to evangelical participation in politics followed the clientelist tradition and sought posts as advisors to the new evangelical parliamentarians. In this way, they hoped to transform themselves into intermediaries of the relationship between parliamentarians and churches in obtaining benefits such as quicker bureaucratic processing of documentation, tax relief, and permits for public meetings.

Two years later, when Fujimori called elections for November 1992 to legitimate his new institutional attangements following his "self-coup," five evangelicals were elected to the Constituent Assembly, all of them Fujimori supporters. Electoral rules had changed; Congress was now unicameral, and the whole country functioned as one electoral district, making it harder for those with merely local or regional support to get elected. The five evangelicals elected included two survivors from 1990 (Gilberto Siura and Gamaliel Barreto), as well as the pastor Pedro Vilchez and the lawyer Guillermo Ysisola from the Biblical Baptists and the adminstrator Tito Chávez from the Independent Baptists. When a new congress was elected in 1995, once more, five pro-Fujimori evangelicals were successful: Siura, Vilchez, and Barreto were reelected, and they were joined by Alejandro Abanto from the Assemblies of God and Miguel Quicaña, an indigenous Peruvian, from the Presbyterians. In the fraudulent election of 2000, only Vilchez managed election to the ephemeral congress that witnessed the fall of Fujimori and lasted less than a year.

How can we characterize the public life of the pro-Fujimori evangelical congressmen? The first thing to say is that they were political novices. Not only that but they acted basically as foot soldiers for a regime that subverted almost every democratic space and became known as the most corrupt in the history of Peru. Nevertheless, Gilberto Siura became well known nationally as one of the most conspicuous defenders of the regime and affirmed that his presence in congress was clearly part of the will of God (Chávez Toro, *Revista USD*, *La República*, September 5, 1997, 10). But despite the fact that all the evangelicals elected to congress in 1992, 1995, and 2000 were pro-Fujimori, it would seem that in the country at large there were evangelicals (a majority of them) who supported the Fujimori regime, as well as other evangelicals who opposed the regime (a minority that grew as the authoritarian character of the regime became more evident). There was no unanimity among evangelicals with regard to the self-coup of 1992, or to the Amnesty Law of 1995 (which benefited military personnel accused of human rights violations in the anti-insurgency campaign), or to Fujimori's unconstitutional second reelection in 2000.

The large evangelical contingent elected to congress in 1990 was taken by surprise by its own success and lack of experience. One of them, Mario Soto, says they lacked "principles of unity and greater coordination" (*Caminos*, December 1990–January 1991, 3–5). Guillermo Yoshikawa feels they "lacked political experience and knowledge of parliamentary procedure" (ibid.). In late 1992, after Fujimori's self-coup, which had arbitrarily closed congress, a group of nine evangelical senators and deputies, originally from Cambio 90 and now styling themselves the Coordinadora Parlamentaria Independiente (Independent Parliamentary Coordinating Committee), evaluated their brief stay in congress, recognizing that they had lacked legilative proposals, group organization and conceptual cohesion ("Participatión de los evangélicos en la vida pública del Perú," mimeo, September 1992, 1). Although the presence of evangelicals in congress had initially raised expectations in several sectors of society due to the idea that they represented a reservoir of moral values, in the end it did not leave any deep mark on national politics. Their presence "was no more than an anecdote in the history of republican Peru. . . . Bereft of any definite social and political project, most of them echoed the government slogans and the rest wandered between isolated acts of protest and silent resignation" (Valderrama 1992, 18–19). However, there were a few exceptions. Victor Arroyo, who was president of the senate committee on cooperatives, self-management, and communities, carried out his task of surveillance of government activities, denouncing cases of "mismanagement" such as that of the Cooperative Credit Central.

When Fujimori quickly abandoned the ideals that he had preached in his campaign and began to implement precisely the neoliberal economic model he had condemned, it soon became clear that there were very different expectations and aspirations among the evangelical parliamentarians of Cambio 90. Carlos García, the second vice president, was marginalized in government and did not have any public function. The members of congress who did not obey the government's directive to shelve the accusations of corruption against the former president Alan García were also marginalized. They then left Cambio 90 and formed the Coordinadora Parlamentaria Independiente. Another group of evangelical parliamentarians opted to support the regime and Fujimori's authoritarian style. Of this group, it was Gilberto Siura who would become, after the self-coup of 1992, one of the most prominent and enthusiastic defenders of the most controversial and unconstitutional acts of the Fujimori government.

With the exception of Siura, the evangelical members of congress of the 1992–2000 period (all pro-Fujimori) were anonymous figures who functioned merely to rubber-stamp Fujimori's laws. They sought to justify their unconditional support of the regime with various arguments. Pedro Vilchez declared that "the president is a friend to those who want to be his friends. And what is more, the evangelicals have never had as much freedom as they have now, so much so that we have one evangelistic campaign after the other" (La Luz 2, 15, n.d., 2). In a less pragmatic and more theological vein, Gamaliel Barreto said: "I believe God put Fujimori in the government of this country. . . . Of course, like all human beings he is not perfect, but God has not called the church to criticise but to pray. Let us pray, then, that God will work with Fujimori and bless him" (1).

One pro-Fujimori congressman, Alejandro Abanto, achieved fame when he presented a bill prohibiting the use of mini-skirts in public institutions. The initiative was ridiculed by the press as "a law against temptation": "Abanto has abandoned his low, almost anonymous and decorative, profile, and leapt to fame" (Vargas, *La República*, February 22, 1998, 26). Pedro Vilchez, on the other hand, was characterized as "a grey evangelical representative of the government who has almost never even given a press interview.... He has presented only a couple of bills in his seven years as a legislator" (Mendoza, *Revista Domingo, La República*, September 19, 1999, 17). However, in 1999 he introduced a bill to punish vagrancy with a prison term and forced labor. The idea had been copied from the Vagrancy Repression Law of 1924, which had been overturned in 1986, and ignored the reality of the enormous number of unemployed and underemployed people in Peru in the 1990s. Vilchez was the only evangelical who was successful in the fraudulent elections of 2000; when a new congress was elected in 2001 after Fujimori's fall, Vilchez once again ran for election, but received a mere 2,300 votes.

The five evangelicals in congress in 1994 all voted for the government's proposed "Cantuta Law," which removed from civil to military jurisdiction the trial of the members of the armed forces accused of the disappearance of nine students and one university teacher. Their support was in spite of the fact that an evangelical, Juan Mallea, had been imprisoned and accused of links with the Shining Path guerrillas, solely because he had been instrumental in the discovery of the bodies of the "disappeared" people.

Gilberto Siura went even further than the other pro-Fujimori parliamentarians in his robust defense of the regime. In 1993, he proposed that the date of the self-coup should become a public holiday and be designated the "day of national defense." He became known as "the ineffable Siura" in the press, someone who "would never dream for a moment of diverging from the official line" (*La República*, 1994). In the case of the "Cantuta Law," CONEP, which represents about 85 percent of the evangelical community, had publicly expressed its concern at the slow and inefficient way the authorities were carrying out the investigations. But Siura not only defended the government's proposed law, but even came up with a theory of "self-kidnapping" to explain the fate of the students and teacher. They had been neither arrested nor "disappeared" by the armed forces, he said. The sister of one of the students publicly challenged him about how he related his Christian faith to such conduct; if we tell the truth, she said, God will help us, and we do not need to fear the threatened reprisals from the military. To which Siura replied: "But I am talking about the army, about a monster which is greater than God" (*Ideele*, March 1994, 17–18).

Siura defended the Amnesty Law of 1995, regarded by opponents as a law of impunity since it exonerated police and members of the armed forces from all responsibility for human rights violations committed since 1980. (There were rumors that Siura was part of a group of congress members recruited and controlled by the National Intelligence Service to defend the regime.) He justified the amnesty law on the theological grounds that Christians should "practice forgiveness above everything." He did not mention the search for truth and the practice of justice, which might also be thought to be important themes for national reconciliation. Another evangelical congressman, Guillermo Ysisola, added, "We who enjoy the grace of God will also know how to exercise forgiveness. Those who think they are free of sin will carry on throwing stones of hatred and vengeance. . . . But today I choose forgiveness, peace and pity. I repeat the words of Jesus to the Samaritan woman: 'No one condemns you and neither do I.'" Despite confusing the Samaritan woman of John 4 with the woman taken in adultery in John 8, Ysisola elaborates a theological justification for his political position. This position was given short shrift in the press:

> The scandal began at midnight . . . when the indescribable Gilberto Siura took the podium to defend a political amnesty bill. . . . It is a minor but significant detail that Siura is the congressman who once declared with a straight face that the disappeared students of La Cantuta "had kidnapped themselves." That Siura and other pro-government parliamentarians intend to justify forgiving the Colina Group [a military death squad] in the name of "reconciliation and pacification" is just another way to mock the citizens of this country. (*La República* March 20, 1994, 20)

The Amnesty Law was repudiated by opposition sectors of the populace and by representative religious organizations such as CONEP. As a representative body of evangelicals with a long history (founded in 1940) and with which the great majority of Protestant churches are still connected, CONEP is almost unique in Latin America. Its public pronouncement on the matter declared that, in the years of political violence, many evangelicals had been killed or disappeared by the armed forces, and several were still in prison unjustly accused of terrorism (López 1998, 229–70; Paz y Esperanza 1999b, 13–110).

Siura was also the author of another controversial bill in 1995, which proposed that congress members should receive a life pension equivalent to their last salary. When the Fujimori regime fell in November 2000, Siura, thirteen other former parliamentarians, and two former government ministers were all declared ineligible for political posts for five years, on the grounds of conspiring against democracy.

The pro-Fujimori parliamentarians from 1992 to 2000 had no political program of their own. Some, like Siura, learned the vices of the traditional politicians very efficiently and did not shirk from justifying their political actions theologically. Most of them, however, were anonymous figures who, at most, appeared only in political anecdotes.

Although the sudden election of nineteen evangelical parliamentarians in 1990 was significant for the collective pilgrimage of the evangelical community in Peru, there has been no repeat of it since. The pro-Fujimori evangelical politicians, far from being the imagined "moral reservoir" of the nation, contributed to the moral deterioration of public life by justifying the undemocratic actions of the regime. This contrasts sharply with the role played by evangelical citizens in social movements and in the struggle to restore democratic institutions during this period. The case of the evangelical parliamentarians of the 1990s shows that good intentions and a good moral reputation are insufficient as a basis for political action. A certain degree of political culture, of knowledge of public questions, and of the operation of the political game, as well as some previous political experience, are also vital. The three evangelical congressmen elected in April 2001 after the fall of Fujimori seemed better grounded in that respect. They were representatives of the new governing party Perú Posible (the engineer Walter Alejos, from a charismatic church) and of one of the main traditional parties, APRA (the teacher Roger Santamaría and the administrator Carlos Chávez, both Baptists). All three were elected as regional political leaders or as longtime militants of a mass party, rather than as specifically evangelical candidates.

Evangelical Parties and Movements

In Fujimori's Peru, various evangelical political movements and parties emerged, usually in the months before an election. Most of these movements and parties did not last long. They were composed both of pastors and laypeople, especially those with higher education. For all of them, the success of evangelicals in the 1990 elections was the starting-point.

Already in 1990, the Renewal Union of Peru (UREP; Unión Renovadora del Peru) had been formed, largely by pentecostals. Later, political movements such as Musoq Pacha (Quechua for "new land") and Christian Presence (Presencia Cristiana) appeared. Both were composed mainly of professional people linked to AGEUP, the evangelical student movement. This organization, and the Peruvian chapter of the Latin American Theological Fraternity, had long been at the forefront in promoting a "holistic" understanding of Christian mission, in which social and political action were regarded as legitimate parts of Christian witness. The biblical doctrine of the Kingdom of God was one of the theological keys in this understanding. Christian Presence was the group that lasted longest, and it presented candidates for congress in 1995 and 2000 in alliance with the nonevangelical parties such as Unión por el Perú (Union for Peru). The former senator Victor Arroyo was among these candidates, as were Nelson Ayllón, former general secretary of AGEUP, and Pedro Merino, former head of CONEP.

There were also other evangelical parties during this period, but they usually emerged without any previous reflection on political theology. In contrast, they were often motivated by a belief that "the moment had arrived" for evangelicals to have their own representatives in public life. One of their objectives was to demand equal treatment for all religious confessions, and they started with the premise that the only ones who could present the demands of the evangelical community were evangelicals themselves. Some of these parties and movements depended on one particular leader with preeminence in a certain segment of the evangelical world; others, however, were more collegial in their organization. The Koinocratic Civic Movement "National Fraternity," led by Guillermo Ysisola (a pro-Fujimori congressman from 1992 to 1995), won several mayoralties in small towns in the Andean region in the municipal elections of 1998, especially where the Independent Baptists were strong. In the 2000 national elections, a group called the Coordinadora Nacional Evangélica (National Evangelical Coordinating Committee) appeared; it was constituted by various small parties (National Fraternity among them). One of its main spokespersons was the Baptist pastor Pablo Correa, who had been instrumental in organizing Cambio 90 in 1990 and giving it strong evangelical links. The Coordinadora sought to negotiate the candidacy of its main leaders with the parties and independent movements who were contesting the elections. Pablo Correa himself and pastor Hugo López of the Christian and Missionary Alliance ran for congress with the Somos Perú ("We Are Peru") slate headed by the mayor of Lima, but neither was elected, even though they claimed to be representing a million evangelical voters. After the fall of Fujimori and the call for elections for April 2001, another evangelical party appeared, the Movement for National Restoration (MRN; Movimiento de Restauración Nacional), composed of leaders from charismatic churches and from the Christian and Missionary Alliance; it also was unsuccessful.

The evangelical parties that arose at election times did not have long-term political objectives. The leaders saw the churches mostly as fields in which votes could be "harvested," and as an interest group for which they claimed, without any consultation, to be the legitimate representatives. They believed they had the right to exercise political hegemony over the evangelical community. The same goes for some candidates in nonevangelical parties. In 1990, one campaign leaflet said: "Vote for your brother, do not vote for an unbeliever" (César Vargas, of Cambio 90). In 2000, one evangelical candidate told voters: "I ask for your support and your vote to be your representative and your spokesman in the congress" (Gino Romero, of Perú Posible). In 2001, two APRA candidates used the slogan "Two pastors for congress." The same idea can be found in the leaflets of the MRN and of National Fraternity; even more, their declarations contained the idea that the evangelicals had a divine right to govern the country, since they had not been called to be the "tail" but the "head." An MRN circular of February 2001 called itself

> a party solidly of 100 percent evangelical inspiration, which serves
> as a space where all the children of God who have the Holy Spirit
> and live according to the principles of the Word of God and who
> have a vocation of service to the nation in the political sphere,
> can develop that vocation with the necessary spiritual and pasto-
> ral cover.

The MRN transmitted the idea that the entry of believers "full of the Holy Spirit" to congress would "restore the moral bases of the nation."

> The political, economic and social crisis which the country is going
> through has its root in a moral crisis, which in turn originates
> in spiritual factors. Only the Christians can discern the way in which
> the "principalities and powers, the governors of the darkness of
> this present era and the hosts of evil in the celestial regions" influ-
> ence events and the situation of prostration of a nation which is so
> rich in resources as ours is. Only the Christians can perceive the
> curses which idolatrous and occult practices bring down on
> our people, and even more so when our very rulers encourage
> them and even practice them.

The irony is that several MRN leaders had supported the Fujimori regime, knowing that Fujimori had introduced "idolatrous and occult practices" into the palace. The pronouncement of the International Fraternity of Christian Pastors (FIPAC; Fraternidad Internacional de Pastores Cristianos, largely composed of charismatic leaders and the main rival to CONEP) before the 2000 elections denied that there was "any one inclination, opinion or position with regard to the forthcoming elections or the candidates, or with regard to the constitutionality or inconstitutionality of the reelection of the current president" (*La República*, February 4, 2000). It was only when the regime fell that they discovered the need for evangelicals in politics to expel such forces. As the MRN did not manage sufficient signatures to register and present its own candidates for the 2001 elections, it concentrated on campaigning for Lourdes Flores, the presidential candidate of the right, whose National Unity Party included several candidates linked to Opus Dei. Two of the main leaders of the MRN and also of FIPAC, Humberto Lay and Roberto Barriger, made a video interview with Lourdes Flores in which they claimed, as representatives of the evangelical community, to have played an active part in the struggle for human rights in Peru, a hitherto unknown activity of such leaders.

The leaders of the evangelical parties that appeared during the 1990s did not take into account the complexity of the political world with its plurality of interests and the latent danger of corruption, or the rules of the political game that requires alliances at certain times. None of the evangelical parties that emerged during this period had any real impact on national politics. In part, this was because they became active only at election times. Another limitation was that they concentrated almost exclusively on winning over evangelical voters, under the false impression that the evangelical vote was captive and homogeneous. They wrongly imagined that church members followed their pastors not only in religious questions but also in political matters.

The Evangelical Vote

Was the evangelical vote a "captive" vote in Fujimori's Peru? Was it directed to favor a certain candidate? It was the 1990 election that created that impression, but the reality was different. The four evangelicals elected to the senate in 1990 received a total of 93,071 votes, and the fourteen evangelicals elected with Cambio 90 to the lower house obtained 97,463 votes. But this represented no more than 20 percent of the evangelical electorate. In the electorate as a whole, about 30 percent of those who vote for a candidate for president abstain from choosing a candidate for senator or deputy; if this also applies to evangelical voters, it would mean that approximately 135,000 evangelicals voted for Fujimori. The evangelicals were just one of the three mainstays of the organization of Cambio 90, the other two being the "informal economy" sector represented by the Association of Small and Medium-Sized Industrialists led by Máximo San Román (candidate for first vice president) and a group of teachers and technicians from the National Agrarian University of which Fujimori had been the chancellor. Grompone is correct to say that "it was not the informal sector, the evangelicals, the lack of a political centre, the discrediting of the parties, the ethnic cleavages and the social differences, which explain isolatedly the triumph of Fujimori, but the fusion of all of these in a moment of political vacuum" (Grompone 1991, 61).

Thus, the entry of Fujimori into Peruvian politics was not exclusively due to the electoral weight of the evangelicals or the supposed mobilization of their corporatist networks. But in public opinion, the idea developed that it had been the evangelicals who had enabled Fujimori to catapult to power. The parties began to see them as a potential electoral hunting ground that they imagined to be homogeneous in its political behavior, and many pastors adhered to the same idea.

In the 1992 elections for a constituent congress following Fujimori's self-coup, the idea of the evangelicals as a monolithic and important voting bloc was still present. In these elections, there were evangelical candidates both in the governing party and in one of the opposition parties, Solidarity and Democracy (SODE; Solidaridad y Democracia). Only five evangelicals were elected, all of them progovernment. The sum of these five candidates' votes, plus those of another progovernment evangelical candidate, comes to 94,439.

The six evangelical candidates in the opposition party, on the other hand, only managed 5,135 votes. Of these, three had been members of the congress elected in 1990 and closed by Fujimori. One of them, Victor Arroyo, received less than 2,500 votes, according to the official results, although a national news magazine speculated that he may have received thirty-five thousand (*Caretas* 1992, 24). Arroyo himself concludes that there may have been vote-stealing within the party to favor another candidate. Whatever the reason, only progovernment evangelicals obtained seats in the new congress.

In 1995, the story was the same: only pro-Fujimori evangelicals got into congress. Of six progovernment candidates, five were elected. Three of these (Barreto, Siura, and Vilchez) were reelected, and they were joined by the indigenous Presbyterian Miguel Quicaña (with by far the most votes) and Alejandro Abanto of the Assemblies of God. The six progovernment candidates totaled eighty-four thousand votes. On the other hand, evangelical candidates in the traditional parties APRA and the Popular Christian Party, both with very little prestige at that time, received only sixteen hundred votes, while the ten evangelicals who stood with the largest of the opposition parties (Unión por el Perú) garnered nine thousand votes, and another thirty-six evangelical candidates in four small parties obtained some three thousand. Once again, veteran parliamentarians from the period 1990–92 were unsuccessful; Victor Arroyo, for example, achieved scarcely more than a thousand votes. The mistake of these opposition candidates was to orient their campaign only to winning the evangelical voters. The government's evangelical candidates did the same, but they had the advantage of the support of the state bureaucracy.

Even in the 2000 elections, the story was basically the same. In this fraudulent ballot, the number of evangelical candidates was again large, all of them seemingly moved by the illusion that church members were obliged to vote for them just because they shared the same faith. In the governing party (by now called Perú 2000), three evangelical congressmen attempted reelection. Only one (Vilchez) achieved his aim, while Siura and Quicaña were defeated. Siura, however, still had considerable support. Over the Fujimori years, he and Vilchez had created clientelist networks in the traditional manner; in exchange for favors, and in spite of their weak congressional input, they had managed to retain significant support among a sector of pastors. Another factor was the strength of the figure of Fujimori among the popular classes, which allowed progovernment candidates without their own electoral base or previous political experience to achieve electoral success.

Among the opposition parties there were thirty-two evangelical candidates. These candidates included members of the Christian and Missionary Alliance, the Pentecostal Church of Peru, the Assemblies of God, the Baptist Convention, the Biblical Baptists, the Presbyterians, the Wesleyan Church, and the Methodists, besides members of independent charismatic churches such as Emmanuel Biblical Church and Strong Tower; however, none of them was elected.

Why was there such a multiplication of evangelical candidacies in this period and such a dispersed evangelical voting pattern? The expectation that 1990 would repeat itself was the key factor. Most evangelical candidates believed that evangelical voters were obliged to vote for them merely on the basis of their common religious affiliation. That is why they oriented their election campaigns toward capturing the evangelical vote. In 2000, for example, the campiagn slogans of the pro-Fujimori candidates were: "Brothers, this is our time. We already know each other, now let's work" (Quicaña), and "Pastor Pedro Vilchez for Congress." Opposition candidates tried the same tack: "A Christian for Congress" (José Serrano, of Perú Posible), and "Fifteen Years in the Lord" (César Madico, of Avancemos). There were attempts to solicit the evangelical vote by offering special favors (such as tax exemptions or public subsidies for evangelical work) to pastors who gave their "spiritual covering" and promised the electoral support of their members. Even though they usually did not say it outright, most evangelical candidates saw the churches as a reserved market for votes, and presented themselves as the only authoritative spokespersons for that community.

However, the evangelical voters did not, on the whole, vote for them. The evangelical electorate grew constantly throughout the Fujimori decade (due to the growth of the churches) and may have reached around a million voters by the year 2000. But we have seen that the votes obtained by the many evangelical candidates in those elections were little more than 10 percent of that total evangelical electorate. What did the rest of the evangelical electorate do? There were those (probably a majority) who supported Fujimori until around mid-1999, and presumably voted for the government's nonevangelical candidates for deputy. On the other hand, there were those who supported the opposition parties, such as APRA, the Partido Popular Cristiano, the Frente Independiente Moralizador, or Unión por el Perú, and who may also have voted for nonevangelical candidates in those parties. Converts to the evangelical faith did not automatically abandon their previous political commitments. There was also probably a considerable part of the evangelical electorate who, following the practice of many other voters, did not exercise their right to choose a preferential candidate for deputy from the party lists but merely voted for a presidential candidate.

Within the evangelical churches there was a plurality of political stances that included one sector (probably a majority, as was the case in the country at large) whose support of Fujimori was constant (at least until 1999), and another sector (a minority that grew as the Fujimori government became more and more authoritarian) that supported the opposition parties. As part of the Peruvian people, the evangelicals did not have a homogeneous and constant political "face," as some suppose.

The parliamentary activities, the founding of evangelical political parties, and the behavior of the evangelical voters at election times are not the only levels at which evangelicals were present in the public scene during the Fujimori period. In the 1990s, as part of the process of growing citizenship on the part of organized sectors of civil society, the evangelicals also went from a marginal position in public life to one of active citizens. In fact, since the mid-1980s, thanks to their numerical growth and to CONEP's active participation in the National Movement for Human Rights, their involvement has attracted the attention of analysts (De la Jara, *Ideele*, November 1998, 9). And in Fujimori's Peru there was a growing number of evangelicals involved in the social movements that confronted the political violence and the economic crisis and fought to reinstate the democratic institutions that Fujimori was dismantling step by step.

Evangelicals and Civil Society

The Spaces for Citizen Initiatives

Evangelicals had varied involvement in citizen participation during Fujimori's Peru. Two areas of experience were linked to the strengthening of democracy in a context in which democracy was being dismantled: the so-called survival organizations (such as Mothers Clubs, the Glass of Milk Committees, the Self-Run Canteens, and the Popular Canteens), and the peasant patrols (or Self-Defense Committees). As in other parts of Latin America, these citizen spaces were the collective vehicles by which the popular classes could express their social expectations and political aspirations during critical periods for their countries (Haber 1997, 36). In a historical context of conflict between state and society, which one author calls "cultures in conflict" (Stokes 1995, 3–15), they demonstrated an enormous potential for recreating civil society and, in so doing, strengthening democracy (Haber 1997, 122). However, with respect especially to the survival organizations, it has been said that they have become attractive for those who would like to control them electorally but have not managed to constitute themselves as articulate social actors (Blondet 2001, 17–20). This was clearly seen by the mid-1990s, when "the leaders of survival organizations, facing the possibility of taking on a pro-active role in local politics . . . ended up fighting among themselves and negotiating individually with the political parties for some part in local power structures, thus losing the support of their own social base" (16–17).

Even so, since the 1980s, the survival organizations and the peasant patrols have been a key factor in strengthening democracy in times of political violence (García Sayán 1988, 18) and in constructing local spaces for building an awareness of citizenship among historically marginalized sectors such as women and peasants (Blondet 1993, 189–90). "The canteens and the women's

Glass of Milk Committees and the self-defence peasant patrols demand the right to survival. They have resisted the recent debacle of social and political institutions because they manage to respond to the two central problems of the moment: the economic crisis and the political violence" (189).

Both the survival organizations and the peasant patrols, as well as the human rights movement, were fundamental on the one hand in putting brakes on Shining Path's hegemonic aspirations to control all the organized sectors of civil society and, on the other hand, in limiting as far as possible the violation of human rights (extrajudicial executions, forced disappearances, torture) by the armed forces (López 1998, 39; M. Smith 1992, 127–45). When Shining Path realized that these popular organizations were interrupting its intended plans for hegemony, it attempted to infiltrate, divide, and destroy them. One of its strategies was to sow rumors about corruption on the part of the leaders of these organizations, to discredit them in the eyes of their members. Another strategy was the assassination of such leaders (Roberts 1998, 259).

One sector of civil society that took an active part in the human rights movement was the evangelical community, via its representative body, CONEP. CONEP had established links with the national human rights movement in the mid-1980s, and in 1994 became a permanent invitee on the National Coordinating Committee for Human Rights. Ernesto de la Jara writes that one of the factors that helped consolidate the national human rights movement was the "active participation of the Catholic Church and later also of the Evangelical Church" (*Ideele*, November 1998, 9).

A significant number of evangelical church members played an active role in the survival organizations and in the peasant patrols. The Fujimori government tried to disrupt and demobilize the survival organizations, and tried to instrumentalize the peasant patrols as cannon fodder in the fight against subversion. At a time when religious communities are more and more recognized as vital factors in the rise of civil society, it is especially important to analyze the participation of evangelicals in these spaces (Rudolph 1997b, 1).

In addition, soon after the self-coup of April 1992, civil society began to organize in various ways to prevent the collapse of democracy. The culminating moments in this process were the demonstrations in defense of democratic institutionality in 2000, before and after the unconstitutional second reelection of Fujimori. Evangelicals were present in this civic struggle through their representative body, CONEP, and through the Evangelicals for Democracy Movement (MED).

Evangelical Women in the Survival Organizations

The participation of evangelical women in these democratic spaces was not institutional or corporatist. Neither CONEP nor any denominational leadership had a strategy for church members to get involved in the Glass of Milk Committees or in the Popular Canteens started by thousands of women in the social sectors that were hardest hit by the economic crisis. Evangelical women were there as citizens who, side by side with their nonevangelical neighbors, got organized and struggled collectively to "survive" in a society that excluded them. The survival organizations that took shape from the mid-1980s onward were spaces not just for "survival" but also for the affirmation of human dignity and for collective responses to political and socioeconomic exclusion. They were concrete examples of a democratization of economics and politics in a social climate characterized by authoritarianism, marginalization, and violence.

From the standpoint of evangelical experience, there were three main reasons why evangelical women made themselves present in these social spaces. (According to the Christian Center for Promotion and Services [CEPS; Centro Cristiano de Promoción y Servicios], in mid-1994 there were about one hundred evangelical women actively involved in popular organizations in the northern zone of Lima alone.) First, the economic crisis forced them to unite with their neighbors to struggle collectively against poverty. Second, their situation of poverty led them to a perception that the love for one's neighbor that they proclaimed daily had to be lived outside as well as inside the church building. Third, in these spaces they discovered solidarity at work to overcome the common problems of the urban peripheries. This was the experience of Benedicta, a Catholic woman who was the leader of a Popular Canteen and of the Glass of Milk Committee in a district of Lima (Levine and Stoll 1997, 63–64); it was also the experience of Paulina, an evangelical woman who had leadership responsibilities in a Glass of Milk Committee in Villa María del Triunfo, one of the poorest areas of southern Lima. Paulina describes her experience thus: "There are poor people, children and the elderly, who need our help.... As Christian women, we have to give testimony to our faith at all times, and especially we have to help needy people. But to carry out this work one needs time, since all things should be done responsibly" (interview with Paulina, May 17, 1999).

In addition, according to another evangelical woman named Paulina, an active neighborhood leader and coordinator of a Glass of Milk Committee in the Lima district of San Juan de Miraflores, the evangelical church itself should be "involved in social work.... It shouldn't be isolated from the community but should serve evangelicals and nonevangelicals alike, without discriminating.... The church is called to serve our neighbor. The church has to follow the way of Jesus who came to serve and not to be served" (interview with Paulina, September 30, 1998).

From the perspective of these evangelical women, they had an advantage in the ethical field over their neighbors. "The neighbors see that we evangelicals are honest and work with honor. They know that we don't lie or steal, and also that we don't marginalize anybody but seek to serve everybody equally" (interview with Paulina, September 30, 1998). This ethical contribution to citizenship initiatives is particularly relevant in a context of systemic corruption of public morals. Evangelical women can become key moral reference points for their neighbors.

These women understand that, just like their nonevangelical neighbors, their economic needs prompted them to organize collectively. The words of Santosa Layme, a popular leader, illustrate this point.

> The hunger and misery of all the families in the area stimulated
> me to found the canteen. First of all, we opened the glass of milk
> program . . . and we distributed one hundred glasses of milk. But this
> was still too little, since many children were left in their hovels
> and did not have any lunch. That led me to found the canteen in a
> community locale (Paz y Esperanza 1999a, 3)

Some evangelicals involved in such initiatives have become well known, such as Doris Mazuelos, a member of an independent pentecostal church called the Evangelical Mission Rose of Sharon; and Fanny Arica, a member of another independent pentecostal church known as Missionary Movement Mount of Holiness. Doris Mazuelos became the president of the District Central Committee of Popular and Self-Administered Canteens of San Martín de Porras, as well as secretary of health of the Federation of Women Organized in Central Committees of Popular and Self-Administered Canteens and Similar Organizations of Lima and Callao. As a popular leader, she was a candidate for congress with the opposition party National Solidarity in 2000, but was not elected because her party was not well supported and her potential electorate opted for other candidates. Fanny Arica was the president, in the 1980s, of the Glass of Milk Committee of Sector 6 Group 10, and health secretary of the Directing Junta of Sector 6. Later she moved to another area and was Governing Lieutenant of Chuquitanta, an area inhabited mostly by people displaced by the political violence. There she became an active leader of the Self-Administered Canteens and of the Glass of Milk Committees. She became the president of the Self-Administered Canteens of Zone D of San Martín de Porras and secretary of the Multisectorial Committee of the Rural Zone of that district. Another case is that of Eulogia Martínez, of the Church of God, who was the founder and president of the Directing Junta of the Mothers Club "the Indo-American Sisters," as well as the secretary of the Coordinating Committee of the Province of Callao for Base Social Organizations.

I have chosen Santosa Layme to illustrate further the experience of evangelical women in these social roles. Santosa took part in a Popular Canteen and a Glass of Milk Committee in San Juan de Lurigancho. She says, "We are accustomed to this work and feel great affection for the canteen. We help each other if anyone gets sick or if a relative dies. We show solidarity. I always tell the other members that God blesses a cheerful giver, even though not all of them are evangelical Christians" (Paz y Esperanza 1999a, 4). According to an article in one of the leading national newspapers, this woman has "acted without vacillation and with great courage, as a leader in her area" (*La República*, March 20, 1994, 6). And the magazine of the Institute of Legal Defense, a body dedicated to the defense of human rights, added:

> Señora Layme is well known and much liked in her district for her dedication to communal activities. She is the president of the Mothers Club of Santa Marta, works in the area coordination of the Glass of Milk, is a promoter of the Peruvian Institute of Responsible Fatherhood and cooperates with the Flora Tristán NGO for the promotion of women. She directs the popular canteen in her district. She has belonged to a pentecostal church for the last sixteen years and, obviously, her rejection of Shining Path is complete. (*Ideele*, May 1994, 33)

Precisely for her leadership, Santosa was arrested by the armed forces in February 1994 and accused of collaborating with terrorism and of having fed members of Shining Path (*La República*, March 20, 1994, 6). She was sentenced to several years in prison by a "faceless court" (a common practice in the years of political violence), but in February 1995 she was pardoned as part of a "rectification process" of the antisubversive policy, the result of national and foreign pressure on the Peruvian government. "Santosa always spoke without fear, in her imperfect Spanish (she never studied beyond the first year of primary school), and convinced us that we had to carry on, we had to persevere, in spite of Shining Path" (*La República*, March 20, 1994).

The experiences of these evangelical popular female leaders varied widely. Some of them were already evangelicals when they joined a Glass of Milk Committee or a Popular Canteen, like Doris Mazuelos and Eulogia Martínez. Others, such as Fanny Arica, joined the evangelical church after previous experience of participation in survival organizations. In some cases, they were obliged by their pastors to rethink their participation. Some pastors could not understand why a believer should be interested in "things of this world," "messing with unspiritual affairs," and "involved in politics" (*Caminos*, June 1994, 9). As a result some women ended up abandoning their responsibilities as leaders of Glass of Milk Committees or other organizations because their commitments in the church gradually began to occupy all the time they had previously used to work with their neighbors; or, in other cases, because the pastor "advised" them to leave all "worldly" activities and "consecrate themselves to the Lord." Nevertheless, there were evangelical women who, without losing their religious identity or their relationship to their local congregation, carried on working with their nonevangelical neighbors.

How did these women contribute to the strengthening of democracy? The honesty and transparency in dealing with public affairs that have character- ized these evangelical popular leaders, above all in a context of systemic corruption, is in itself an important contribution. In addition, their presence in these activities shows that there has been a growing awareness of civic responsibility in a religious community that was for many years regarded as a "refuge of the masses" engaged in a "social strike" (D'Epinay 1968). But this change has not happened in a vacuum; it has accompanied a process of growing awareness of citizenship on the part of organized sectors of civil society.

Evangelicals in the Peasant Patrols

The peasant patrols (*rondas campesinas*), which started in the mid-1980s in the Cajamarca region and spread in the 1990s with the growth in political vio- lence, have been particularly strong in Ayacucho, an Andean zone especially affected by the "dirty war" between the guerillas of Shining Path and the Peruvian armed forces. In 1994, the number of peasant patrols in the Aya- cucho and Apurimac regions was estimated at 1,665, with some sixty-five thousand members (Degregori 1996a, 24).

In this context of violence (twenty-five thousand dead, hundreds of forced disappearances, thousands of displaced people), a transformation of the reli- gious field occurred in the rural zones of Ayacucho. Due in part to the almost total absence of Catholic priests, many small evangelical churches, mostly pentecostal ones, appeared (Klaiber 1997, 247). The peasants found an al- ternative religious solution to their problems, in opposition to the "religion of violence" propagated by Shining Path (Palmer 1992a, 6). Denominations such as the Assemblies of God, the Pentecostal Evangelical Church of Peru, and the Presbyterian Church have seen rapid growth in recent years. In the department of Ayacucho, evangelicals

> were 3.7 percent of the population in 1981, but today they are 10.15 percent. In the provinces most affected by the violence, growth has been significantly higher. In Huanta evangelicals went from 4.1 percent in 1981 to 14.95 percent in 1993. In La Mar, they went from 7.8 percent to 16.3 percent, and in Cangallo from 4.3 percent to 20.25 percent. There are no exact figures, but in rural zones the percent- age of evangelicals is even higher, nearing 40 percent in a census of five communities in Huanta. (Degregori 1996a, 20)

Degregori observes that in rural areas of Ayacucho, the evangelicals stayed in the "dirty war" zones, whereas the Catholic pastoral agents left for safer places (1996a, 20). (It should be stressed that in other regions affected by political violence, such as Puno and Cajamarca, the Catholic Church had a different role. There, the progressive sector of the church predominated, influenced by liberation theology, and there was greater pastoral commitment in the rural areas. But in Ayacucho, the diocese was extremely conservative and governed by bishops linked to Opus Dei.) Aguiló says that "in Ayacucho, parishes and convents 'put chains' on their doors in the face of the wave of urban and rural terror, and pastoral visits were reduced to the point of disappearing totally" (1994, 43).

In the opinion of some analysts, the peasant patrols were developed and oriented by members of the evangelical churches, and the armed clashes were principally between Shining Path and pentecostals (Österlund 2001). Several patrols were led by pastors. There were cases in which 80 percent of the members of peasant patrols were from evangelical churches (Díaz, *Revista Domingo, La República*, June 9, 1991, 20). One historian, referring to the options that peasants had in this climate of violence and death, described the evangelical "option" thus:

> For the peasant who had not been a Shining Path guerilla but who also did not want to be a *montonero* [a member of the peasant patrols], if he wished to stay alive the only remaining option was to flee as quickly as possible to some refugee encampment in Ica or in Lima ... unless a blind faith (such as in the case of some evangelicals) helped our hypothetical peasant to stay and defy all the subsequent tribulations. (Flores Galindo 1988, 405)

It was not really a case of "blind faith," of course. Rather, one needs to understand the evangelical mentality, and especially the way the pastors understand their pastoral vocation and their calling to remain alongside their flock in all circumstances. But it should also be pointed out that there were variations in the origins of the peasant patrols, especially in the Ayacucho region. Some were the initiative of the armed forces, who wanted peasants as "human shields" or cannon fodder against armed subversion in a region that they did not know well (Degregori 1996a, 23–26). In this case, the patrols were part of a counterinsurgency strategy (Starn 1996, 229). But other patrols were started as a survival strategy by the peasants themselves, to defend themselves against Shining Path terror (Degregori 1996a, 26). Shining Path destroyed communities and took many villagers away by force for indoctrination and incorporation into their units. There were also cases in which peasant patrols were founded out of mutual necessity on the part of peasants and the armed forces against the common enemy, through a convergence of peasant will and counterinsurgency policy (Coronel 1996, 105).

Evangelicals seem to have taken part mainly in those peasant patrols that were started on the intitiative of the peasants themselves. "In Apurimac the evangelical churches, especially the pentecostal ones, have played a very important role in the struggle against Shining Path. In a social context plagued by poverty and sickness and among a population of Andean migrants partially disconnected from their old communities, the evangelicals recreated utopian horizons" (Del Pino 1996, 118).

Del Pino also describes what was, in his opinion, the ideological catalyst for the evangelicals to confront Shining Path.

> From 1984 onwards, the Pentecostal Evangelical Church began to grow strongly. Its message was: we live in apocalyptic times, on the eve of the second coming of the Holy Spirit. It is urgently necessary to "choose the way of life," the "true Christianity," to guarantee salvation and eternal life. For Shining Path, it became hard to break these communities, so they decided to combat them. The evangelicals then elaborated an ideological response which translated into practical action: for the final judgement, the earth should be cleansed of "demons." So it was necessary, under the protection of God, to fight against the forces of evil. In this way, the bloody repression carried out by Shining Path met with a response in the armed action of the evangelicals, and the political war was converted to some extent into a religious war, since the evangelicals did not see themselves as fighting against a run-of-the-mill enemy, but against the Anti-Christ himself. (1996, 118)

For Del Pino, the armed confrontation between evangelicals and Shining Path can be explained as a conflict of worldviews. If for Shining Path the armed violence was seen as the only way to build a "classless society," the evangelicals had another way of interpreting this violence, as a sign of the last times and an indication of the approaching Second Coming of Jesus (Isbell 1992, 76).

> Both [Shining Path and the evangelical churches] arrived in the valley [of the River Apurimac] to conquer the hearts and souls of the needy. Shining Path offered the revolution; the evangelicals offered paradise.... The war completed the ideological counterpoint: for Shining Path, killing evangelicals was finishing off the "traitors of the people"; for the evangelicals, confronting Shining Path meant struggling against the demons, against the Anti-Christ. Both were ready to die for their holy books: the guerillas for the *Thoughts of Gonzalo* [Abimael Guzmán, the Shining Path leader], and the brethren for the Gospel. (Del Pino 1996, 167)

Thus, the way the evangelicals interpreted the terrorist actions of Shining Path can explain their struggle to put an end to the wave of violence and death that this Maoist group started and that was depopulating the rural areas. In this confrontation there were two components. The ideological component was the hegemonic mentality that both sides shared that led both to seek to be

the only proprietors of the geographical space. The "proselytistic" component was each side's interest in gaining the greatest number of followers.
The struggle between them was with "no quarter given." While Shining Path
sought to kill evangelicals, whom it considered to be its ideological competitors and a hindrance to its plans of territorial dominance, the evangelicals
fought against the "terrorists," whom they saw as a clear manifestation of the
Antichrist and a sign of the last days of history. What attracts attention here is
the way they read those parts of the New Testament that talked of the signs of
the last times, in order to classify the actions of Shining Path as manifestations of the approach of the Antichrist.

The militant way in which evangelicals in the Andean communities adopt
their religious commitment and the defense of their faith is also a key internal
factor in explaining both the discipline and the cohesion they showed in facing
up to adversity. Certain characteristics of the community life of evangelicals
(such as their respect for the spiritual authority of their pastors, and the solidarity and companionship of their congregational life) help to explain their
participation in the peasant patrols. They saw themselves as the army that
God had raised up to put an end to the "terrorists" and as those chosen by the
Lord to punish those who did not respect human life. While the fighters of
Shining Path were ready to "offer themselves" without reservation for "the
party" and for "President Gonzalo," the evangelicals were ready to die fear-
lessly for Jesus Christ and their faith. When Shining Path tried to control the
personal and collective life of the peasants, including their religious practices,
it came up against a rival power that told it they could not "serve two masters."
This rival power provided the strength needed both to resist Shining Path
indoctrination and violence and to organize and fight against them. In the
end, they were successful.

The peasant patrols, then, were the social vehicle through which many
evangelical peasants of the Ayacucho region expressed and channeled their
commitment to a constitutional ordering of society. These evangelicals fought
both for their own survival and for their religious convictions; and, even if they
did not realize it, they were contributing to the strengthening of democracy in
a political context in which it was being undermined by both Shining Path
and the armed forces.

Evangelicals and the Struggle to Restore Democratic Institutions

In Fujimori's Peru, critical evangelical voices could be heard mainly from two
directions. On the one hand, there was the institutional voice that spoke
through the more politically aware leadership of CONEP. On the other hand,
there was a collective voice, organized by a group of anti-Fujimori pastors and
leaders, that by the time of the 2000 elections had adopted the name Evangelicals for Democracy Movement (MED). Both of these voices were critical of

Fujimori's authoritarian regime and of the parliamentary behavior of the pro-Fujimori evangelical congress members. There were five main occasions on which these critical voices were able to make their positions public: (1) the election of 1990; (2) Fujimori's self-coup of 1992; (3) the referendum on the new constitution in 1993; (4) the passing of the so-called Amnesty Law of 1995; and (5) Fujimori's unconstitutional second reelection in a fraudulent election in 2000.

EVALUATIONS OF THE EVANGELICAL ROLE IN THE 1990 ELECTION. In the only democratic period under Fujimori (1990–92), political discussions among the CONEP leadership centered around the concern that Shining Path might discern a connection between the government and the evangelicals, and thus justify their aggression against churches in the regions where armed conflict was going on. Before and after the 1990 election, in successive pronouncements prepared by a sector of the CONEP leadership that did not support Fujimori's candidacy, the emphasis was on delegitimating any political attempt to claim the right to represent the evangelicals as a whole. Later, in its general assembly of 1991, a document called *Evaluation of the Electoral Process of 1990* was unanimously approved. It stated that in the election there had been a "lack of ethics" on the part of some evangelical candidates who had manipulated the churches in order to get votes, and in several churches there had been a "shameful use of the pulpit" for party political propaganda (CONEP 1991, 1). Apart from this, in Fujimori's democratic years, CONEP's public posture was one of vigilance toward the actions of government, especially as "the image of evangelicals as honest citizens who were responsible in their use of public resources was at stake; and indirectly the image of the churches themselves was at stake also, since public opinion regarded them as having been the decisive factor in Fujimori's victory" (Verástegui 1992, 7).

THE SELF-COUP OF 1992. This posture changed noticeably after the self-coup of April 5, 1992. The divergent opinions within the evangelical community became clearer from then on; when CONEP called a general assembly three days after the coup, opinion among evangelical leaders was divided. The sector that supported the regime argued that the evangelicals had no business expressing their opinion publicly on these matters. The anti-Fujimori sector argued, on the other hand, that the evangelical churches had to fulfil a prophetic role by publicly denouncing the regime's actions. After a lengthy discussion, a consensus was reached on a pronouncement that characterized the self-coup as a "rupture of the constitutional order" ("Pronunciamiento público del CONEP," April 9, 1992). Even that was too much for some pastors, who believed that the churches should limit themselves to their spiritual task of prayer and verbal proclamation of the gospel, avoiding social and political questions. However, the evangelical senator Victor Arroyo immediately

resigned from the ruling party, Cambio 90, for its break with the constitutional order, and Carlos García, the Baptist pastor who was the second vice
president of the republic but totally marginalized by Fujimori, said that "to
justify this passing roughshod over the constitution and the laws, the dictator
has used the pretext of the inefficacy of the legislature and the corruption of
the judiciary" (García, *Ideele*, May 1992, 10).

It should be pointed out that the CONEP pronouncements up to 1992
were written by pastors and leaders who had been critical of Fujimori and of
the pro-Fujimori evangelical members of congress from the very beginning.
Their theological thought and political reflection had been influenced over the
years by their involvement with the Peruvian evangelical student organization
AGEUP and the Latin American Theological Fraternity (a regionwide organ of
evangelical thinkers). Their opinions were influential among evangelical
university students and graduates and among the small nucleus of "organic
intellectuals" of the evangelical world who would later found the MED. But
their influence in the broader evangelical community was limited. The latter
tended more to follow the general course of public opinion, identifying with
the Fujimori regime, which had (as public opinion believed) solved the two
major problems of national politics: the political violence and the economic
crisis.

THE REFERENDUM OF 1993. After the self-coup, the newly elected constituent
congress, dominated by Fujimori's allies, prepared a new constitution that
was then submitted to a national referendum on October 31, 1993. The yes
vote won the referendum by 52 percent. In the evangelical camp, anti-Fujimori leaders made their defence of a no vote clear in a "Christian Manifesto to
Public Opinion" on July 2, 1993:

> Without claiming to be official representatives of the evangelical
> community, we manifest to our compatriots that . . . ever since the
> *coup d'état* of April 5 last year, with the rupture of the democratic
> order and contempt for the norms of democratic life, the acts of the
> government have been based on an authoritarian style disguised as
> beneficent populism. . . . As evangelical citizens we do not support
> this policy or the style of government imposed on us, nor do we
> support those who seek to justify it "Christianly" from the public
> offices which they now enjoy. . . . The project of constitutional re-
> form . . . would mean approval of an undemocratic, unpopular, auto-
> cratic and centralising judicial order. (*La República*, July 10, 1993)

The document was signed by pastors and leaders of various denominations (including the Assemblies of God, the Christian and Missionary Alliance, the Presbyterian Church, the Peruvian Evangelical Church, the Nazarene Church, and the Baptist Convention) as well as by representatives of

diverse institutions affiliated with CONEP. It was also signed by several former Cambio 90 senators and deputies from the 1990–92 period, and by the former second vice president Carlos García.

The pro-Fujimori evangelicals did not make public pronouncements, but

> with equal conviction, did not lose any chances to show their approval
> of the new constitutional proposal. Echoing the official arguments,
> they said that the constitution would guarantee the overcoming of the
> verbal paralysis of politics, and would assure the development of
> the country within the new rules of the game set by the free market.
> (Goto, *Caminos*, December 1993, 8–9)

THE AMNESTY LAW OF 1995. In a statement entitled "Justice and Truth for Reconciliation," CONEP published its opinion on the so-called Amnesty Law of 1995. CONEP spoke of its

> deep pain and indignation because of the content and the way
> in which the said law was approved. We express our concern that
> those who were the authors of crimes against the life and dignity of
> people are escaping any sanction, and above all our concern for the
> implications of this on the consolidation of democracy and the pro-
> cess of pacification. ("Pronunciamiento público del CONEP,"
> June 20, 1995)

Anti-Fujimori evangelicals also produced a statement that asserted that the new law confused diverse situations and cases, and benefited those who, going beyond their legal functions, had committed grave crimes against humanity. And they stressed that the members of congress who professed to be evangelicals and had approved the new law did not represent the thinking of the church, and still less the ethics and morals of the Scriptures (*La República*, June 19, 1995).

Fujimori retained considerable support in the country as a whole until mid-1999, and the same held true in the evangelical churches. There was a sector that had established a clientelistic relationship with the pro-Fujimori evangelical congressmen, besides sympathizing with the neoliberal economic model and with the authoritarian style of Fujimori. They frequently expressed their disagreement with the pronouncements of CONEP. Several of them had credentials as "honorary advisors" to the evangelical congress members and became intermediaries between the churches and the congress in obtaining mutual advantages such as speeding up church requests going through the state bureaucracy, and setting up networks of political support inside the churches. Thus, when they invited the evangelical congress members to their public rallies and asked them to greet the crowd and lead a prayer, these pastors were giving tacit recognition of the value of their public role.

By mid-1999, when the political panorama was changing and many organized sectors of civil society were starting to take to the streets to protest against the increasingly authoritarian nature of the regime and against Fujimori's intention to win an unconstitutional additional term in office, the balance of forces inside the evangelical community also began to change.

THE 2000 ELECTION. In two rounds of elections held on April 9 and May 28, 2000, Fujimori claimed victory and a further five years in power. But national and foreign observers were unanimous in characterizing the elections as illegitimate and fraudulent. The People's Defense (Defensoría del Pueblo), the only state institution not under the control of the central government, said the election had suffered from a "deficit of legitimacy" and "the basic standards for free and competitive elections" had not been respected (Defensoría del Pueblo 2000, 67). The end result was a country split down the middle. On both sides of the split, obviously, there were evangelicals. Subsequently, a series of events sparked off a profound political and moral crisis in the country. One of these events was the revelation of a video in which the presidential advisor and power behind the throne, Vladimiro Montesinos, was seen bribing an opposition congressman to switch to the ranks of the government. Another event was the resignation of Fujimori in November, while on a visit to Japan. The evidence of corruption within the government was by that time overwhelming.

What was the reaction to these events within the evangelical community? Before the 2000 election, CONEP published a statement entitled "Why Christians Should Reject the Second Reelection of Mr. Fujimori." The statement gave the following reasons for this position:

> The absence of values in governmental administration, such as
> truthfulness, honesty, justice, freedom, human dignity and solidar-
> ity; the concentration of power which prevents the full exercise of de-
> mocracy and blocks the development of the regions; the lack of the rule
> of law; the withdrawal of Peru from the sphere of the Inter-American
> Court of Human Rights; the growth of poverty and misery; the in-
> ability of the government to solve the problem of unemployment...;
> the segregationist character of the economic model; the corruption;
> the religious discrimination; the lack of freedom of opinion. ("Pro-
> nunciamiento público del CONEP," January 10, 2000)

In fact, this pronouncement had been written by members of Christian Presence, the evangelical political movement that would soon become part of the founding group of the MED. The response of progovernment evangelicals was quick in coming and came through two routes. One of these consisted of the public declarations of two foreign pastors, one an exiled Cuban and the other an American. They were both from churches whose leaders were generally seen by members as "anointed" by God and endowed with un-questionable authority. Their opinions were published in the daily newspaper *Expreso*, well known for its pro-Fujimori stance. The Cuban González Cruz declared that Fujimori "had obtained international recognition and had man-aged to regain the confidence of investors in the country" (*Expreso*, January 26, 2000). González added: "I know how my people think...and I know many other evangelical leaders who think as I do.... The opinion of a leader like me counts for a lot, but I don't want anyone to think that I am getting involved in politics. I am apolitical" (*Expreso*, January 30, 2000). The other statement was from an American missionary, Roberto Barriger, linked to a charismatic church: "Functionaries of international organs, when speaking of Peru, refer to 'the Fujimori miracle'...I don't know if human rights are not respected. I haven't seen anything. Nor do I know if he is a dictator." Eduardo Yaipén, an evangelical leader, said, "This group [CONEP] is not representa-tive. It is just a small group of traditional pastors" (*Expreso*, January 31, 2000). The following year, in the 2001 elections, Roberto Barriger and other pro-Fujimori pastors campaigned for Lourdes Flores, the presidential candidate of the Peruvian right.

The other route of response to CONEP's questioning of Fujimori's re-election attempt was through the public communiqués of the Christian and Missionary Alliance Church and of FIPAC, an organ that unites mainly char-ismatic pastors and churches that are not in CONEP and that utilize the dis-course of "prosperity theology" and "spiritual warfare." The Alliance commu-niqué of February 6, 2000, said that "the Christian and Missionary Alliance Church of Peru does not take part in any action of political proselytism, since as a religious institution it is distant from all party politics" (*El Comercio*, February 6, 2000, B11). Notwithstanding, when Fujimori was forced to call new elections for April 2001, the Alliance leaders, together with others linked to FIPAC who had for years been opposed to political involvement by believers and had criticized the human rights work carried out by CONEP, founded the new party MRN, with the intention of fielding its own candidates. In their failed attempt to get the requisite number of signatures to register the party, they did, in fact, make use of the pulpit for party political propaganda; and when some of their intended candidates ran for election with other parties, they received the "authorization and spiritual covering of the party's Pastoral Supervision Junta," headed by the main leader of FIPAC ("Carta circular del MRN," January 21, 2001).

Much more explicit in its condemnation of the CONEP stance was the communiqué of FIPAC, dated January 28, 2000: "[We lament] recent political declarations made in the name of the evangelical people, with critical opinions regarding the current government.... Such declarations...reflect only their own opinion, but certainly not that of the evangelical Christian people in general." Days later, the president of FIPAC said in a letter to CONEP:

We understand that CONEP is the representative body of its associates . . . for institutional purposes. However, CONEP should be respectful of the plurality among the evangelical people regarding their political opinions and positions. . . . For that reason, CONEP does not have the right to issue communiqués with political declarations . . . which certainly do not reflect the thought and opinion of the evangelical people in general. We ask you, therefore, to limit yourselves to your rightful function, which is to be representative in the institutional and ecclesiastical sphere, and abstain from issuing political statements that compromise and polarize the church of Jesus Christ. (letter to CONEP, January 31, 2000)

These statements, declarations, and letters, using "apolitical" language and with a "pastoral" tone, were aimed at delegitimizing the public stance adopted by CONEP. It became evident that there were two blocs, each one claiming to be the authoritative voice of the evangelical community. On the one side, CONEP formally represented some 85 percent of evangelicals. On the other side, FIPAC was an association of (mainly) charismatic pastors, principally from large churches in Lima. Since the mid-1990s, due in part to an institutional crisis in CONEP as well as to the rapid growth of these charismatic megachurches with their discourse of "spiritual warfare" and prosperity, there had been an undeclared war between the two organs.

The institutional crisis of CONEP had begun in 1992 and worsened in 1995, debilitating its social work and its presence in civil society. Sectors close to the pro-Fujimori congressmen had gained control of the organ's key posts. But in early 2000, in a changing political environment, there was another change in the key personnel. Two pastors linked to anti-Fujimori sectors were elected to important posts on the directorate. Later, the former senator Victor Arroyo became the executive secretary, and in 2001 other leaders of the MED were elected to the directorate.

The role of CONEP, in many moments, extended to pastoral orientation for evangelical voters and to denouncing the fraudulent and unconstitutional elements in the electoral processes. In successive public pronouncements, CONEP called for justice and transparency from the competent authorities, and called on voters to take part with civic maturity in the elections. This role of active vigilance over the electoral processes earned CONEP the recognition of the Defensoría del Pueblo, which praised its efforts to "promote the vigilance and defense of the citizen vote" (letter of May 22, 2000); and of the representative of the National Democratic Institute and the Carter Center (letter of May 18, 2000). This reflected the position CONEP had gained in civil society over several years for its participation in the national movement for human rights. Subsequently, when a transitional government was installed after Fujimori's resignation, CONEP was invited to take part in an

Inter-Institutional Working Group convoked by the new government, with the aim of proposing measures leading to the formation of a truth commission to investigate the years of political violence. CONEP was also invited to be part of a Roundtable to Fight Against Poverty. In addition, it has observer status, together with the Peruvian Catholic Bishops Conference, on the National Council of Human Rights.

Besides CONEP, another key evangelical institutional actor at this time was the MED. It was founded in January 2000 by various entities linked to the anti-Fujimori sectors of the evangelical community, although its origins go back to the reaction to Fujimori's self-coup of 1992. The founding organizations of the MED included Peace and Hope (CONEP's human rights organ); the evangelical student movement AGEUP; the Peru branch of the Latin American Theological Fraternity; and the Peace-Peru Project of the Latin American Council of Churches. The MED took part in several protest marches with the anti-Fujimori opposition (such as the historic "march of the four *suyos* [a Quechua term for the four regions of the country]" in July 2000), and organized a "Vigil for Democracy" on June 3, 2000, in front of the offices of the Organization of American States (OAS) in Lima. After the fraudulent elections, the MED wrote to the OAS insisting that new elections be held, echoing the OAS's own stance that "representative democracy is an indispensable condition for the stability, peace and development of the region" (MED letter to the OAS, June 2, 2000). The MED's position contrasted, for example, with that of the evangelical Radio del Pacífico, which a day before the first round of the elections gave an indirect sign of support for the Fujimori regime by saying in a radio broadcast that there are "biblical mandates which one must obey; the authority is placed there by God for our good."

Conclusions

Various themes have emerged from this examination of the evangelicals' search for political representation in Peru from the mid-1950s onward and of their civil society activities in the 1990s. On the basis of their experiences up to the 1980s, many evangelicals concluded that they needed their own channels in order to make their voice heard in public life. Two of their justifications for entering parliamentary life were, first, that only the evangelicals themselves could be relied upon to present their own social and political claims; and second, that the best channel for this was a large-scale entry into congress. However, the evangelicals did not articulate alternative spaces for participation in formal politics or develop a different political ethic. Rather, the pro-Fujimori parliamentarians from 1992 to 2000 reinforced traditional politics, adopting all too easily the vices of the old political class such as clientelism and nepotism. In addition, they were not prominent legislators or well known for their surveillance of the executive. On the contrary, they were inexperienced politicians who gave support to the dismantling of democratic institutions.

The evangelical presence in civil society presents a different picture. As part of the rise of various segments of civil society, they delineated new ways of doing politics. At the same time, the public voice of CONEP was especially important throughout the 1990s, as was that of the MED in 2000. CONEP publicized its view of the self-coup of 1992 as a rupture of the democratic order, deplored the Amnesty Law of 1995, and opposed the unconstitutional reelection of Fujimori in 2000.

Peru is going through a period in which, as in many countries of Latin America, the political expectations and aspirations of evangelicals have increased greatly. There is a growing awareness in various sectors of the churches with regard to their social position. But there are also problems with regard to many leaders' understanding of their social role, and they show little awareness of the political potential of the evangelical community to stimulate new forms of democratic life. The evangelicals only unite circumstantially to deal with questions of interest to the whole group or when freedom of religion is under some threat. They have not yet understood the need to build a broad network of relationships, especially outside the limits of the evangelical world.

The political parties do not yet see evangelicals as an autonomous social force, but rather see them as a growing electoral market that can be easily captured by employing a religio-political discourse that appeals to their traditional agenda of freedom of religion and religious equality. Perhaps the problem is not so much the politicians' use of religion as the form of religion (and religious leaders) that the politicians find it easy to exploit. But politicians as a whole seem not to have fully understood that the evangelicals constitute an ambiguous and multifaceted social phenomenon. Electoral results show that decisions by hierarchies or by charismatic religious leaders are not necessarily followed by the people at the grassroots. Recent history also shows that the evangelical vote is not "captive"; it does not have proprietors who can negotiate its destination. However, the Peruvian case tends to show that most evangelicals still see democracy in terms of participation in periodic elections and as a means to achieving a share in temporal power and its benefits. The examples of the presence of evangelicals in social movements and the action of representative organs such as CONEP within civil society may constitute alternative forms of political practice with great potential for contributing to a sustainable democracy.

5

Religion and Democracy in Brazil: A Study of the Leading Evangelical Politicians

Alexandre Brasil Fonseca

We no longer want a democracy of participation; we are no longer content with a democracy of deliberation; we need a democracy of liberation. Democracy is the subordination of social organization, and especially political power, to a goal which is not social but moral: the liberation of all. Democracy is not just a set of institutions, however indispensable, but above all a demand and a hope.

> —Alain Touraine, *O que é a democracia?*
> [1994] (1996)

Setting the Scene

The significant beginnings of Protestantism in Brazil go back to the arrival of Anglican English and Lutheran Germans in the early nineteenth century (Freston 1995). The first conversionist churches using Portuguese (Presbyterians, Baptists, Methodists) date from the second half of that century. All the foregoing are usually referred to as *historical Protestants*, to distinguish them from the pentecostals who arrived in the 1910s with the Christian Congregation and the Assemblies of God. A fresh wave of pentecostal churches began in the 1950s, followed by a third wave from the late 1970s typified by the Universal Church of the Kingdom of God.[1] Pentecostals now comprise 68 percent of all Protestants. By 2000 (according to the official census), there were twenty-six million Protestants in Brazil, or 15.5 percent of the population, and they were disproportionately represented among the poor. All Protestants are usually known in Brazil as *evangélicos*; I shall refer to them often as *evangelicals*, since the vast majority come within the Anglophone sense of the term.

The evangelical presence in Brazilian politics gained visibility with the election of a Constituent Assembly in 1986. Before that, participation was small, with most segments of Protestantism adopting the slogan "Believers don't mess with politics." But for the 1986 elections, the first after a twenty-one-year military dictatorship, some pentecostal denominations presented their own official candidates, leading to the election of thirty-two evangelical federal deputies. This new involvement was justified partly by the allegation that the new constitution might declare Brazil a Catholic country, and partly by the desire to influence the process of redemocratization. Many of these thirty-two deputies were subsequently bought off by the government in key votes during the Constituent Assembly, in exchange for funds and especially concessions to operate radio and television stations.

Recent events have painted a more complex picture of evangelical participation in politics, with an ever-increasing number of congress members linked to the churches. With an already extensive literature on the subject, this chapter will seek rather to build on what we know by focusing on the period 1998–2001.[2] Sources include monitorings of the written and electronic media, interviews, and participant observation in political events (whether oriented toward evangelicals or not). My objective is to describe the new phase in relations between evangelicals and electoral politics that emerges in these years and its implications for democracy.

Evangelical presence in Brazilian politics at the very end of the twentieth century has been characterized by a discourse of opposition to the federal government, with greater prominence of evangelical politicians who regard themselves as on the left or center-left. I shall focus especially on the postures of two especially prominent politicians at the time of the 2002 presidential elections: the Liberal Party federal deputy Bishop Carlos Rodrigues, then political coordinator of the Universal Church of the Kingdom of God; and the former governor of the state of Rio de Janeiro, Anthony Garotinho, a Sunday school teacher from the Presbyterian Church and (until late 2003) a member of the Brazilian Socialist Party.

Until recently, evangelical participation in politics had been disproportionately linked with conservative groups or with a subservient progovernment posture. But in the late 1990s, two important leaders emerged "from above," adopting an oppositionist discourse, making agreements with left-wing parties, promoting electoral debate within the churches, and contributing (in their own way) to the politicization of impoverished segments of society that are usually apolitical. By whetting the taste for politics among believers through a discourse that values political means, criticizes current powerholders, and denounces the plight of large sectors of society (i.e., a discourse similar in tone to that of left-wing parties), as well as by activating evangelicalism's peculiar power of association (Putnam 2000; Tocqueville [1835] 2000), these actors may be making an important contribution (albeit often through unintended consequences) to democratic consolidation in Brazil.[3]

The Evangelical Supporting Cast in Rio de Janeiro Politics

Anthony Garotinho, the evangelical governor of Rio de Janeiro from 1999 to 2002, was only converted to Protestantism in 1994, and his political action among evangelicals depended considerably on three key intermediaries: his deputy governor, Benedita da Silva; his junior secretary in the office of the governor, pastor Everaldo Dias; and the federal deputy (from 1991 to 2002) and radio entrepreneur Francisco Silva. Besides being evangelicals and politicians, all three of these have in common their experience of poverty in childhood.

Benedita da Silva

Benedita da Silva characterizes herself politically as a woman, black, shanty-dweller, pentecostal, and member of the Workers Party.[4] Elected city councillor in Rio in 1982, she became the first black woman federal deputy (from 1986 to 1994). She was elected to the Senate in 1994, became deputy governor of the state of Rio in 1998, and in 2003 became the minister for social action in the new Workers Party (PT; Partido dos Trabalhadores) government led by Luís Inácio Lula da Silva.

She is the daughter of a bricklayer and a washerwoman, and was sexually abused when seven years old. At seventeen she had her first child. At twenty, she interrupted her fifth pregnancy by abortion. She is currently married for the third time, having been widowed twice. Her husbands have always been nonevangelicals involved in social movements. She began her working life as a domestic maid and street vendor, but at forty managed to complete a course in social work. Since 1955, she has been part of the Neighborhood Association in the Chapéu Mangueira shantytown where she lived until recently, and was elected president of the association in 1978.

Benedita says her political education was through daily experience of social inequality. Liberation theology, the ideas of educator Paulo Freire, and the action of the Communist Party in the shanties were other factors in her political involvement.

As the daughter of a *mãe-de-santo*, a female leader in the Umbanda religion, she followed this religion until she was eighteen years old. Then, through her links with the Shanty-Town Pastoral, she became a Catholic. But poverty and her husband's alcoholism led her to join an evangelical church in 1969.

I felt unhappy and needed a little peace. So when I was 26 I joined the Assemblies of God. My religious option gave me calm to reflect and make decisions. What I really needed was to find a foothold in things that were outside my control. Any religion can generate this feeling. In my case, it happened in the evangelical church. (Benjamin and Mendonça 1997, 96)

In the church she adopted the peculiar customs of pentecostal believers, which would make her stand out even further as a politician. When she became a parliamentarian, she pressed for greater female participation in politics and defended minorities. Although Benedita became a reference point for left-wing evangelicals, she did not at first orient her electoral campaigns toward the evangelical vote. It was only after her contact in 1992 with pastor Everaldo Dias that she began to campaign among the evangelical community. Previously, she had felt that a woman in a left-wing party would find little space in politically narrow churches. She would also stress the desire not to be seen to use the church as an "electoral instrument." But this posture changed after meeting Everaldo.

Everaldo Dias

Benedita says that evangelicals who support her do so either because they are already politically "progressive" or because they see in her "spiritual sincerity." Pastor Everaldo fits both categories. Born in a working-class family in one of the poorest and most violent districts of Rio de Janeiro, his mother was a lay leader in the Assemblies of God. Everaldo graduated in accountancy and at twenty-seven managed to open his own insurance brokerage. In 1990, he became an ordained pastor in the Assemblies and ran the denominational magazine.

His political activity, he says, was at first linked to "brothers in the faith," with "no ideological implications." His main political admiration was reserved for Leonel Brizola, a left-wing populist politician. Everaldo organized the electoral campaign of his denomination's candidate for federal deputy in 1986, but broke with him when the latter supported the presidential aspirations of Fernando Collor in 1989. (Collor, the first democratically elected president after the 1964–85 military dictatorship, was impeached in 1992 for corruption.) Instead, Everaldo supported Brizola for president, and in the runoff election followed Brizola in supporting the Workers Party candidate Lula. Similarly, in the 1992 municipal elections, he supported Benedita da Silva in the runoff election for mayor of Rio. Everaldo was one of few Assemblies of God pastors to side with Benedita on that occasion.

Even I had reservations about the radicalism of the PT [the Workers Party], but supported Benedita as a sister in the faith who fought for the same social causes that we experience as pastors in the Assemblies. Our churches are among the poor, so this aspect of improving the situation of the people a bit helped us identify, with our common origin as survivors with God's help in this terrible world. (interview, February 20, 1995)

With Benedita running out of resources in her campaign, Everaldo's financial help was timely. In the circumstances, Benedita's narrow defeat for the mayoralty was considered a victory. In 1994, Everaldo organized an Evangelical Committee to support Lula's candidacy for president and Benedita's for senator. He then worked in her office in the senate, and in 1998 became one of the campaign coordinators for the gubernatorial slate that united Anthony Garotinho of Brizola's Democratic Labor Party and Benedita of the Workers Party. The two main left-of-center parties were united in an attempt to capture the state government, and both presented evangelical candidates. It was then that Francisco Silva came onto the scene.

Francisco Silva

As a federal deputy since 1990, Francisco Silva's parliamentary presence was always poorly evaluated; his electoral success had been due to his ownership of radio stations (Fonseca 2003). He owns Radio Melodia, which has the second or third largest audience in Greater Rio. Silva's mother was a member of the Christian Congregation. After a difficult childhood, he became a typical self-made entrepreneur. When asked, he usually claims to belong to the Christian Congregation, but never reveals which local church he attends. In fact, his religious affiliation is a mystery. The Christian Congregation prohibits political activity and the use of electronic media. Silva probably has no links with a local church and has even on occasion styled himself "an evangelical of all the churches." However, he has significant support from pastors and leaders of large denominations such as the Assemblies of God and the Baptists.

During the first year of Anthony Garotinho's state government, Silva was the state secretary of housing, despite belonging to a conservative party. This was the result of a preelection agreement, as Governor Garotinho explained to me:

Deputy Francisco Silva is a friend of mine. We were introduced by Benedita da Silva, who told me: "If you give your testimony on Radio Melodia you will win over all the evangelicals in Rio. There is only one problem. Silva is in the PPB [a right-wing party] and has placed allies of his in the Housing Department of the current state administration." So we set up a meeting. Silva told me: "For my electorate I would like to support you. If the current governor takes these jobs away from me, will you give them back when you're in power?" I replied that that depended on Benedita because we had agreed that all social questions would be in her domain. So Benedita said it was all right. But after we had won, she went back on her word, and I had to insist that we kept the agreement. So I made him housing secretary so he could nominate whoever he wanted. (interview with Anthony Garotinho, April 10, 2001; unless otherwise indicated, all quotations from Garotinho are from this interview)

Silva's help was vital for mobilizing the evangelical multitudes who went to the musical events that his radio station promoted. Garotinho thus departed from Benedita's political practice, choosing the evangelical electorate as his preferred target through the articulations of Everaldo Dias and Francisco Silva.

An Evangelical Governor in Rio de Janeiro: Anthony Garotinho

Born in Campos, a large city in the state of Rio de Janeiro, in 1960, Anthony Garotinho is of modest origins. His lawyer father had gone bankrupt, and he was brought up by his grandfather, a small trader of Lebanese origin. Becoming a "teenage rebel," he channeled his energies into amateur theatre and student politics, joining the Communist Party. During the period of military rule, he wrote and acted in plays with a social message. He became a radio presenter at a young age and adopted the nickname Garotinho ("little boy"). He married one of his theatre colleagues, and they now have nine children, five of whom are adopted.

Garotinho incarnates what Sennett (1988) calls the "personalization of politics," related to a populism in which "the political leader achieves credibility and legitimacy with a certain segment of society not by the content of his political acts or his political programmes but by the type of man he shows himself to be" (Saes 2001, 73). Characterizing Garotinho as populist is justified both in terms of his political origins in Brizola's Democratic Labor Party and in terms of his own practice.

But for Garotinho, it was his *popularity* (not *populism*) that helped him to organize the first strike of sugar-cane workers in Campos when the military regime began slowly to redemocratize. The rural workers' union was his first political base, and he was a candidate for city councillor in 1982 with the Workers Party. The following year he met Brizola and joined the Democratic Labor Party (PDT; Partido Democrático Trabalhista), calling the Workers Party in Campos "a tiny sect." He was elected state deputy in 1986 and mayor of Campos in 1988, uniting the opposition parties against the sugar-cane oligarchy. His city administration was very popular, and in 1994 he ran for state governor. But Brizola's reputation was by then suffering from association with crime and administrative incompetence. Garotinho tried to dissociate himself from Brizola. While campaigning, he suffered a bad car accident, and while recovering in the hospital he had an experience that drew him toward the evangelicals: "At three in the morning, in the hospital bed, I saw the accident before my own eyes as if in a film. I felt it was something supernatural, from God. It made me cry convulsively for hours on end and I felt something burning inside me."

An Assemblies of God member, visiting the hospital, assured him that the burning inside was the Holy Spirit and that he had to "give his life to Jesus" (Garotinho 2001, 36). The accident harmed his campaign at a crucial moment, and he narrowly lost the runoff election. At the time he did not divulge the experience, thinking that, so soon before the election, "the evangelicals will not believe it is true and I will lose the Catholic vote."

Garotinho subsequently sought out a well-known evangelical pastor, Caio Fábio, who told him he needed to accept Jesus in his understanding, since he had already done so in his heart.[5] Garotinho attributes his reticence in coming out publicly as a *crente* (believer) to his Marxist background and to the influence of the party and his wife. But after weekly Bible studies with Caio Fábio, he was baptized in the Presbyterian Church in 1995.

In 1996 he again ran for mayor of Campos, winning in the first round with 74 percent of the votes. For the gubernatorial elections of 1998, the Workers Party opted for alliances with other left-of-center parties, making possible the Garotinho-Benedita slate. The Workers Party in Rio, however, was split over the alliance strategy. But Garotinho needed the support of the Workers Party in order to overcome his poor 1994 showing in the state capital. A large part of the urban middle and upper classes rejected him as a young upstart from the interior of dubious cultural taste.

Garotinho played the religious card heavily. He took part in events promoted by Radio Melodia, but did not get official support from any denominational leaders. Both the Assemblies of God and the Universal Church of the Kingdom of God came out in favor of his main rival. Garotinho later reflected on this:

> I think evangelicals in general were used by their leaders for objectives which were not really political except in appearance. In my election for governor all the denominational leaders were against me, but the evangelicals voted for me because of my message. Why were the leaders against me? I still don't know. Perhaps institutional interests made the other candidate more attractive, but the evangelical people realized that for the interests of the people of God my candidature was more attractive.

Breaking with Brizola's usual practice, Garotinho did present proposals in his campaign, especially on the theme of public safety. His proposals tried to balance preventing crime with combating it, thus seeking to avoid the left's usual lack of a policy on crime due to its concern for human rights, while also avoiding the repressive policy then in force, which paid a bonus to policemen who killed more people. Garotinho impressed the electorate with his approach to this vital question of criminality, and was elected governor in the run-off with 58 percent of the votes.

Two Years, Two Crises

I shall examine Garotinho's first two years as governor (1999–2000) through a discussion of the images presented by the press and in official publications. In opinion polls published in the press, his administration always had over 70 percent approval, at times being the most highly ranked of any state government. His financial administration was particularly praised initially (although not in the last year of his government), having renegotiated the state debt and placed its finances on a healthy footing.

In his own statements, Garotinho refers to God as responsible for his success: "I am a Christian and I can't forget what the Bible says in Mark 9:23: Everything is possible for him who believes" (*IstoÉ*, December 8, 1999). In an April 9, 2001, press conference for the evangelical media, Garotinho's explanation of the debt renegotiation (he was in opposition to the federal government so it was reluctant to help the state of Rio) throws light on how he lives out his faith:

> In the negotiation process I was very patient. I held out until the very last day permitted by law. [Federal finance minister] Malan told me: "I'm going to sign this contract [revising the debt and thus favoring the state of Rio], even though I don't want to. It will be very good for Rio, but there's something making me sign it." It was half past eleven and the deadline was midnight. [Still Malan delayed signing.] At a quarter to twelve I left the room and went to the bathroom and prayed: "My God in heaven, I've been negotiating for nine months. Break this man's heart." I went back and a few minutes later he said: "I don't know, I think I'll sign . . ." It may have been a coincidence; after all, the deadline was approaching, but it may have been my prayer.

Garotinho was on the cover of one of Brazil's main news magazines, *IstoÉ*, in 1999, in a pose that imitated the famous photograph of John Kennedy at his desk with his baby on the floor in front of him. In the first months of his administration, the press praised his capacity to negotiate, conciliatory style, and public safety policy: "Garotinho unites a type of charismatic religiosity which is increasingly popular with an also popular facility in using the mass media. If he can conciliate his discreet populism with efficiency, he can really become a national name in politics" (*Folha de S. Paulo,* June 25, 1999).

After six months of government, the first negative evaluations appeared in the press, particularly with regard to lack of success in the vital area of criminality. Public policy in Rio had oscillated in the 1980s and 1990s between repression (right-wing administrations) and an emphasis on human rights for the poor (left-wing administrations). Neither policy had managed to reduce the crime statistics, but the latter was seen as leniency toward the criminals and drug mafias that hide out in the poorer districts of Greater Rio.

Garotinho nominated a leading anthropologist, Luís Eduardo Soares, to coordinate policy in the area of public safety. He attempted a "civilizing process" by means of profound changes not only in physical and technological structure (reform of the police stations) but also in police mentality when interacting with minorities. But Soares felt marginalized within the existing structures on the one hand and pressured by Garotinho for results on the other. Resistance to Soares's initiatives from within the police increased, reaching the point of death threats against Garotinho and Soares and their families by the "Astra Group," a segment within the police well known for its violent and "unorthodox" methods.

Soares was eventually dismissed in early 2000. He left saying that Garotinho's presidential ambitions had made him opt for the "easy way out" of an agreement with the Astra Group. But some analysts felt Soares's project had suffered from a "reformist messianism" typical of intellectuals who were ignorant of the reality of trying to reform in one fell swoop the notoriously violent and corrupt Brazilian police.

Soares's sacking was the last straw for the ailing alliance with the Workers Party. One section of the party had never accepted the alliance at all and had refused to participate in the state government. Garotinho had handed the social area to the group faithful to the deputy governor Benedita da Silva. Some versions claim that Garotinho had consistently undermined Benedita's capacity to act, while others point to Benedita's own lack of administrative ability. When I asked Garotinho about his deputy governor, he merely commented: "I would just reply biblically: what a man sows, he shall also reap."

The opposition current within the Workers Party was fierce in its criticism of Benedita's postures and methods. In the run-up to the municipal elections of 2000, there were claims that the Evangelical Nucleus of the Workers Party (led by Pastor Everaldo Dias) had encouraged hundreds of evangelicals to affiliate so that Benedita would be chosen as the party candidate for mayor of Rio. The veteran leader of Garotinho's Democratic Labor Party (PDT), Leonel Brizola, called Benedita a "Queen of Sheba" living in luxury.

The crisis in the alliance surfaced when Garotinho said publicly that the Workers Party (PT) should rename itself the PB, the Party of the Big Appetite, due to its supposed thirst for benefits in government. When Soares was dismissed, the party renounced all its posts in the state government after a year and three months of strained collaboration. In the opinion of Lincoln Araujo, an evangelical member of the Workers Party and former junior secretary of education and member of the Methodist Church, the problem was the "patrimonialist and populist concept of public administration" of the bureaucrats of the PDT (interview, May 8, 2001).

Garotinho not only lost the support of the Workers Party but also came into increasing conflict with Leonel Brizola, the veteran head of his own PDT. Brother-in-law of the last president before the 1964 military coup, Brizola had returned from exile with redemocratization, founded the PDT, and twice governed Rio de Janeiro. He was well known for his personalistic leadership, so many younger leaders had to leave the party when their own charisma had begun to affect that of Brizola.

After a few months of Garotinho's administration, Brizola began to criticize him publicly for not respecting party processes and for his excessive involvement with the evangelicals (*Folha de S. Paulo*, October 28, 1999). Above all, Garotinho's obvious presidential aspirations were not welcome. When the Workers Party left the administration, Garotinho was for a time obliged to depend heavily on the PDT and even declared he would not run for president in 2002. But when Brizola announced his candidacy for mayor in 2000, Garotinho was once again on a collision course, having already defended Benedita da Silva's mayoral candidacy in a left-wing alliance that would be the quid pro quo for the gubernatorial alliance of 1998.

Brizola renewed his attacks on Garotinho, calling him Judas and Brutus and attacking his political approach to the evangelicals. "I don't like this project of exploiting the evangelical movement for the sake of his candidacy.... It shouldn't be made into an electoral platform. This is an obscurantist maneuver. How much blood humanity had to shed before the separation of Church and State! Why go back to this now, to separating people between those who belong to God and those who don't?" (*Folha de S. Paulo*, October 28, 1999). "Ours is a secular party. Our rulers have to be more or less ecumenical. They can't be exalting one religion to the detriment of others. [The evangelicals] have a different training and are not prepared for political life.... We must overcome these deformities to avoid returning to a type of fundamentalism" (*Folha de S. Paulo*, December 17, 1999).

Garotinho counterattacked, repudiating what he saw as Brizola's constant disparaging of his evangelical faith and vowing to fight for control of the party. For several months Garotinho attempted to wrest control of the party from Brizola, but by November 2000 he concluded he had no option but to leave. He took with him a number of federal and state deputies and mayors, many of

whom accompanied him the following month in joining the Brazilian Socialist Party (PSB; Partido Socialista Brasiliero). Garotinho defended his new
party, saying he had always understood his previous affiliation with "labor" as
the route to socialism.

Public administration had been characterized in Rio for many years by
the formation of fiefdoms within the institutions. The difficulty of changing
these structures of domination and favor was Garotinho's great challenge. He
had a centralizing tendency himself, but he adopted modern administrative
practices and a conciliatory policy that valued the legislature.

The main criticisms of Garotinho have been for adopting a popular style
in his daily life, as well as his evangelical affiliation and habit of quoting the
Bible. Two images of him have prevailed: on the one hand the competent
politician, on the other hand the centralizer who undermines others' initiatives, cuts down potential competitors, has no patience with collective forums,
and is more concerned with his own ambitions than with lasting achievements.

He was careful in his choice of new party, opting for the most "credible"
one available. Despite problems in some regions, the Socialist Party is regarded as a left-wing party with traditions and some serious members. When
participating in party forums, Garotinho always emphasizes the importance
of grassroots involvement. He presents himself as representing a political left
that believes it can come to power peacefully, promote social justice, and pave
the way for socialism.

Two meetings on the same day in May 2001 illustrate the differences in
Garotinho's discourse at meetings of the Socialist Party on the one hand and
in meetings with pastors on the other. Among the pastors, at a meeting to give
account of his state government, he spoke of those programs that had greatest
popular appeal (such as the Citizen Voucher and the Popular Restaurant,
discussed later), defended his identification with the poor, and reaffirmed his
evangelical identity. But at the Socialist Party meeting, he responded to criticisms of his government that would deny it the title of left-wing. He reaffirmed his position as a socialist (having defended himself publicly as a
"social democrat" prior to joining the Socialist Party); he defended participatory forms of politics and a project to train youthful leadership in shanty
communities, and declared that the Citizen Voucher program was only
temporary. The emphases in his discourse were socialism, grassroots participation, and social transformation. He declared:

> The profile of our government is very clear. It is a govern-
> ment of solidarity, a human government, a government of social
> justice, in other words a left-wing government. Being left-wing is
> more than words. I've seen leftist governments here in Rio de Janeiro
> send the police out to attack the workers. But in our government,
> whenever there's a demonstration outside the palace, the secretary

calls the people inside for a coffee. A serious left-wing government has got to stop waffling, roll its sleeves up, and solve the people's problems.

The Actors on Stage: From Rio to Brasília

No sooner had Garotinho arrived in the state government than his campaign
for the presidency in 2002 began, using not only the usual stickers and badges
but also a website (www.2002garotinho.com.br). Two groups were especially
involved in promoting this hoped-for transfer from Rio to the federal capital,
Brasília: the so-called Republic of Campos, the intimate friends of the governor; and the evangelicals. The connection between Garotinho's presidential
ambitions and his relationship with the evangelicals was the object of criticism
from many quarters.

One of the main ways of publicizing his presidential aspirations was
through the radio program *The Peace of the Lord, Governor* (A Paz do Senhor,
Governador), chaired by federal deputy Francisco Silva. The daily program
lasted ten minutes, and I monitored fifty-one programs broadcast between late
1999 and mid-2000. In the last fortnight of December 1999, the program
mentioned a possible candidacy. Silva would say "mark my words" whenever
a letter from a listener talked of the idea of Garotinho as president, to which
the latter would reply good-humoredly: "Take it easy, you're in too much of
a hurry. . . . You'll end up making things difficult for me." Both men are
experienced in the use of radio and manage to entertain at the same time that
they are making a mailing list of thousands of addresses for future election
campaigns.

The program consisted of letters, Bible readings, prayers, rhymes, comments on the government's actions and plans, and invitations to events connected with his government or with his preaching trips. Analysis of the letters
read aloud shows that 40 percent were written by Assemblies of God members and 20 percent by Baptists, which is similar to the radio station's audience profile (Fonseca 2003). Just over half the letters were from the state of Rio
and the rest from other states. Apart from radio programs, Garotinho also made
frequent preaching trips, averaging one per week during his period in the state
government. The churches visited were not just in his own state but all over
the country. Most visits were to Assemblies of God and Baptist churches, and
to events organized by Adhonep (the Brazilian equivalent of the American-
initiated Full Gospel Businessmen's Fellowship International). Everaldo Dias
controlled the agenda for these trips, and the intention was to make Garotinho
nationally known. He was usually accompanied by well-known singers of
evangelical music and he sold copies of the book containing his testimony.

Besides talking of incidents from his government and of how he was converted, Garotinho also spoke of the need to "change people in order to change the world," using a parable I shall recount later. This discourse of "changing people in order to change the world" would seem to be irresistible to the evangelical community, especially as he stressed his church links and referred to himself as a Sunday school teacher who preaches regularly. The sum of these characteristics had the potential to earn him broad support among the evangelical electorate, despite all its theological and political divisions. At one point in Rio, his acceptance among evangelicals was 20 percent higher than among nonevangelicals.

His religious activity was sometimes very intense (as in late 1999) and less so at other times (as during the process of changing parties at the end of 2000). From April 2001 he revived his religious activity to coincide with the publication of a book containing the testimony of his religious experience. This activity provoked criticism from sectors of the media and from politicians. A comment from a leading Workers Party figure is typical: "Humanity fought to separate the state from religions. Garotinho has dangerously tied his government to a segment of the evangelicals (not to all). The enormous influence the evangelicals have is a deviation" (Jorge Bittar, *Folha de S. Paulo*, April 16, 2000). Garotinho's characteristic response was along the lines that he had "a clear position about church and religion: I am in favor of a secular state. I do not mix politics and religion" (*República*, September 19, 1999).

At the same time, he promoted his candidacy within the Socialist Party, tried to encourage politicians to affiliate to the party, and attempted alliances with other parties that would increase the free television time available to him during the election campaign. (Candidates are allotted a certain amount of time according to the number of seats in congress held by their party or coalition of parties.) The Socialist Party alone would allow him very little time, so in 2001 he approached the Liberal Party (PL; Partido Liberal), dominated by the Universal Church of the Kingdom of God. However, in late 2001, the Liberal Party seemed more inclined to support Lula, the presidential candidate of the Workers Party.

Another key actor in Garotinho's presidential drive was pastor Everaldo Dias. He was responsible for the state government's basic income program called Citizen Voucher. This program is carried out in partnership with religious organizations and was initially criticized for distributing most of its benefits through evangelical churches. Over time, more Catholic parishes and Spiritist centers were included. The program distributes vouchers worth about 40 dollars that can be exchanged for food in supermarkets; recipients must prove low income levels, and their children must be enrolled in school. Despite criticisms from some sectors of the Catholic Church, Bishop Mauro Morelli, a leading defender of liberation theology in the episcopacy, has praised initiatives such as this and the Popular Restaurant (which serves lunches for 40 cents) as giving dignity to poor citizens and helping them fight poverty and hunger.

Thanks to the administration of this program and his links with Bendita da Silva, pastor Everaldo Dias managed to get his brother elected as city councillor for the Workers Party. Everaldo controlled Garotinho's preaching agenda and his flow of contacts with the evangelical world in general.

Garotinho and his team were much more effective in their campaigning among evangelicals than the other presidential hopefuls. An opinion poll shortly before the October 2002 election showed Garotinho to have more votes among evangelicals than any other candidate (37 percent), well above his 17 percent average in the population. This success was due both to Garotinho's own capacity as a communicator and to his team's competence in knowing what image to present to the evangelical voter. The starting-point seems to have been when Benedita da Silva heard him speak in a church about his conversion and advised him to do this regularly since his words transmitted "great sincerity." In love with the microphone since his preconversion days in radio, his preaching trips consist basically of an enthusiastic recounting of his evangelical testimony.

To what extent is all this an electorally motivated abuse of religion? It is interesting to recall the words of Catholic priest and historian José Oscar Beozzo regarding former president Tancredo Neves's relationship with lay Catholic brotherhoods: "It wasn't an abuse. Tancredo was a profoundly religious man. Of course, he was also a politician, and that is why he visited all the brotherhoods" (in Dines, Fernandes Junior, and Salomão 2000, 56). The same phrase can be applied to Garotinho's relationship with the evangelical churches. His staff's perception of the electoral importance of this activity, allied to Garotinho's obvious pleasure in it, have helped his political acceptance among evangelicals.[6]

By May 2001 Garotinho had reached 11 percent in the opinion polls for president, but six months later he had fallen to 9 percent after an unproven accusation of corruption against him (referring to an incident before becoming governor) in the media. For reelection as governor of Rio, the same opinion polls gave him 68 percent. In the end, Garotinho opted to run for president and presented his wife as his candidate for governor. She was victorious in the first round of the election, defeating Benedita da Silva. (The two main candidates for the governorship of the state of Rio de Janeiro, the least Catholic in Brazil, were both evangelical women in left-wing parties.) Garotinho himself nearly got through to the runoff election for president, finishing third with 17.9 percent. This was a satisfactory result, considering his weak party base and lack of resources. His strong showing among evangelicals was fundamental in this, and his strategy of "evangelizing" the campaign almost paid off. However, his campaign strategists were counting on far more than

37 percent of the evangelical vote; indeed, their expectations of 60 or 70 percent would have been enough to put him in second place.

The difficulty with this strategy is that, in reality, the voters' choices take into account a variety of values and concerns that cannot be limited to the religious sphere. For the Garotinho campaign, there were two dilemmas: how to disseminate his evangelical profile so as to maximize the evangelical vote; and how to do that without at the same time avoid accentuating the rejection of his candidacy among nonevangelicals, especially in the major cities. It is impossible to have the best of both worlds. In a candidacy for president (or indeed for state governor or for mayor of a municipality), religionizing one's political discourse is only useful within one's own religious community. Garotinho rejected the label "candidate of the evangelicals," yet his campaign made use of his religious identity. This made his candidacy viable, but at the same time ultimately limited its appeal. Even among the evangelical electorate, it is noticeable how his campaign met resistance; the majority of evangelicals, it seems, either did not know of his religious affiliation or did not feel that that in itself was sufficient to override other political considerations.

Supporting Cast in the Federal Congress

Apart from Anthony Garotinho, the other major evangelical political actor in recent Brazilian politics has been the Universal Church of the Kingdom of God (UCKG), coordinated politically by Bishop Carlos Rodrigues. Born in 1958, Rodrigues is a cofounder and one of the main leaders (under the overall leadership of Bishop Edir Macedo) of the UCKG, the most controversial and visible religious phenomenon in Brazil today, which has also spread to some eighty countries around the world (Corten, Dozon, and Oro 2003). Before talking about the leadership of Bishop Rodrigues, I shall analyze his supporting cast.

Members of Congress for Jesus

After the election of thirty-two evangelical federal deputies for the Constituent Assembly in 1986, the evangelical community awakened to politics. There were more candidates, which was one reason for the smaller number of evangelicals elected in the following elections. But the total once again rose sharply in the 1998 elections, thanks to the growing strength of the UCKG (tables 5.1 and 5.2). The changing strength of the main denominations can be seen in table 5.2.

The Assemblies of God, which had overtaken the Baptists in the number of congress members in 1986, was itself overtaken by the UCKG after 1998. The Baptists themselves have also grown, despite not having any organized plan of political action such as the UCKG has. Evangelical parliamentary politics, dominated overwhelmingly by members of historical churches until

TABLE 5.1. Number of Evangelical Congress Members (Federal Deputies and Senators) in Each Legislature, 1983–2001

Legislature	Congress Members Elected	Total (Including Substitutes Who Took Office)
1983–1987	12	17
1987–1991	32	36
1991–1995	23	35
1995–1999	32	38
1999–2003	51	57*

Sources: Fonseca 2003; Freston 1993a, 1996, 2001; Tribunal Superior Eleitoral, www.tse.gov.br; Câmara dos Deputados, www.camara.gov.br.

*Until May 2001.

1986 (Presbyterians, Baptists, Methodists, Lutherans, etc.), is now predominantly pentecostal. Whereas only 5 percent of evangelical congress members before 1986 were pentecostals (Freston 1993a), 65 percent were in 2001.

In geographical terms, the state of Rio de Janeiro has sent the most evangelicals to congress since 1982. In the 1999–2003 legislature, it had ten evangelicals, followed by the state immediately to the north of it, Minas Gerais, which had eight.

There has been an important change with respect to the number of evangelical congress members in parties associated with the opposition to the federal government of the day (table 5.3). From 1999, there was a significant increase in evangelical opposition politicians. But table 5.3 does not show everything. Switching of parties is common in Brazil, and during the 1999–

TABLE 5.2. Evangelical Representation in Congress, by Denominations, 1987–2001 (Including Substitutes Who Took Office)

Denominations	Number of Parliamentarians			
	1987–1991	1991–1995	1995–1999	1999–2003*
Assemblies of God	13	13	10	10
Universal Church of the Kingdom of God	1	3	6	16
Brazilian Baptist Convention	7	5	4	10
Charismatic Baptists	3	0	1	5
Presbyterians	4	1	4	3
Four-Square	2	1	1	2
Lutherans	1	2	2	4
Other Historical Denominations	4	5	1	3
Other Pentecostal Denominations	1	1	1	3
Total Number of Denominations	14	12	11	13

Sources: Fonseca 2003; Freston 1993a, 1996.

*Until May 2001.

TABLE 5.3. Evangelical Congress Members and Their Position in Relation to the Federal Government (Party Affiliation at Time of Taking Office)

1987–1991		1991–1995		1995–1999		1999–2001	
G	O	G	O	G	O	G	O
31	5	28	3	34	1	45	12

Sources: Freston 1993, 1996; Fonseca 1997.

G: progovernment parties; O: opposition parties.

2003 legislature, switching by evangelicals was further encouraged by our two main actors, Bishop Rodrigues and Anthony Garotinho. By mid-2001, twenty-five evangelical congress members were in opposition parties and only thirty-two in progovernment parties.

There are three main types of opposition parliamentarian. First, there are the evangelical militants of social movements. Second, there are some who switched from progovernment parties in order to support Garotinho for president. And last, there are the UCKG deputies who converged on the Liberal Party–Social Liberal Party coalition.

By mid-2001 the Liberal Party was the party with the largest number of evangelical members of congress (twelve, two more than the large progovernment parties, the Party of the Brazilian Democratic Movement (PMDB; Partido do Movimento Democrático Brasiliero) and the Liberal Front Party (PFL; Partido da Frente Liberal). The Liberal Party was actually founded by a practicing Catholic who died in 1999. The UCKG's decision to place several of its parliamentarians in the party was due to the lack of a strong successor as party leader, and to the fact that the party was well established throughout the country. UCKG politicians have become presidents of the party in several states, and the church has campaigned to increase party membership inside and outside the denomination. In 2002, in alliance with the tiny Social Liberal Party (PSL; Partido Social Liberal) (also dominated by the UCKG), the Liberal Party controlled twenty-nine votes in congress, making it medium-sized by Brazilian standards.

Looking at current evangelical members of congress in general, there are three main career profiles. One is that of the politicians who are supported by the leadership of their denomination: the national leadership in the case of the highly centralized Universal Church, and the local or state leadership in the case of other pentecostal denominations. Examples of the latter include Mário de Oliveira and Josué Bengtson of the Church of the Four-Square Gospel; Salatiel Carvalho and Silas Câmara of the Assemblies of God; and Glycon Júnior of the charismatic Baptists.

A second common profile is that of the parliamentarians who are linked to the mass media or are gospel singers. The relationship between the media and electoral potential has been often commented on by the social sciences, and the evangelicals have made the link even stronger. In this group we have the gospel singers Matos Nascimento (Assemblies of God) and Magno Malta (Baptist), as well as the owners of radio stations Francisco Silva, João Caldas (Assemblies of God), and Arolde de Oliveira (Baptist).

A third common profile is of evangelical militants in organizations and social movements who have launched an electoral career based on such connections. This group includes Miriam Reid, member of a new charismatic church and a social worker who was active in student politics; and Paulo Baltazar, a Methodist doctor from the interior of the state of Rio who became a town councillor in 1989, mayor of his town in 1992, and a federal deputy in 1998. Baltazar says that when working as a doctor in poor districts of the town and seeing the "indifference of many politicians who did nothing to diminish the suffering of so many people, I felt obliged to get politically involved." This group also includes the congressmen connected with the Evangelical Progressive Movement (MEP; Movimento Evangélico Progressista).

Evangelicals and Progressives

In 2000, Carlos Alberto Bezerra Júnior was elected city councillor in São Paulo with twenty-six thousand votes and reelected in 2004 with thirty-eight thousand votes. He is the son of the founder and leader of a large charismatic church called Grace Community. His election campaign was devoted to the question of ethics, as the city administration had been mired in corruption scandals. As a doctor who runs the church's social projects, he was concerned with the question of poverty and defended evangelical political involvement. He is a member of the Party of Brazilian Social Democracy (PSDB; Partido da Social Democracia Brasileira), a party that defines itself as social-democratic but in 1994 had allied with parties of the right to get into government. But Bezerra's advisors include several evangelical leaders renowned for their left-wing postures, and he has identified with the MEP.

Bezerra's example is repeated in many smaller municipalities throughout Brazil. The MEP was founded in 1990 and has encouraged dialogue between evangelicals and leftist parties, as well as evangelical participation in trade unions and social movements. In recent years, it has also encouraged candidacies by evangelicals in the left or center-left parties, based on "an attitude of ethical indignation and commitment to wide-ranging social reforms" (Machado 1997, 81). The MEP's political postures include "an involvement in grassroots causes and support for the proposals presented by parties on a range between social democracy and democratic socialism. It also defends ... a political culture which emphasises participation" (81).

There are currently several federal deputies linked to the MEP, as well as city councillors in various state capitals, and one mayor and one deputy mayor

of medium-sized towns. Most members of the MEP are not prominent ecclesiastical leaders (although one of the main founders is now an Anglican
bishop), and this is reflected in the way the movement attempts to influence
the evangelical vote, in contrast to evangelical political movements that have
the open support of (especially pentecostal) denominational leaders. But the
growing number of left-wing municipal and state-level administrations has
meant that more and more left-wing evangelicals have gained positions in
such administrations.

Gilmar Machado is a black Baptist educator from the state of Minas
Gerais who has been involved in the MEP since its early days. In 1990 and
1994 he was elected state deputy, and in 1998 he became a federal deputy
with the Workers Party. Another Baptist, Joaquim Brito, from a small state in
the Northeast, has been a leader of the main trade union confederation in his
state and for a while in 1999 was a stand-in as federal deputy. He was national
president of the MEP in the mid-1990s. Another Baptist trade unionist,
Walter Pinheiro, from the state of Bahia, was the leader of the Workers Party
congressional caucus in 2001.

The number of left-wing evangelicals in congress grew with the conversion to evangelicalism of a well-known Workers Party senator from the Am-
azonian state of Acre, Marina Silva. In 2003, she became minister for the
environment in President Lula's new government. Marina had begun her political career in ecological movements in the Amazon region, strongly influenced by liberation theology and Catholic organizations. But personal anxiety
due to ill health caused by mercury poisoning (not uncommon in the region)
led her to an evangelical church seeking, as she put it, "the blessing of God
and not the God of the blessing" (*Revista Graça*, n.d., 22). She was later converted and began attending the Church of Grace. A woman of very poor origins, illiterate until the age of fifteen, she began to articulate the connection
between her new faith and her politics.

> Today, with all respect to my Catholic partners, I am an
> evangelical. . . . I would say the evangelical churches are just
> beginning to make the connection between the ethical princi-
> ples of Christianity and the principles that should guide our ac-
> tions in secular life. There are several people who are starting to say:
> "Look, it's not just a question of ethics from the moral point
> of view." This ethics also has to be in our relationship to public
> institutions, and especially when we have some sort of role such as
> a congressman or mayor. (Dines, Fernandes Júnior, and Salamão
> 2000, 390)

Besides those politicians who convert after their political careers have
already gotten under way (as with Marina Silva and Anthony Garotinho), there
is a new generation of evangelicals active in social movements who are also

choosing the electoral route. These people view the church as, among other things, a space for gaining valuable experience that can later be transferred into politics. One example is that of Cabo Júlio, a policeman who led a police strike in 1997 and was elected to congress the following year with the highest number of votes of any federal deputy from his state. He is also a pastor of a charismatic community church, and the rhetorical, organizational, and leadership experience he gained in the church was vital for his role in the strike and subsequent election campaign. Another example is Lincoln Araújo, the Methodist mentioned earlier as former junior education secretary in Garotinho's administration in Rio and also deputy mayor of the Greater Rio municipality of Nilópolis between 1996 and 2000.

> My political involvement basically grew out of two institutional experiences. One was with my local church, through involvement in the Sunday School, in the church and in the youth group. The other was in the student movement.... Exercising leadership in the church, you learn to speak and to organize in the church assemblies. The church helped me a lot to maximize my potential in this way. (interview, May 8, 2001)

Generally speaking, evangelical growth in recent years has allowed growing participation in more and more sectors of society. There are now organized evangelical groups for athletes, entrepreneurs, university students, police officers, and the military, for example. There are also ecological groups and groups of liberal professionals. Broadening the spectrum of participation in society also has the effect of opening up new possibilities for electoral success based on involvement in diverse social sectors.

The Congressman-Bishop: Carlos Rodrigues

In 1976 a young man of eighteen stood in a square in a poor district of Rio de Janeiro listening to an enthusiastic preacher asking his listeners to accept Jesus as savior. The young man was Carlos Alberto Rodrigues, and the preacher Edir Macedo was starting what was to become one of the major religious phenomena of the late twentieth century in Brazil.

The following year Rodrigues, Macedo, and a handful of others cofounded the Igreja Universal do Reino de Deus (Universal Church of the Kingdom of God; UCKG). One of the other cofounders was Marcello Crivella, Macedo's nephew, who in the mid-1990s was to lead the UCKG in its rapid expansion in Africa before returning to Brazil to direct the New Canaan project, a huge social project based on irrigation of a dry region in the Northeast. Crivella is also a very popular gospel singer and was elected senator from the state of Rio in 2002. (His total of over three million votes means that he was supported by many people from outside the Universal Church, and in fact must have received many votes from nonevangelicals.) The UCKG now has a large communications empire (the third largest television network in Brazil, scores of radio stations, and a daily newspaper in the city of Belo Horizonte).[7]

In politics, successful UCKG candidates included one federal deputy in 1986 and three federal and three state deputies in 1990. In 1994, the UCKG doubled its number to six federal and six state deputies, besides supporting winning candidates from outside the church for some state governorships, which enabled it to get some nominations in state administrations.

In 1998, the UCKG concentrated on its own candidates. It supported twenty-eight candidates for federal deputy and thirty-nine for state deputy, managing to elect eighteen and twenty-six, respectively. Although its representatives are dispersed in many parties, they can act together when necessary, making the church into a medium-sized "party." For the 1998 elections, the UCKG candidates were dispersed among a broad range of parties (thirteen), with a slight concentration in the progovernment center-right PFL. Rodrigues alleges that this was due less to ideological preference than to a desire to "contaminate" the PFL, which, according to him, is strongly influenced by the Catholic clergy.

Shortly after the 1998 elections, several of the UCKG's newly elected representatives switched to the Liberal Party, a medium-sized centrist party that, according to Bishop Rodrigues, "gives us space to manifest our point of view." Another party also attracted several UCKG members of congress, the small PSL, which in congress allied with the Liberals. While the deputies elected were originally distributed in seven parties, they later concentrated in five: the PL-PSL bloc, plus three large progovernment parties (PFL, PMDB, and the Brazilian Progressive Party [PPB; Partido Progressista Brasileiro]). It is presumably easier to obtain advantages individually via the latter parties, while the PL-PSL bloc is brought into play for the more "complicated" issues.

This tactic has created a larger political *locus* for the UCKG without the need to found an evangelical party. The latter would only harm the UCKG's electoral chances, due to the Brazilian electoral system. Thus, besides its influential television and radio network, it also became a significant new political force. In states where the UCKG presents more than one candidate, it ensures the best possible distribution of its members' ballots by instructing each local church which candidate to vote for, attempting to guarantee the election of all its candidates in that state. It also chooses the party affiliations of candidates carefully, to maximize its electoral potential.[8]

In 1998, many of the UCKG candidates were clergy. Previously, only two of its six federal deputies were pastors. But Bishop Rodrigues declared, in the denominational journal, that it was time "to send the parents and no longer the children" into party politics. Of its forty-four parliamentarians elected in 1998, only nine were not pastors or bishops. In an interview, Rodrigues also gave me another explanation for this clericalization of the UCKG's caucus:

> Sometimes we'd elect a fellow and he went to parliament to look after his own interests. If he was a businessman, he would look after his businesses and ally with other entrepreneurs. If he was a lawyer, he would start looking after the affairs of his large clients. He developed a calling to ask for favors, requesting an audience with a minister but not to talk about poverty or ask for a hospital or something for the shanty-town. So we realized that if you put a pastor that isn't so likely to happen. (interview with Bishop Carlos Rodrigues, May 7, 2001; unless otherwise indicated, all quotations from Rodrigues refer to this interview)

Rodrigues's grammar and way of speaking still betray his lower class origins. Bishop Marcello Crivella, however, is different. One of the few UCKG leaders with higher education (an engineering degree), the articulate Crivella is from a middle-class family and represents a socially more palatable face of the Universal Church. The "aesthetic veto" that Garotinho has suffered from the Rio elite applies even more to the UCKG. Press treatment of the UCKG was initially very hard-hitting, especially for its "unconventional methods" aimed at "deceiving the people" and "squeezing their money out of them." Rodrigues himself experienced the harshest side of this "aesthetic veto": when he was responsible for establishing the church in São Paulo in the 1980s, he was arrested and charged with charlatanism. "Suffering for love of the gospel" has become common among UCKG pastors; Bishop Macedo himself was imprisoned in 1992 when accused of charlatanism. The church media frequently uses photos of Bishop Macedo behind bars reading the Bible to illustrate, as Macedo says, that the UCKG is like an omelet: the more you beat it, the more it grows.

In 1982 Rodrigues suggested to Macedo that the youthful UCKG should try to elect a city councillor in Rio and should support Sandra Cavalcanti for state governor. Cavalcanti was a practicing Catholic and very conservative, and the aim was to prevent the "communist" Leonel Brizola from winning (Justino 1995). Today, Rodrigues says that supporting Cavalcanti was a mistake; if she had won, "it would have set our state back years in human rights." But this initiative marked the beginning of Rodrigues's work as political coordinator of the UCKG. At election times, he would leave his pastoral duties to work full-time for the church's official candidates. Over the years, Rodrigues also led the church work in several Brazilian states and founded the UCKG in Argentina and Spain, before becoming bishop in Portugal.[9] From there, he went to Africa, where he worked in Angola, South Africa, and Mozambique. In Mozambique, the UCKG has a television station; Rodrigues has always been a great advocate of church investment in the media. Like Garotinho, he himself has worked as a radio presenter and has declared that "even if we are building a church or a cathedral, we interrupt everything to be able to buy or lease a radio or television station."[10]

The role of political coordinator was more structured from 1996 when he started an "Evangelical Parliamentary Advisory Office" to assist evangelical members of congress and to keep the evangelical community informed of what was happening in Brasília. A constant concern of his was to win over voters outside his church ("I want to broaden my reach and win over those who aren't evangelicals for my political side"), however unlikely that may seem. At the same time, through the structures of the Liberal Party ("the party that gives a chance to evangelicals") rather than through religious institutions, he offered space to evangelicals of other denominations.

Going beyond the frontiers of the UCKG (which is already starting to happen through agreements with pastors of other denominations) would be a significant advance. In the municipal elections of 2000, Rodrigues supported a Liberal Party candidate for deputy mayor who is an Assemblies of God pastor. However, Ronaldo Didini, a former UCKG pastor and television presenter who broke with the church, saw only limited possibilities of broadening the political base, since "the Universal's parliamentarians are elected to defend the business and economic interests of the Universal Church and not of the evangelicals in general" (*Época*, July 6, 1998).

As part of his activities as a "religious lobbyist in defense of the evangelicals," Rodrigues managed, by dint of pressure on parliamentarians, to alter a bill that required a minimum distance between buildings belonging to different religions. He was also influential in persuading the president to veto certain clauses in a new law on the environment that included severe fines and even imprisonment for the leaders of "noisy" churches. (Many pentecostal churches would have been affected by this so-called law of silence.) In a 1998 interview, Rodrigues seemed rather uneasy when explaining the negotiation process.

We voted in favor of the law allowing the reelection of the president because it was an agreement to overthrow the "law of silence."[11] They demanded our votes in congress. Is that political blackmail? I don't know. That's what it's like there: when you want to stop one bill, you have to vote for another. [The leader of the government] said: "You people vote for the government in the reelection question and the president will veto the law of silence." There were a couple of other questions in the agreement as well, but I can't remember what they were. So we did it. Is it just? Is it right? I don't know. At the time, it was what we were able to do. (*Eclésia*, October 1998)

Three years later, I again questioned Rodrigues—already with some parliamentary experience as a deputy—about the agreement. He replied: "I won't say it was good. But the bill had already passed and was about to become law. There was nothing else we could do. Today I would defeat the bill before it reached that stage. Today I'm there in congress and I see the bills as soon as they are born."

Rodrigues's activities within the UCKG were a special target of criticism from some former leaders who left the church. Ronaldo Didini described him as "the typical Pharisee described in the New Testament." Mário Justino wrote of his "notoriety for being tough with pastors and helpers." In weekly pastors' meetings, "we were psychologically raped by Rodrigues's cynicism and sarcasm" (Justino 1995, 61). In his parliamentary activities he was similarly criticized, by evangelical and nonevangelical colleagues. The veteran Assemblies of God deputy Salatiel Carvalho claimed that he was a poor negotiator, being accustomed to give orders (a not uncommon criticism regarding evangelical pastors in first terms in parliament). More severe was the verdict of the president of the tiny Social Labor Party (PST; Partido Social Trabalhista), a party that for a short time contained several UCKG deputies: "That shitty bishop, idiot, demon, liar . . . he doesn't respect anyone. How can he run a sect and talk of Jesus? He doesn't have anything of Jesus" (IstoÉ, October 19, 1999). This, in response to Rodrigues's accusations that the party had taken money to allow in the then mayor of São Paulo who was embroiled in charges of corruption.

Rodrigues's own evaluation of his first year as a parliamentarian in 1999 emphasized his difficulty in gaining acceptance as leader of the "evangelical caucus." "It was hard to make the more experienced deputies see that it is no reflection on them to follow the leadership of a new parliamentarian."

From the Right to the Center, with an Eye to the Left

Rodrigues spoke of three stages in the public trajectory of the Universal Church. Initially, undergoing police surveillance and with several leaders charged or in prison, the church resisted through the judiciary, using good lawyers and always obtaining favorable verdicts. Three charges were commonly made against the church: fraud, charlatanism, and quackery. In the early twentieth century, it had been common for such charges to be brought against Afro-Brazilian religions and spiritism, and as with the UCKG in the late 1980s and 1990s, there were attempts to label members pathological and to deny the status of religion to the accused group on the grounds that it was using methods such as "brainwashing" and "psychological pressure" (Giumbelli 2000, 225).

As these lawsuits did not stop the growth of the Universal Church, Rodrigues said, a second phase of attacks took place through the media. As part of its reply, the church developed its own media empire. This led to a third stage of attacks, the elaboration of laws that would harm the UCKG (and by extension all evangelicals) and the church's response through the strengthening of its parliamentary "watchtower."

With the worst of these battles now over, Rodrigues concluded in 2001, his political role could be more wide-ranging. "Now that I no longer need to fight for the freedom to preach the gospel, which is virtually complete, I can fight for civil society, for the poor, for what I think is just."

One characteristic of the new phase of evangelical politics is precisely the emphasis given to this discourse regarding justice. From the time of the Constituent Assembly of 1987–88 until the legislature of 1994–98, the evangelicals in congress were overwhelmingly in progovernment parties, and such an emphasis on justice was unthinkable as one of their defining characteristics. On the contrary, their main concerns were moral questions, bills establishing "the Day of the Bible," and a desire for recognition of the "importance" of the evangelicals, always combined with subservience to the powers that be. But in the legislature elected in 1998, the center of gravity shifted. Corporatist demands (protection of evangelical institutional interests) were still present, but were balanced with wider concerns.

Senator Marina Silva, for example, argued that it was possible to invoke grounds of conscience for objecting to bills that go against one's religious principles, as happened when she voted against an abortion bill. To this harmony in moral questions among evangelicals of different ideological hues, there has also been a growing trend toward what may become an evangelical social discourse.[12]

What Garotinho and Rodrigues say about paying more attention to the poor and about the need for social justice could find an echo among evangelical parliamentarians, most of whom are elected by poorer voters. There are, of course, other interests involved as well, but we should not neglect the influence of an ever better informed and active electorate.

Another traditional element of evangelical politics that seems to be changing is unconditional obedience to whomever is in power. Besides its ideological component (especially during the military regime), this posture has often been defended theologically by Brazilian evangelical leaders by citing chapter 13 of the New Testament book of Romans. The UCKG, on the other hand, defends a posture of independence. Rodrigues illustrated this. "I wasn't elected to say amen. I have always been an independent person. So I joined the opposition and I think I'm right. I'm not a radical oppositionist, though; if something is good I'll vote for it."

This is a considerable change, since in the presidential elections of 1994, the UCKG had campaigned actively against the Workers Party, mainly through its journal *Folha Universal*. The action of the party was routinely associated with the devil and with other religions. "Lula appeals to Candomblé" (an Afro-Brazilian religion), said one headline (July 10, 1994); on another occasion, the party was "a product of the Roman clergy" (June 2, 1994). Lula supposedly supported liberal laws on abortion and homosexuality, as well as being "a specialist in strikes [and] inconsequential radicalism" (August 21, 1994).

By late 1995, this radical anti–Workers Party posture was being abandoned, and replaced by overtures to the left. In his interview with me in 2001, Rodrigues defined himself as a centrist. In other interviews, he called himself a leftist (Cruz, *Noticia e Opinião*, October 10, 2000) or center-leftist (Dines, Fernandes Júnior, and Salomão 2000), and in a publication from his parliamentary office he again used the latter self-definition.

To what extent can the UCKG's changing political posture affect other evangelical segments? Many still doubt its sincerity, regarding it as merely a ploy to strengthen the church's defense of its corporate interests. In late 2001, the UCKG was engaged in serious negotiations with the Workers Party regarding support for Lula's 2002 presidential bid. The Workers Party preferred to refer to these negotiations as being not with the UCKG but with the Liberal Party. In any case, Workers Party leaders, even those regarded as more radically left-wing, all affirmed the possibility of a close association with the evangelicals. As one said, "We accept all religions. It was socialism that was harmed most in the fight between socialism and religion. The evangelicals are welcome." Or in the words of another party leader, "the evangelicals can also help in developing an anticapitalist awareness" (*Valor*, October 16, 2001).

Rodrigues's oppositionist discourse was somewhat diffuse.

> The group that's in power has been there for thirty years, fifty
> years. If you can't do anything in thirty years it's time to get out
> and give others a chance. I don't know if they'll be better or not,
> but you've got to give them a chance to prove themselves, and
> if they're no good we can turf them out after four years. But you can't
> have one group in power for thirty years, a group of bankers and
> industrialists. . . . Do we really live in a democracy? I don't think so.
> A democracy in which power doesn't change hands in fifty years,
> what sort of democracy is that?

Given his background and aims, it may be too much to expect articulate progressive proposals from Rodrigues. A man of action, his pragmatism could be summed up in the word "independence." With the UCKG's vast financial and symbolic capital, he "owes no one anything." His denomination already enjoys a level of legitimacy that allows it to diversify its positions, while always keeping the defense of its corporate interests as its basic reference point.

Perhaps one of the church's greatest concerns in politics is expressed vividly by Rodrigues: "Our priority is simply to perform well politically in order to put an end to this negative image concerning us." The idea that the

UCKG gets rich by exploiting the poor is very common among the middle class and the press. By initiating social projects and taking a more critical political posture, the church may be investing in a sort of social and political marketing campaign to improve its image. In addition, it is clear-sighted about the Workers Party's chances of electoral victory and, by pledging support or at least benevolent neutrality, is seeking to guarantee some degree of direct involvement in any future Workers Party government's telecommunications policy. The church also has an eye to increasing its parliamentary caucus, thanks to judicious electoral alliances that will improve the chances of its candidates being elected.

Whatever the reasons, one should not underestimate the effects on the denomination's ethos of a discourse of concern for the poor, together with social projects offering material support, professional training courses, or literacy classes. As Mariz says, pentecostalism gives its members access to modernizing experiences, both by demanding "a new ethic in everyday life and by emphasizing verbality, the use of the word, the study of the Bible and the intellectual systematisation of faith"—elements that reinforce rational choices and "develop attitudes and skills which are relevant to the situation of the poor in modern capitalist societies" (1996, 178–80).

Nor should we underestimate the importance of the experience of daily contact between church leaders and left-wing politicians. Bishop Rodrigues's speech in congress when the Workers Party was commemorating its twentieth anniversary on February 9, 2000, illustrated the potential of such contact.

> [The Universal Church] used to fight ferociously against the Workers Party [because] we thought they would close the churches.... But when we got to know our *companheiro*[13] Lula ... Walter Pinheiro, who is our evangelical brother from the Baptist Church, Gilmar Machado [another evangelical deputy], and other *companheiros* of the Workers Party, we started to dialogue and listen to their speeches, and we saw that our truths were lies, that our fears were groundless, and that there was no justification for persecuting those in our own institution who were members of the Workers Party or for excluding from leadership all those who had respect and affection for the party. Through dialogue we came to understand that you fight for the same thing we fight for. And in my first parliamentary term I am achieving something I am really proud of, that my Liberal Party is following the Workers Party in 90 percent of the votes in this house.

Rodrigues's statement brings us to a key question for our analysis. What is the nature of his leadership among the other deputies, and how far does it really go? When starting the speech just quoted, he said he would be speaking "not only for my party but also for the institution I helped to found over twenty years ago" (the UCKG). He then said he was "proud" of getting his party to follow the Workers Party in most congressional votes. How far does the parliamentary action of "the institution he helped to found" extend, and what was his role as deputy leader of the Liberal Party?

Leader of the Evangelical Caucus: What Caucus?

Besides being ever-present on the opinion page of the denominational weekly *Folha Universal*, Rodrigues usually reappeared on the pages dedicated to politics. While Bishop Macedo and other leading bishops generally write about religious themes in the journal, Rodrigues always wrote openly about political questions. He frequently touched upon electoral themes in his articles, with occasional analyses of current affairs. The general tone of the articles in 2000 was of constant criticism of the federal government (a theme that overflowed at times into the editorial column). On occasions the Workers Party was praised. The growth of the Liberal Party was often mentioned, alongside the importance of evangelicals becoming more effective in their "Christian faithfulness in politics," which would happen when evangelicals "vote for their brothers." Many articles talked of persecution suffered by the church. Others condemned clientelistic practices to buy the evangelical vote, since evangelicals want "clean elections," "looking straight in the eye, greeting your voters, and promising nothing at the personal level" (*Folha Universal*, September 17, 2000).

Bishop Rodrigues's supposed leadership of the "evangelical caucus" of over fifty members of congress was much commented on in the main national newspapers and even in specialist evaluations of the current congress. But in fact, an analysis of the behavior of evangelical members of congress shows that this "caucus" is a myth. So far, it has only had any sort of corporate existence when moral issues are being voted on, such as bills on abortion and civil unions for homosexuals. Even then, Rodrigues was not responsible for the concerted action, but rather the common religious convictions that also helped mobilize a "Catholic caucus" of some one hundred deputies.

While it is not surprising that evangelicals from other churches who had had no help from the UCKG in their election were reluctant to follow Rodrigues's leadership, it is curious to find the same phenomenon even among the eighteen who owed their election to the Universal Church (fifteen being members of the church, and three from other denominations). On the one hand, in UCKG publications one could read proclamations of support for a large raise in the minimum salary; on the other hand, ten out of these eighteen deputies voted against this large raise. Table 5.4 shows how they voted on this occasion (in which government and opposition were severely divided), as well as on the question of approving a petition for the opening of a parliamentary inquiry into corruption in the federal government.

TABLE 5.4. Voting Behavior of Congress Members Supported by the UCKG

Federal Deputy	Party[a]	Government's Proposal for Minimum Salary[b]	Petition for a Parliamentary Commission of Inquiry into Corruption	Evaluation of Parliamentary Performance as a Whole
Aldir Cabral	PFL	yes	no	very good
Bishop Rodrigues	PL	no	yes	very good
Bishop Wanderval	PL	no	no	very good
Costa Ferreira[c]	PFL	yes	no	good
De Velasco	PSL	no	no	very good
Gessivaldo Isaías	PMDB	yes	—	average
Jorge Pinheiro	PMDB	yes	no	good
Jorge Wilson	PMDB	yes	no	poor
Luiz Moreira	PFL	yes	yes	average
Magno Malta	PL	no	yes	good
Marcos de Jesus	PSDB → PL	yes	yes	poor
Oliveira Filho	PTB → PL	yes	yes	poor
Paulo Gouveia	PL	no	yes	average
Pastor Lincoln Portela[d]	PSL	no	yes	very good
Reginaldo Germano	PFL	yes	no	average
Valdeci Paiva	PSL	no	no	good
Wagner Salustiano	PPB	yes	no	good
Vote of progovernment parties	PSDB, PTB, PPB, PMDB, PFL	yes[e]	no	
Vote of the opposition parties	PT, PDT, PSB, PL, PSL, PCdoB, PPS, PV	no	Yes	

Source: "Olho no Congresso" (supplement to Folha de S. Paulo, March 22, 2001).

Note: Only seventeen deputies are included. The eighteenth, Almeida de Jesus of the PL, left his seat in July 2000 to occupy a place in the municipal secretariat of the northeastern city of Fortaleza. On the question of the minimum salary, he had voted with Bishop Rodrigues.
[a]PSDB = Party of Brazilian Social Democracy (of president Cardoso); PTB = Brazilian Labor Party; PPB = Brazilian Progressive Party; PMDB = Party of the Brazilian Democratic Movement; PFL = Party of the Liberal Front; PT = Workers Party; PDT = Democratic Labour Party; PSB = Brazilian Socialist Party; PL = Liberal Party; PSL = Social Liberal Party; PCdoB = Communist Party of Brazil; PPS = Popular Socialist Party; PV = Green Party. Note that the names of Brazilian parties often indicate very little about their ideological position (the PPB, for example, is right-wing).
[b]On this vote the progovernment parties did not vote uniformly; the PSDB voted in favor and the others against.
[c]Member of the Assemblies of God elected with the support of the UCKG.
[d]Pastor of the Renewed Baptist Church (charismatic) elected with the support of the UCKG.
[e]About one hundred deputies in progovernment parties defied the government and defended a higher raise.

The righthand column also shows the general evaluation given to each parliamentarian periodically by a leading national newspaper. During the debate over the minimum salary, the Folha Universal (May 28, 2000) ran a full page of articles under the general heading "Evangelical Caucus Repudiates the Minimum Salary of Only 151 Reais" (the government proposal). It included photographs of five evangelical deputies from the PL-PSL bloc. But the righthand side of the page contained a column of short items on the doings of other Universal Church politicians, including two from progovernment parties who later voted in favor of the minimum salary supposedly "repudiated" by the "evangelical caucus."

In other congressional votes, it is equally hard to discern a pattern. The UCKG deputies were usually split, with between six and nine voting with the opposition and the rest with the government. But the division does not consistently follow even party orientation.

In May 2001, the opposition was attempting to get the necessary 171 signatures to open a parliamentary committee of inquiry into denunciations of corruption in the federal government. For some reason, three UCKG deputies in the PL-PSL bloc did not sign the list. Rodrigues himself, under pressure from the government not to sign, had waited until the last minute before signing and declaring that he and his party would all sign. Rodrigues's declaration got headlines in the press and earned praise from many nonevangelical opposition deputies. The following speech illustrates the climate of events.

> For the first time, I see the evangelical sectors of our country raising the flag of ethics in politics. Previously, it was other religious sectors who led these movements. Now I can glimpse a new cycle of morality, a new period of intolerance of corruption in government, with the evangelical nation taking to the streets to demand a committee of inquiry. (Deputy Batochio, April 18, 2000; www.camara.gov.br)

When I queried Rodrigues about the UCKG deputies who had not signed the petition, he replied that he does not force anyone's hand, but merely reminds the deputies that they will have to "face the streets" later. But the problem with this reply is that the voters' room for maneuver is still very small and it is unlikely that a candidate for reelection who is really supported by the UCKG would in fact be rejected by them.

In short, congressional voting behavior does not point to a real UCKG caucus. On the whole, the deputies follow their parties, although there are fairly widespread exceptions. This policy was part of Rodrigues's strategy and consolidated his leadership even further. Having deputies in both opposition parties and progovernment parties, he could broaden his range of action. When necessary, he could activate the "caucus," as in the election of the president of the lower house, but by not forcing uniformity in everyday questions he avoided unnecessary erosion of his prestige.

Rodrigues has had no qualms about characterizing his church as authoritarian. In the church, he expected his pastors to say amen to everything he says; but in politics he negotiated with them. He claimed to have no difficulty in living with this duality: ecclesiastical space and political space are different, he said. If a deputy wants to vote with the opposition he should join an opposition party, whether the Liberal Party or one of the others. All he needs to do is inform Rodrigues of this wish. Not all the UCKG deputies followed him into opposition, simply because they did not want to, he claimed.

This points to an interesting balancing act between parliamentarians, church, and parties. Why have all UCKG parliamentarians not joined the Liberal Party to show their independence? Because this would mean a smaller number of successful candidates in elections and a reduced bargaining flexibility in congress. For example, with the current electoral rules, if all the UCKG candidates in the state of Rio de Janeiro had run for the Liberal Party, their votes would have been sufficient to elect only three of them, instead of the six who got in through several different parties. While individual preferences may count for something, the overall strategy of the church must take into account the possibility of keeping doors open in both government and opposition. Tension and broad dialogue are fundamental. The sophistication of UCKG politics is such that even in the church newspaper its deputies can take up progovernment or opposition positions. For example, in late 2000, an article entitled "Sources for Raising the Minimum Salary Generate Polemics among Deputies" had photos of two deputies on one side and on the other side two others (including Bishop Rodrigues) with the caption "The Other Side of the Question." In the text, both opinions were represented. The denominational journal openly mentions a difference of opinion within the supposed caucus, and thus increases the church's range of action in parliament.

Regarding the frequency with which church deputies appear in the journal, pride of place goes clearly to Rodrigues, who was present in every edition in 2000. At the other extreme was Costa Ferreira, the veteran Assemblies of God politician who managed to return to congress in 1998 with UCKG support, who did not appear at all. In between, all the others appeared with greater or lesser frequency. The most frequent were the leader of the PSL, Lincoln Portela (a charismatic Baptist elected with UCKG help), and Aldir Cabral of the PFL, who could perhaps be considered the leader of the UCKG within the government.

The leading national daily newspaper *Folha de S. Paulo*, in its evaluation of the performance of all members of congress, placed the UCKG deputies slightly above the average (59 percent were judged "very good" and "good," against a general average of 53 percent). Five were "very good," including Rodrigues, Portela, and Cabral, the three most often mentioned in UCKG publications. Three were considered "poor," including one (Jorge Wilson) who appeared very little in the *Folha Universal*, but also Marcos de Jesus, who appeared quite frequently.

This "coverage" was undoubtedly taken into account when the church defined its candidates for the October 2002 elections. The selection process started at the level of the UCKG bishops in each state, who forwarded a list of names to Rodrigues. He eliminated some and decided how many candidates the church should present in each state, based on the electoral quotient of the parties (i.e., the number of votes likely to be necessary to elect someone of that party in that state) and on the number of people who frequent the church in that state (the assumption being that about 70 percent of the eligible voters who frequent the church will actually vote for an official church candidate). The chosen candidates were then assigned regions of the state, to avoid any competition for votes between them.

Before 1998, UCKG candidates were often professional people of some success and some education. But in 1998 a new policy was introduced, preferring bishops and pastors. Successful candidates' faithfulness to the church is measured in the first instance in the question of staff. The new deputy is supposed to allow the church to nominate his or her staff; Rodrigues stressed that the church does not allow nepotism, and this criterion is said to have led to a break with a few UCKG politicians over the years (although a 1999 list of deputies accused of nepotism included two from the UCKG who are still in good standing with the church, including Aldir Cabral; *Folha de S. Paulo,* October 17, 1999). In addition, candidates agree to vote according to the church's wishes in matters that affect its institutional interests, and in moral questions.

If at first politics meant "defending the work of God" (*Eclésia,* October 1998), today it means defending "the causes of civil society" (Dines, Fernandes Júnior, and Salomão 2000). The "discovery" of the need to "do what is just" seems motivated not just by ideological conviction but by the constant contact of the church with the poorest sectors of Brazilian society, by contact with diverse expressions of progressive thought, and perhaps also by a strategy to improve the church's public image.

Rodrigues asked for patience. When in only twenty years a church comes from nowhere and gets politically established all over the country, with the reach of a medium-sized party, it attracts attention and great responsibilities. Rodrigues's presence in parliament could be understood as a clearer commitment to a politics that is also concerned about those who share the material privation that most UCKG members experience. Rodrigues promised a renewal of the caucus for the next legislature and stressed that it was difficult for a deputy who has been in the right-wing PFL for twelve years suddenly to switch to the Workers Party. While Rodrigues's discourse here may sound like a sanitized version to be presented to a university researcher, there is more at stake. Besides the (seemingly genuine) discovery that the Workers Party is not "at the service of the devil," there is also the perception that a posture of subservience to conservative parties has not ensured the guarantees that the church would have liked.

If on the one hand he respects "individual preferences," on the other hand Rodrigues left no doubt that there was church control over parliamentary behavior, and this seems to be a significant contribution of the UCKG to

Brazilian democracy. The Council of Bishops carries out a formal evaluation of the performance of each of its parliamentarians, making a dossier with all pertinent information such as frequency of attendance in congress, speeches, votes, and so on. On this basis, the council decides whether "he deserves to be reelected or not."

We thus have a sort of indirect election in which a "council of the enlightened" defines for the "masses" which politicians deserve their votes. The bishops' role is self-attributed, not granted by the church faithful. But Rodrigues suggested that this did not mean passivity on the part of the members. While a recommended candidate may be virtually guaranteed election the first time, reelection is more difficult. A church deputy once claimed, "Our voters are faithful; we could get a lamp-post elected" (quoted in Freston 2000, 299). To which Rodrigues replied, "We may elect it the first time, but if the lamp-post doesn't work, the people won't want it any more."

Like every social organization, a church is influenced by changes in the larger society. The UCKG leadership could not ignore the great desire for change among most of the population after eight years of the Cardoso government. Along these lines, the UCKG deputy Marcos de Jesus said, "I can't go against the voice of my people, who want Lula for president." Relations between the church and its members are two-way, and at some point religious leaders are obliged to meet many demands and desires of their followers.

To what extent, though, would the faithful really be able to boycott a candidacy approved by the bishops? In 1998, twenty-three of the sixty-seven UCKG-supported candidates for federal or state deputy were not elected: did the leaders get their calculations wrong (or take some calculated risks in states where the church is weaker) or did the faithful simply not vote as anticipated? We do not know, but Rodrigues was emphatic that the UCKG caucus would go on increasing.

In fact, in 2002 the UCKG caucus did grow by about 30 percent, electing twenty-two members of congress out of a total of about sixty evangelicals elected. Meanwhile, UCKG politics is only a very limited space of democratic education for the mass of poor people affiliated with the church. If the UCKG were to open more space for participation, the implications would be enormous; but this would almost certainly mean the end of the institution as we know it today and perhaps the end of its headlong expansion. That, at any rate, is Rodrigues's opinion:

> Democracy in the church doesn't work. You can't have an assembly to ask whether the pastor should buy an organ or start a radio or television program. None of the democratic denominations grow. The sheep shouldn't give orders to their pastor. There's no democracy in the home either. A father doesn't ask his son: "what should I do with this money?"

So, while the UCKG discourse has shifted markedly to the left and into opposition to the federal government, the UCKG structure has no place for democratic practices in its everyday functioning, which limits its contribution to Brazilian democracy.

Evangelicals, Political Participation, and Democracy in Brazil

The evangelicals, in organized fashion and by different routes, have been intensely active in electoral politics in recent years. Are they making a contribution to the consolidation of Brazilian democracy?

The economist Carlos Lessa (2000) believes they are. In a book on the city of Rio de Janeiro, he identifies two movements that offer real possibilities of facing up to inequality: the evangelical communities and the funk movement! Evangelical potential is due to the evangelicals' bipolar structure of religious community and religious institution. This structure confirms the believer in his or her self-worth and superiority to others, which has implications for democratic life. "Basic democracy, the feeling that you are 'someone,' which is often sought in bars, is achieved many times over by the believer in his church" (343).

Lessa claims that when evangelicals move beyond their churches they will transfer the values inherent in their religiosity, which will mean progress toward greater social equality. I have identified this movement in the UCKG, although it is not yet clear how far this goes and what impact it can have on society. The same may be happening with the evangelical group around Anthony Garotinho. This is what Lessa foresees:

> The believers will find it easy to learn about civic rights and duties. In the civil sphere, they will feed the demand for an effective functioning of the judicial system and for a reduction in arbitrariries by the security organs. In the social sphere, they will tend to give priority to better quality in the public services, education and health. In the mercantile sphere, thanks to their cohesion, the believers may act as a counterweight to business, as purchasers of their products and users of their services. . . . If the defense of civil and social rights outside the church are understood as a duty, the evangelicals will become a vanguard element in the struggle for full citizenship. (2000, 443)

How do our actors perceive this process? Garotinho situated evangelical action within the religious sphere. "Change people in order to change the world" was the motto of his sermons throughout the country. He often used a parable to illustrate this. An overburdened geography teacher, busy correcting exams, tries to give his small son something to keep him occupied. He cuts up a map of the world, gives the pieces to the boy, and asks him to piece it back together. Thinking this would give him hours of peace and quiet, the teacher is surprised to see the boy come back very quickly with the task completed. He asks the boy how he managed to do it. His son replies that he had no idea where to start, until he noticed that on the back of one of the pieces was a picture of a man's arm. Seeing all the pieces had a part of a man on the back, he just went on *putting the man back together*, which resulted in the *world* being put back together as well.

Thus the only way to put the world to rights, concluded Garotinho, is through Christian preaching, which through the new birth produces new men, who are then fit to make the world more just. For him, the main contribution of the evangelical churches to democratic consolidation would be precisely the transformation of individuals through conversion. However, at the same time, Garotinho also pointed to the need for greater commitment from evangelical leaders. We can summarize his viewpoint as an encouragement for the faithful to continue preaching, plus an appeal to church leaders not to use their religious communities to guarantee "institutional interests" to the detriment of what is best for society.

Bishop Rodrigues, on the other hand, thought that Garotinho had to preach the message of "changing people in order to change the world" because he was newly converted and needed to win the confidence of the evangelical electorate. Rodrigues himself had no need to do this because, as a preacher of twenty-five years' experience, he had "already won over his audience." His "message" emphasized political participation, the need for "people of good will" to be involved politically. He claimed that Nilson Fanini, former president of the Baptist World Alliance and the leading figure in the Brazilian Baptist community, had been persuaded by his influence to consider a candidacy.[14] Unlike Garotinho, Rodrigues's political preaching was conspicuous by the absence of a conversionist discourse. He was much more sparing in his use of Bible verses (only quoting one in our two-hour interview). His basic religious concern could be described as the need to exorcise politics of the demonic practices of corruption, and to build a more effective presence of the church in society: "A state secretary who is a drug addict, who uses cocaine, who is a liar, demon-possessed, [spiritually] perturbed (and there are many like that), kills a lot more people than a crook with a gun. Because he kills continually.... This can be combated out here [outside the church] as well."

Confronting the demon-possessed "out here" was Rodrigues's theological motivation. Evil is regularly exorcised inside the church. But evil "out here," in the public sphere, requires intervention in that sphere with all its specificities. Seeing the world as peopled by evil forces that lead individuals to "the bottom of the well," the church is disposed to exorcise the political sphere. Its basic motivation is to remove people who reproduce the evil that dwells in their own lives in their everyday actions in public life. Corruption is understood as "a diabolical practice that destroys people and nations"; consequently, those who have "the fear of the Lord" do not get involved in it.

While Garotinho, a new convert, was excited about the possibility of verbalizing his faith, Rodrigues seemed jaded after twenty years of dedication to preaching and founding churches in various cities and countries. He increasingly believed that his religious practice had to have repercussions in other areas and could not remain within "four walls." These repercussions did not amount to a theocracy, but rather to a status in society that he considered Catholics to have.

> I understand that people are worried that we are going to make a confessional state, but I think there is great maturity among us and we know that that is not possible. We are going to do the same as the priests who become ministers, governors, vice presidents. Marco Maciel [then vice president] is a priest. Paulo Renato [then minister of education] was trained by Catholic Action, José Serra [then minister of health] also. There are several Supreme Court judges who were seminarians, who are priests. In fact, they are more priestly than the priests.

The contrast between two well-known religious singers illustrates the changes in the relationship between Brazilian politics and the churches. In 1999, the Catholic priest Padre Marcelo Rossi and the UCKG bishop Marcello Crivella were both prominent in the media. They both signed contracts with important recording companies (Universal and Sony). Rossi is aligned with the Catholic charismatic renewal, and his songs and his "Jesus aerobics" have been a tremendous commercial success. The words of his songs are superficial; one of them says "the little animals went in two by two. The elephant and the birds with the children of God. Raise your hands and give glory to God." On the other hand, bishop Crivella of the UCKG recorded his CD to raise funds for a large new social project in the arid Northeast that the church was opening. The words are very different from Rossi's: "My God, what is happening here in my country? There are so many people suffering. In the cities, in the countryside, our people go through hunger and unemployment. . . . Lord, there is so much crisis and nowhere to flee to. He who governs without faith can do very little."

Ten years earlier, it would have been unimaginable to see a Catholic priest on television imitating elephants and birds and saying he sees angels (in the words of another of his hits) and a pentecostal leader dedicating himself to disseminating a project of social development based on volunteering, and whose lyrics demand action from the authorities in the fight against poverty and unemployment. In 2002, the singer-bishop Crivella of the UCKG was elected senator, and by the end of 2003 he was in fourth place in opinion polls for the 2004 elections for mayor of Rio de Janeiro.

As for Garotinho, he claimed not to have had contact with the MEP but he had read books by one of its key founders, Robinson Cavalcanti, a political scientist and former professor at the Federal University of Pernambuco and now an Anglican bishop. Cavalcanti's theology is that of "holistic mission," and Garotinho reproduced part of this.

> I believe we cannot be negligent. Jesus said: you have to be the
> salt of the earth and light of the world. When you have a society with
> such grave problems as Brazilian society has, the evangelical
> doesn't have the right before God to avoid combating this inqui-
> tous system that our country is living under.... I think that although
> we know things here on earth will never be totally put right, we
> can perfectly well start building the Kingdom of God here on earth.

It was often said (by segments of the media and by political opponents) that Garotinho would be a danger to democracy because he would want to unite church and state. But in his declarations we can detect a bringing to-gether, not of church and state, but of religion and politics, a common practice in Brazilian history. He seems distant from any sort of theocratic aspiration. For him, "it is perfectly possible to reconcile the secular state, a state with-out a religion, a lay state, but one in which each one individually has his or her faith. Believe in God, and you can live in a plural society." In Demerath's terms (2001), Garotinho's model is that of a secular state with religious politics.

The lack of sophisticated theological thinking may be one reason why evangelicals are often viewed with a certain suspicion as regards their part in democratization. But as Stoll (1990, 329) reminds us, Latin American evan-gelicals are largely in a redemptive phase (saving one's soul) rather than a transformative one (changing the world). They may now be entering the latter phase, but still lack greater democratization of their institutions and their discourse. Gaskill (1997), however, sees this new phase as unlikely as long as the evangelicals are enjoying numerical and financial growth under neolib-eralism.

In this regard, Baptist federal deputy Gilmar Machado of the Workers Party and the MEP felt the Universal Church's interest in supporting Lula's candidacy for president in 2002 was in part motivated by an understanding that the growth of the church is harmed by the current situation, both by high levels of governmental corruption and by the economic policies and the appalling income distribution resulting from them (interview, November 17, 2001). An improvement in economic conditions is thus seen as potentially positive for church growth; which is not so far from the reasoning behind certain entrepreneurial groups that have also come out in favor of Lula. Another factor is the social origin of pentecostal leaders, as illustrated by Rodrigues's discourse.

> Democracy was elaborated for the people and not for the elite. The evangelicals today are the closest to the people. Most evangelical leaders are from the grassroots; their origin is in poverty, in the poor peripheries, or in the lower middle class. It seems to me the evangelicals who come from this class origin fight for this class.... We evangelicals have an enormous desire for change. Change is part of our message anyway. Nonconformity. Our intellectual and spiritual training, which is from the church, is geared to change. To a break with certain values. The evangelical is democratic by philosophy.

As for Garotinho, a member of a historic Protestant church, democratic principles have been easily identifiable in his discourse and practice. "The democratic churches teach people to act politically, to participate. I voted to choose my presbyters who then choose the pastor. The Presbyterian Church is parliamentarist. This is good because people get experience of political practices."

In the political sphere, both Garotinho and Rodrigues adopted a discourse of opposition to the Brazilian economic model and stressed the need to fight poverty and promote greater equality—themes that are traditionally associated with being "left-wing" (Buarque 1992; Sader 1995). Both for Rodrigues and for senator Marina Silva (Dines, Fernandes Júnior, and Salomão 2000), the traditional evangelical link with conservative thinking was related to the fact that Protestantism was largely implanted in Brazil by American missionaries, who were obliged to avoid the theme of politics in order not to harm their right to preach. Thus, evangelicals came to be associated with an apolitical stance and with progovernment postures on the theological principle of "submission to the powers that be."

In the years following redemocratization in Brazil (post-1985), the Catholic Church through the Ecclesial Base Communities was in clear possession of the oppositional space within the religious field. As Bourdieu (1989) says, the real is relational. In the face of the established forces in Brazilian society in the 1980s, it was unlikely that evangelical institutions would find much space on the political left. Local-level case studies have shown that, where the Catholic Church did not occupy the oppositional space, evangelical groups were able to fill in the vacuum on the religious left (Burdick 1993; Novaes 1986).

Today, a movement of evangelicals toward a more critical political participation would seem to be favored by a certain vacuum in the religious field. Both the Catholic base communities and the Protestant ecumenical groups, which have traditionally occupied the religious left, are losing important institutional spaces. In Christian Smith's words, new perspectives are opening up for the evangelicals.

> If the Catholic Church in Latin America were to continue to head in a politically conservative direction, emphasizing spiritual devotion over social engagement, this would open the door for Protestants increasingly to explore political participation and democratic social reform without threatening the anti-Catholic dimension of their identity (1994, 136)

Our protagonists agree that Brazil at the beginning of the twenty-first century has what political science has come to call "procedural democracy" (Dahl 1971), in which economic concentration is the greatest impediment to democratic deepening. O'Donnell (Reis and O'Donnell 1988) points to Latin America's need for "another democratic transition" that goes beyond the existence of objective procedures.[15] This transition would be a continuous process in which, despite having reached political democracy, democratization is sought also in economic, social, and cultural spheres. As Moisés (1995) says, we should not fall into the "electoralist fallacy" as indicative of an egalitarian situation.

Huntington (1991) talks of structural factors that favor the establishment of democracy. Most countries of the "third wave" (which established or returned to democracy in the 1970s and 1980s), including Brazil, had in common a rise in per capita income. But Huntington rejects an "overdetermination" in the link between democracy and economic performance, also stressing sociocultural factors. He then points to religion as an important element: if the "first wave" of democracy was mainly in Protestant countries, the "third wave" has been mainly in Catholic ones. The *aggiornamento* of Vatican II and the diffusion of liberation theology in Latin America assisted the adoption of a human rights discourse that was fundamental for confronting authoritarian regimes.

Beyond procedural conditions, institutional and political structures can favor the dissemination of a political culture that is favorable to an egalitarian society. "What defines democracy is not just a set of institutional guarantees or the kingdom of the majority. . . . Democracy does not rest only on laws, but above all on a political culture" (Touraine [1994] 1996, 26).

Even with free elections, Brazil is far from this sense of democratic consolidation, which, according to Putnam (1993), depends on the production and reproduction of social capital to "make democracy work."[16] To understand why some democratic governments succeed and others fail, Putnam looks at the conditions for creating and maintaining representative institutions in society. Inspired by Tocqueville's work on civic associations and by studies of civic culture, Putnam considers civic community essential "to stable and effective democratic institutions" (1993, 11). Through the habit of meeting in associations (which Tocqueville regarded as common among the Americans), individuals contribute to the effectiveness and stability of democratic government. First, the "internal effects" of union create habits of cooperation, solidarity, and public-spiritedness. Second, the "external factors" of aggregation in different associations of a vast network contribute to effective social collaboration, to establishing norms, and to disseminating confidence among participants. Through the daily experience of mutual help in associations, citizens invest in social capital, which accumulates in similar ways to financial capital but is a public good. Trust between citizens can be fomented through civic communities.

Evangelical churches contribute to this by offering an environment of solidarity that has historical roots and that over time could result in the establishment of a democratic government. Religion in American society is said to have played a central role in this civic undergirding (Tocqueville [1835] 2000). In a later work, Putnam points to the collapse of community in modern America. Bowling Alone (2000) is motivated in part by the privatization of religion. Churches had been responsible for forming much social capital by opening up meeting spaces as well as by philanthropy and volunteerism. "Churches provide an important incubator for civic skills, civic norms, community interest and civic recruitment (66). But a lot of this was lost in the last decades of the twentieth century, not only in membership numbers but in the qualitative reduction of meeting spaces offered by religion. Catholicism and evangelicalism are still growing in the United States, but the former does not tend to foster meeting space due to its nominal character, and the latter is more concerned with the home than with the broader community. Both thus illustrate, for Putnam, a larger problem: the decline of civic infrastructure. Privatized religion builds less social capital and contributes less to democracy.

Is this the situation of Brazil today? The sociology of Brazilian religion has not produced enough empirical data to analyze the Brazilian situation in the light of Putnam's ideas. It is possible that the prevalence of Catholicism has something to do with the fragility of Brazil's democracy. The argument of a link between Protestantism and democracy could be brought back in, not via theological propensities but via Protestantism's organization, which supposedly foments greater social capital. The pratice of mutual help and solidarity has become more widespread in Brazil only in the 1990s, with "citizenship campaigns" calling on the population to get involved in associations against hunger and poverty. While the 1970s in Brazil were characterized by the so-called Gerson's law ("the important thing is to come off best in everything"), the epitome of egoism and lack of solidarity, today community values are more respected, even though the population's associational urge is still timid. Data shows that evangelicals' involvement in trade unions, political parties, and associations is similar to the national average, being lower in sporting and cultural clubs and higher in churches and neighborhood associations (Fernandes et al. 1998, 120).

Churches represent a space for strengthening this incipient associationalism in Brazil. A strong lead was given by the Catholic base communities in the 1980s, a major focus of production of social capital. Today, political parties, especially opposition ones, also have an important role in this, as well as trade union initiatives and civic campaigns, such as that which helped bring about the impeachment of President Collor for corruption in 1992.

In the Brazilian context, the pentecostals seem destined to have an important role in developing civic community. One of the greatest barriers to egalitarianism and solidarity is widespread poverty.[17] Associational options among the poor (over half the population) are practically nonexistent. It is in this context that pentecostal churches are active, promoting meeting space and creating bonds of solidarity demarcated by religion. While this network can easily be limited to the "brothers and sisters in the faith," there are signs that this might be overcome. If trust is still largely restricted to the religious group, some initiatives are facilitating acts of solidarity in the broader community that are not motivated merely by proselytistic aims. Both the Garotinho government's Citizen Voucher program, via the churches, and the UCKG's diverse social programs organized by its philanthropic arm, known as the Christian Beneficent Association, have broadened church members' vision of their role in society and formed new networks. Novaes comments:

> Besides changing trajectories and increasing the amount of "self-esteem" [among shanty-dwellers], the evangelical presence can also be detected now in the construction or reconstruction of local associational life. In Rio de Janeiro, there are already a significant number of pastors and ordinary evangelicals in the leadership of local organizations in the shanty-towns. (2001, 73)

The hierarchical and authoritarian structure adopted wholeheartedly by the Universal Church, together with the *caudillo*-type personalistic leadership of many other denominations, may be seen as a strong impediment to any contribution to democracy. While this may in fact inhibit participation, it may also create a situation similar to that of American Catholics in Tocqueville's time: "I think it is wrong to regard the Catholic religion as a natural enemy of democracy.... Among the different Christian doctrines, Catholicism appears to me, on the contrary, one of the most favorable to equality of conditions.... The priest alone is raised above the faithful: everything is equal below him" ([1835] 2000; vol. 1, part 2, chap. 9, 275).

The question now is whether Brazilian pentecostals can see the possibility of trust toward other social actors who do not share the same faith, even of taking part in networks with those who are currently demonized.[18] This is certainly the greatest limitation on the social capital produced in this context, making it difficult to establish broader and more diversified networks. An atmosphere of tolerance and respect is fundamental in order for the training offered within these civic communities, accessible to the great mass of people who are excluded from most other forms of community, to be translated into sufficient social capital to deepen Brazilian democracy.

Just as evangelical religion is talked about as a refuge from urban violence (Ventura 1994), a space for rehabilitation of prisoners (Varella 1999), and a means for combating *machismo* (Brusco 1993), the experience of associationalism among the evangelical poor and their recent "taste for politics" may help democratic consolidation.[19]

Inequality will not diminish as long as neoliberal-inspired policies hold sway. This impedes the consolidation of democracy beyond a proceduralism that interests mainly the national elite. A stable democracy will only be achieved by means of political action that gives priority to the struggle against inequality. The rise of urban violence illustrates what is at stake. In the meantime, the evangelicals offer a definite option of participation, albeit limited by many religious restrictions, corporatist interests, and clientelistic practices, and they have brought about greater religious plurality in important spheres of society and politics.

Postscript

In 2004–5, Bishop Rodrigues was implicated in the denunciations of corruption that involved the Workers Party and the Lula government. The UCKG immediately removed him from his functions as political coordinator and bishop, and Rodrigues later resigned his congressional seat. Garotinho, however, continued in the political limelight, joining the centrist Brazilian Democratic Movement Party (PMDB; Partido do Movimento Democrático Brasileiro), and positioning himself to run as the PMDB candidate in the 2006 presidential election. However, his party decided not to field any presidential candidates. He later endorsed Geraldo Alckmin of the PSDB, who lost to Lula in the October 2006 runoff election.

With the fall of Rodrigues, the UCKG's political line may undergo changes. The main figure is now Senator Marcello Crivella, nephew of the church founder. Despite his unproven political capacity, Crivella's public image and electoral potential currently surpass that of the UCKG itself, and he placed third for governor of the state of Rio de Janeiro in the first round of the October 2006 election, with almost 19 percent of the vote.

ACKNOWLEDGMENTS

My thanks go to my research assistant, Flávio Conrado, and to Lenildo Medeiros, advisor to Everaldo Dias, without whose help this study would not have been possible.

NOTES

1. According to the government census of 2000, we have the following ranking of Brazilian Protestant churches: Assemblies of God (32 percent of all Protestants); Brazilian Baptist Convention (12 percent); Christian Congregation (9 percent); Universal Church of the Kingdom of God (8 percent); Four-Square (5 percent); Adventists (5 percent); Lutherans (4 percent); Presbyterians (4 percent); God is Love (3 percent); Methodist (1 percent).

2. This literature includes Burdick (1993), Fernandes et al. (1998), Freston (1993a, 1993b, 1994, 1995, 1996, 2001), Mariano and Pierucci (1992), Novaes (1986), Pierucci (1989), and Pierucci and Prandi (1996).

3. As the sociological tradition stresses, an action can produce consequences not intended by the actor. In Weber's words (in Gerth and Mills 1946, 140), "the final result of political action frequently . . . has a totally inadequate and even paradoxical relationship to its original meaning."

4. Harvey Cox talks of the profound impact Benedita had on his perspectives regarding Latin American pentecostalism. She "was a six-foot three-inch detonator who exploded books full of theories and generalizations in minutes. . . . I was puzzled. What about all those articles I had read that told of the 'otherworldliness' of pentecostals? What about the accusations that pentecostalism itself is the product of calculated right-wing North American effort to woo Latin Americans away from Catholic liberation theology and radical social movements?" (1995, 165).

5. Respected in the 1990s in the civil society of Rio and among intellectuals for his social activities and left-wing politics, Caio Fábio fell from grace in 1998 because of an extramarital affair and because he was accused of receiving money to sell a dossier with supposedly damaging revelations regarding president Cardoso and cabinet ministers (Fonseca 2003).

6. "You must see me preach," he enthused during our interview. When I told him of an occasion I had seen him preach, he replied: "That was my first time, that doesn't count. Now I'm much better."

7. On the history and structure of the UCKG, see Freston (1993, 1999), Mariano (1999), and Corten, Dozon, and Oro (2003). Abroad, the church has done especially well in Portugal, Argentina, South Africa, and Mozambique. Its media include the weekly *Folha Universal*, with a circulation of over 1,100,000.

8. A candidate with a lower number of votes in a party (or coalition) with a high total may get elected, whereas a candidate with many more votes in a weak party may not.

9. While in charge in the state of Bahia, Rodrigues gave an interview to anthropologist David Lehmann. In Lehmann's words: "During our interview he was advising a distant colleague by telephone on how to avoid tax by conducting a financial transaction in a certain way and on what sort of transmitting equipment to buy for his radio station; he signed a cheque for US$17,000 in payment for a church he was taking over, and conducted various other real estate transactions. All this with a keen eye for legal and financial detail worthy of a dynamic business executive" (1996, 122).

10. Rodrigues claims the Universal Church only began to grow after it obtained a fifteen-minute radio slot just before an Umbanda program. It then became part of church strategy to lease slots just before or after Umbanda slots (Fonseca 1997).

11. The law limiting Brazilian presidents to only one term was changed in 1997, thus allowing the reelection of incumbent Fernando Henrique Cardoso. Resistance to the change in congress was overcome by a process of intense bargaining.

12. As the journalist Angélica Cruz wrote in the early days of this new phase: "Like the Marxists, the UCKG seems to be going through a period of revisionism. Lately, its media appears to be dominated by some sort of progressive demon-possession. In the *Folha Universal* the editorials look like something written by the PSTU [a party of the extreme left]. Between quotes from the Bible, they cry out against the effects of globalization and hit out at the Cardoso government and its economic team. In the early morning programs on TV Record, viewers are greeted by pastors and bishops in an oppositionist trance. All this has come out of the head of Bishop Rodrigues" (Cruz, *Noticia e Opinião*, October 10, 2000, available at www.no.com.br).

13. *Companheiro* is the word used by left-wing activists to refer to each other.

14. It is, however, true that rumors regarding Fanini's electoral aspirations predate the public reconciliation between him and the Universal Church in 1994 (Fanini having previously been one of the Universal Church's severest critics).

15. See Diamond, Linz, and Lipset (1989, 16): "In this study, then, democracy— or what Robert Dahl terms 'polyarchy'—denotes a system of government that meets three essential conditions: meaningful and extensive 'competition' among individuals and organized groups (especially political parties) for all effective positions of government power, at regular intervals and excluding the use of force; a highly inclusive level of 'political participation' in the selection of leaders and policies, at least through regular and fair elections, such that no major (adult) social group is excluded; and a level of 'civil and political liberties'—freedom of expression, freedom of the press, freedom to form and join organizations—sufficient to ensure the integrity of political competition and participation.'

16. "Social capital refers to features of social organization such as trust, norms and networks that can improve the efficiency of society by facilitating coordinated actions" (Putnam 1993, 167).

17. Adding up all those who earn less than two dollars per day, plus those classified as functionally illiterate, we reach a figure of almost one hundred million people, well over half the population. For a long time Brazil has had the most, or one of the most, unequal distributions of income in the world.

18. In the southern city of Londrina we see an example of this. The city council organizes a weekly celebration in the town hall. Even though the event is coordinated by an evangelical pastor, Catholics also participate. Each religion takes turns to preach the sermon. The event is transmitted live on a local evangelical radio station, which means its listeners sometimes tune in to priests and nuns preaching liberation theology.

19. Certain sectors of Brazilian Catholicism have in recent years "maintained a negative idea of politicians, parties and politics, which clearly limits their commitment to democracy" (Moisés 1995, 72).

Conclusion: Evangelicals and Democracy— the Experience of Latin America in Context

Daniel H. Levine

My first encounter with an evangelical street preacher in Latin America came in 1968, in the Guatemalan market town of Solalá. The market was in full swing, and in the midst of people buying, selling, and bargaining, a Protestant preacher was working the crowd. The majority of Guatemalans are Indians; the audience was entirely made up of Indian men and women, and the speaker, I remember, was preaching the gospel in Kakchiquel, the language of the region. Holding a Bible in his hands, he illustrated his sermon by pointing to a hand-painted canvas that depicted heaven, hell, the judgment of the nations, the temptations of this world, and the ways of the righteous and of the sinner. The canvas made me think of *The Pilgrim's Progress*. I found the scene stirring enough to save the slide for more than three decades, but at the time it seemed little more than an interesting sideshow. None of it fitted into any accepted scheme of things at the time.

In retrospect, it is easy to see this preacher as a precursor of the wave of Protestant, especially pentecostal Protestant, religious expansions that swept Guatemala and all of Central America in subsequent years. The religious experience was new, as was the leadership: ordinary, often nonwhite, and barely lettered men using a popular language, who recall the circuit-riding preachers of nineteenth-century North America. The signs were there, but they slipped by most observers.

Twenty years later, at rush hour on a Friday evening in the Venezuelan capital of Caracas, a friend dropped me off at the Petare Metro station, one of the busiest in the city. Petare is also the gateway to a vast collection of poor *barrios* spread out over the hills in the eastern edge of Caracas. Walking into the station I found myself in the midst of a large and enthusiastic crowd: not a concert, not a political meeting, not a market, but rather a pentecostal revival. There were preachers, there was music, and young men and women, courteous and well-dressed, circulated through the crowd inviting passersby to join them in prayer and to come to church. The atmosphere was warm and charged with energy and enthusiasm. I still remember the human warmth, the cultural effervescence, and the emotional power on display there.

I already knew intellectually about the advance of the Protestant churches, especially in poor neighborhoods. I had even, on a few occasions, heard the music, the clapping of hands, and the enthusiastic hymn-singing of the faithful, praising God late into the night. But never before had I directly experienced the human warmth, the cultural effervescence, the freshness, and the emotional power that I felt that evening in Petare. It reminded me of scenes I had experienced elsewhere, among groups inspired by the theology of liberation: neighborhood organizations, cooperatives, women's groups, health committees, and many others. Here as well, one encountered a sense of openness, an atmosphere of hope and cultural creativity, and the same strongly popular and working-class make-up of the crowd. That night in Petare, waiting for the train, I remember thinking: this is really the future of religion. The future is here, in these kinds of places, in these social spaces, with ordinary men and women like this. This is where the future of religion will be built.

Encounters like these could be repeated endlessly. As discrete moments, each has interest, color, and warmth. Taken together, they provide a window into the experience of change in religion, and in the place that religion claims and holds in society and politics across the region. The first point to make is that change is normal; the second is that religion is itself an important source of change. Not long ago, these statements would have been shocking to most students of religion. Religions were widely assumed to be carriers of "tradition," consigned by reigning theories of secularization to privatization, decline, and disappearance. Theoretical blinders play no ideological favorites: such views helped scholars and observers miss the religious roots of the civil rights movement in the United States just as they misread the surge of the Iranian revolution. Tocqueville's comment is apt. "The philosophers of the eighteenth century," he wrote, "explained the gradual weakening of beliefs in an altogether simple fashion. Religious zeal, they said, will be extinguished as freedom and enlightenment increase. It is unfortunate," he continued, "that the facts do not accord with this theory" ([1835] 2000; vol. 1, pt. 2, chap. 9, 282).

Patterns of Change in Latin America

When I first went to Latin America to study religion and politics, over thirty years ago, the great transformations with which we are all now familiar were just getting underway. To speak about religion at that time meant to speak about the Catholic Church, and "everyone knew" that Catholicism was a conservative and profoundly antidemocratic force, closely linked with the interests of oligarchies and power holders. The theoretical perspectives that guided most studies of religion and politics remained anchored in nineteenth-century stereotypes, according to which religion was by definition static, incapable of change, and condemned to at best privatization and more likely disappearance with the advance of science and modern culture. From this vantage point, when religion did surface in politics (in political rhetoric, or perhaps as a tool of mobilization) such instances were dismissed as undesirable hangovers from the past, when not explained away as the by-products of supposedly more basic casual factors such as social class or economic interest.

The very idea of studying religion and politics required special justification. Economics, which must be the religion of our times, was the preferred focus of attention and analytical model. At that time, when I was starting out, it was a major effort to convince others (including funding agencies!) that religion, and religion and politics, were worthy subjects of study. Now the effort is not so arduous. The repeated pressure of events that ran counter to expectations (the tragedies of Jonestown and Waco, the unexpected rise of the Christian Coalition to political prominence, and the Iranian Revolution, to name only a few) has impelled scholars to rethink long-established paradigms, abandon old theories, and slowly accept that what they see in the news is no short-term aberration, but rather the leading edge of something new. Theoretical changes have freed us from the blinders imposed by modernization theory: we now have new tools to understand religion's multiple roles in the public sphere.

For those of us who work and study in Latin America, the events just noted simply confirmed what was already present in our experience: that something really new, of possibly great significance, was being created in the relationship between religion and politics. We have had plenty to work with for a good half-century now. This book is a testament to how "hot" the topic of religion and politics has become, and to how vital the reality of the matter is throughout the world. It was not always so.

In the three decades or so since I first went to the region to study religion and politics, both Catholicism itself and scholarship on the relationship of religion to society and politics in Latin America have experienced a series of major transformations, "paradigm shifts," if I may be permitted to use that overworked term. On the ground throughout Latin America, four underlying trends have given shape and substance to change. To begin with, by any measure there is now *more religion, more instances and variety and accessibility of religion* than ever before. Where a typical town or neighborhood once could be safely assumed to have one church, sparsely attended at that, one now finds multiple, competing religious offerings: evangelical chapels and charismatic movements, street preachers and radio or television programs. One cannot get off a bus, exit a train station, turn on a radio, or stand in a public square almost anywhere in the region without encountering some kind of preacher.

The multiplication of religious instances and the greater accessibility of religion are concrete signs of religious pluralism: the five-hundred-year Catholic monopoly is gone. A story that not long ago could be told with confidence about how Catholicism supported and reflected the established order became a story in which religions (not only Catholic but also Protestant) have become sources of new ideas about how to organize society and politics, and how to lead the good life. The Catholic Church is no longer alone in speaking for religion: other churches compete for public voice and access. At the same time, a plurality of voices can be heard within both the Catholic and Protestant camps: different organizations, groups, and programs, often with autonomous resources and international funding.

These changes have been accompanied by fundamental transformation in the substance and focus of scholarship on religion, society, and politics. At the beginning of the period, there was in place a well-established tradition of legal and institutional studies, working with laws, treaties, and documents that dealt with the relation of states and church institutions. This was the stuff and substance of religion and politics for that school of thought. Many of us starting out at that time sneered at this work as excessively legalistic and hampered by a narrow understanding of politics, but much of great value remains from that body of work, most notably the insistence on the presence of church institutions and their relation to legal structures and political power. In the late 1950s and 1960s, a new kind of scholarship emerged that sought to link transformations in Catholicism, already underway in the region, to "development" and democracy. The idea was to explore the uncoupling of church institutions from longstanding alliances with state, political, and social elites and the construction of new norms and a new normative consensus in favor of democracy and development. Part of the impulse here came from attention to a series of new, lay-driven groups, most notably Christian Democratic political parties, who, it was hoped, would make possible a different, more assertively democratic kind of space of religious activism in politics. The emergence of these movements and parties, more independent of clerical control than earlier Catholic Action groups, and much more committed to democracy, was seen as a critical step in the creation of a different and much more progressive presence for religious leaders, organizations, and guiding values in the process of social change.

Just as these movements were getting under way, with added legitimacy from the Second Vatican Council, the ground was shifting in important ways throughout the region. In political terms, democracy was under siege, and military regimes took power in a number of major countries. The Cuban Revolution opened up new horizons for the left, and soon revolutionary movements began to pick up steam in Central America, and later in Peru. Within Catholicism, this is of course the period in which liberation theology first emerged with a sustained critique of inequality and injustice in society, politics, and the church itself. There was considerable enthusiasm in Catholic circles throughout the region for the vision liberation theology promoted (not development but rather basic change and liberation) and for the kinds of movements and alliances it promoted (grassroots communities, outreach, alliances with the left). Great hopes were placed in the possibilities for revolutionary change in Central America, hopes that gained new impetus with the 1979 Sandinista victory in Nicaragua. These hopes were matched elsewhere by expectations about the potential of new grassroots groups to become the seedbed for a new kind of politics, and the breeding ground for a new, active, and able citizenry. Terms like "civil society" and "social capital" only came into widespread use later, but expectations about the potential of civil society to change politics are what was at issue. Underlying all these hopes and expectations was a mostly unstated faith that once "the people" gained awareness and organized themselves, their united power would be unstoppable.

The gradual accumulation of empirical studies and the evolution of the movements themselves has revealed a very different kind of reality. These past decades have witnessed not an irresistible tide of the people "erupting" into churches and other institutions, but something more like a rising and then receding tide of movements. In case after case, movements proved fragile and vulnerable: dependent on the protection and sponsorship of sympathetic clergy, hierarchies, or religious orders, on transformations in the political sphere well beyond their control. Political allies turned out to be unreliable, and movements often divided, following divisions at other levels. In general terms, the autonomy of religiously inspired or supported groups (like many in "civil society") was greatly exaggerated, and they turned out to be exceptionally vulnerable to changes in church leadership, and to betrayal or abandonment by political allies. Many also proved vulnerable to openings in the political arena: as civil wars were gradually resolved and civilian politics returned, activists and resources flowed into other channels for action, such as political parties. By now it is clear that early hopes for a new politics will not be fulfilled. Everywhere in Latin America, transitions to democracy have been accompanied by demobilization and marginalization of popular movements. It is easier to hold groups together against a common enemy like the military than to choose among competing parties in an election (Oxhorn 2001, 1994).

The fact that political opening came accompanied by economic crisis put a premium on the availability of existing church and church-related networks and the presence of leaders and activists experienced at reaching across class lines to mobilize and deliver services assumed new prominence. In many cases, grassroots groups were supplemented or even replaced by NGOs, often with important transnational connections. The range is astonishing: human rights organizations, Catholic religious orders, missionary societies, and Protestant churches of all kinds, relief organizations and development agencies, research and educational foundations alongside environmental groups and efforts directed at specific sectors such as rural or urban trade unions, housing, or children. Groups like these organized throughout the region to make plans, broker resources, and provide services ranging from education to surplus food, health and agricultural extension to legal advice, cooperatives to housing projects. Although only a small proportion of the groups in question were explicitly religious in origin and sponsorship, many had clear links with religious groups. They shared ideas, agendas, personnel, and resources. Much of the staffing for such efforts came from the ranks of ex-clergy. It is not that churches or linked groups "stepped into the breach." What happened is better described as the widening of existing gaps, the weakening of state agencies, and the disappearance of other groups, leaving these organizations with fewer competitors.

The energy and commitment of members also turned out to have limits. It is never easy to move from the local and particular to the general and political. This transition was made all the more difficult by the fact that these were years of severe economic crisis throughout the region, a time when the struggle for survival of self and family made it hard for ordinary people to find time and resources for collective action. Most groups were overwhelmingly female. That women comprised the vast majority of the membership of grassroots religious groups has less to do with the supposedly greater piety of women than with the appeal of religiously sanctioned organizations to people for whom organization and activity outside the home was something new. Women quickly took the opportunities and became active in new ways across the region. Because church organizations are culturally sanctioned vehicles for women, they draw hitherto silent voices into public spaces. But many women remain wary of specifically political activism and constrained by family obligations, including pressure from male relatives to stay out of politics, which is seen as "men's work." Together these characteristics shape the kind of activism that most members are disposed to support. Group members would commit themselves with enthusiasm and bravery to local issues but resist recruitment for broader agendas; they would filter out activist and conflict-centered messages. The result was that they followed leaders only so far, but no further. Moreover, many activist women faced resistance from families and spouses: the choices were difficult, and often led to ultimate abandonment of activism (Blondet 1991; Drogus 1997b).

At the same time, throughout this period there was a steady and mostly unnoticed growth of Protestantism. All across the region, but with special force in Central America and Brazil, new churches proliferated, membership numbers took off, and chapels, storefront churches, and larger, more impressive edifices began to change the landscape. This movement gathered force through the 1980s and, once free of the Cold War pressures so notable in Central America, burst on the public scene with enormous energy and creativity in the 1990s. New churches and movements, many of them fundamentalist or pentecostal, soon overwhelmed the historical, immigrant-focused Protestantism long present throughout the region. As with Catholicism, existing scholarship about Protestantism in Latin America quickly became outdated, and new concepts were required to make sense of the new order of things that was being created in country after country.

Before the recent surge of growth, most scholarship was either intradenominational (historical or apologetic) or given to seeing new churches and conversion to them primarily as a "haven for the masses," offering solace and escape from the pressures of intense change and conflict. This body of work was joined in the 1970s and 1980s by a wealth of studies, often polemical, that depicted the growth of Protestantism in Cold War terms, as part of the outreach of the North American religious right. A related line of work depended on deducing political positions directly from a reading of theological texts, while another strove to fit the possible social, cultural, or political possibilities of religious change into a framework provided by certain conventional dichotomies, such as tradition versus modernity or patron-client relations. There was an obsession with what one might term the "numbers game," tracking the geometric growth of Protestantism throughout the region.

Landmark studies by Stoll (1990) and Martin (1990) helped put the issue of Protestantism, society, and politics in Latin America on the academic map in fruitful new ways. Eschewing the numbers game and moving confidently beyond the presumption that escape and solace exhausted the meaning of religious transformation, these and other authors (Garrard-Burnett 1998a; Peterson, Vásquez, and Williams 2001; Steigenga 2001) directed attention instead to the social changes that were creating a new potential base for the Protestant message and for its delivery, and to the long-term cultural and political transformations that these changes might entail (see Levine [1995] for a review of the issues).

Through the 1990s, these transformations in scholarship coming from the First World were pushed and pulled along by the emergence of a body of creative new thinking and academic work by scholars and activists from Asia, Africa, and, not least, Latin America. These new developments are well represented in the array of questions and data provided by Paul Freston and his collaborators, which add up, I think it fair to say, to a data-oriented, practical problem–focused kind of work that is directed less to the construction or validation of some theory of religious change, or the creation of a new kind of politics than to a close analysis of the formation of churches and groups, sources and patterns of leadership, alliances, and issues. This is an understandable and useful strategy, particularly given the exaggerations and often romantic expectations of much earlier work. But any scholarship that claims to want "just the facts" and nothing but the facts easily runs into trouble when it comes to explaining what facts are relevant and why. In addition to thinking about empirical patterns that the authors have turned up, and the kinds of data they have uncovered, it is also important to examine the explanatory assumptions they bring to bear: the theories, implicit or explicit, that situate any data effectively in context, and make for comparability across cases, so that we can say, with some confidence, that "evangelicals" on any range of issues have something in common apart from their self-proclaimed status as evangelicals.

The Chapters in This Volume

This brings me, at long last, to the chapters themselves. A number of important common themes are elaborated in detail in the conclusion of Paul Freston's *Evangelicals and Politics in Asia, Africa and Latin America* (2001) and are present, in greater or lesser degree, in all the chapters. From many, I have selected four:

- A concern to map the careers of activists and especially of politicians, candidates, and office-holders who are evangelicals
- A concern to explore the relation between evangelical growth and democratization, not only through what we might call direct politics (regime transitions, elections, legislative politics, participation in government) but also indirectly, through the creation and defense of instances of civic life and civil society
- As a spinoff from the theme of evangelicals and democracy, a beginning edge of concern for the other side of the coin, that is, how politics and involvement in politics affect evangelicals
- A broad interest in the role that new churches can and do play in the creation of "civil society" and "social capital" (these are, of course, notoriously elastic terms: one wag suggests that civil society is the chicken soup of democratic theory: whatever the difficulty, civil society is assumed to be good for you; it is no surprise, therefore, that usage varies here, but this is a theme that deserves a closer look)

These common themes are knit together into a coherent package by several shared commitments: a commitment to "get the facts," that is, to accumulate numbers and organizational details (of churches, denominations, and related organizations, of explicitly evangelical political parties or coalitions, candidates, or office-holders) as a foundation for future work; a commitment to steer clear, for now, of "grand theories"; a commitment to use knowledge to enhance the potential contribution evangelicals can make to the construction and survival of democracies; and finally, of course, a broad commitment to discover what it all means for the evangelical movement as such, and for its future.

The authors provide us with a remarkable wealth of information about how evangelicals have gotten involved in explicitly political activities. Fonseca works on the recruitment and experience of activists and leaders, building in creative and ingenious ways from biographies of individual politicians to a sort of collective portrait of evangelical legislators. He then uses this material deftly as an entry point for a rich analysis of alliances and coalitions. The Brazilian case is especially interesting because, in contrast to every other of which I am aware in Latin America, evangelical politics in Brazil has developed its own dominating presence: the Universal Church of the Kingdom of God, or simply, the Universal Church. In little over a quarter of a century, the Universal Church has accumulated followers, trained leaders, acquired legitimacy, created a formidable media empire, begun transnational outreach, and developed a self-conscious and very practical political strategy. Rather than establish a party of its own, the Universal Church has hedged its bets by maintaining a presence in many parties, counting on strong internal discipline to provide coherence. To ensure reliability, rank-and-file believers, including many professionals, were replaced as candidates by bishops and pastors.

In Brazil, political figures and office-holders identified as evangelical are present in political parties all across the ideological spectrum, from the left (the Worker's Party, in government since 2003) to the right and in between. This very diversity, along with the monolithic character of the Universal Church itself, suggests two points. Hopes for a confessional state are no longer on the table: at issue is more religious involvement as salt and light to politics, rather than an open church-state alliance. The Brazilian pattern also raises questions about how recruitment to politics as such may go counter to or constrain the internal democracy of churches and church involvement locally. Earlier scholarship saw churches as building public space and civil society as a contribution to democratization: church control across parties and associations raises questions about the depth, extent, and possible long-term viability of such democratizing influence.

Samson's work on Guatemala shows us another side of the recruitment issue. This is a case where the possible involvement of the churches in politics was so skewed by Cold War issues and by the dominating figure of General Efraín Ríos Montt (not to mention the subsequent political disgrace of evangelical president Elías Serrano) that in the wake of war and a slow consolidation of civilian politics, we find *no* evangelical parties, no block of self-identified evangelical deputies, and little or no expectation about "the new Israel." Present instead is a diverse collection of lower level activities with an important involvement of churches in core issues such as human rights, ethnic reconciliation, and peace.

The overall record suggests that evangelical political parties, defined and marketed as such, have not done well. They have not been able to "deliver" the evangelical vote, they have not attracted masses of voters of any kind, and, perhaps most damaging, they have proven no more resistant to corruption than any other kind of political party. Hopes that the involvement of evangelicals would moralize and sanitize political discourse and the political order have clearly not been realized. Darío Lopez explores this matter in the Peruvian case, drawing a clear and valuable distinction between on the one hand a small group of evangelical politicians, legislators, and office-holders (most of whom were thoroughly corrupted by the Fujimori-Montesinos regime, which corrupted most groups and leaders) and, on the other, the rich involvement of activists and ordinary people in civil society, in survival associations in the cities and Rondas Campesinas in the countryside. His work fits well with a large body of writing that shows how such organizations in civil society moved from defense (of life, health, or neighborhood and family) to a broader agenda of self-government and activism, pulling many hitherto silent voices into political action.

The second general theme is the relation of evangelicals to democratization and to the consolidation of democracy. Evangelicals did not play a particularly prominent role in most of the region's transitions to democracy, and I think it fair to say that with the exception of cooperation in human rights work, and (in the Central American cases) cooperation in helping broker an end to armed conflict, the weight of evidence suggests that the potential impact of evangelicals on democracy is greater through indirect means. With the gradual consolidation of competitive civilian politics, the presence of evangelicals, self-consciously identified as such, in ordinary political activity (campaigns and elections, office-holding, associational life, lobbying) has become a well-established fact throughout the region, with greatest prominence in Brazil. This is something very new in Latin American experience, and raises a host of questions, including one of great importance that is not discussed in most of the chapters. The question is this: how and why did a religious discourse that historically viewed politics as alien, corrupted, and dangerous, that instead focused individual and community energies on spreading the good news and winning souls and on building communities of faith, come to see politics as a legitimate and even necessary field of action for the faithful? The children of light may once have been enjoined to avoid those of darkness: now they see politics, despite dangers and temptations, as part of their mission and responsibility. How did this happen? Such a question is of course not unique to the evangelicals of Latin America. The same can and has been asked about the rise of the religious right in the United States, as well as about the transformation of Iranian Shi'ism from quietism to activism, or the emergence of so-called fundamentalist Islam.

A simple answer is, of course, that not every one has changed: separationist groups remain. Where activism and involvement in politics have emerged on a grand scale, as in the United States or Iran, a sense of threat combined with a perception of moral crisis was a spur to getting involved. In these and other cases, the subsequent development of sustained organization and mobilization aligned in some way to religion has depended on lengthy, and for the most part unnoticed, periods of institution-building and the accumulation of resources and skills. Perceptions of threat and moral crisis are certainly understandable in Latin America, given the well-known political, economic, and social disasters the region has experienced in recent decades. Anyway, recruitment to the new churches has been so intense, and the curve of growth so steep, that all kinds of people, with already established understanding, connections, and skills, joined the new churches, bringing themselves and their previous lives into the new communities. People do not necessarily give up all other ties when they take up a new one, even if that may be a stated goal. They may continue to belong to unions, read newspapers, and have political opinions. This reality undercuts fears of a monolithic "evangelical bloc." Most of the survey studies I have seen make it absolutely clear that evangelicals are, broadly speaking, similar to their nonevangelical counterparts in terms of their distribution of opinion, memberships, and so on.

The third general theme, how politics can affect the evangelicals, could well be subtitled "politics bites back." On the evidence of these chapters, evangelicals are learning to play the political game, and that can be a mixed blessing. This is particularly vivid in the portrait of Bishop Rodrigues of the Universal Church, who is, to put it plainly, very willing to wheel and deal, and very good at it. This same ability and disposition is also evident, in less savory terms, in the careers of evangelical politicians corrupted by the Fujimori-Montesinos regime in Peru, or in the downfall of Guatemala's evangelical president Elías Serrano. If nothing else, these and similar cases remind us that evangelical politicians are also subject to the temptations and woes of politics. Indeed, many have been eager to be used, hungry for the recognition that political figures can provide them, without always calculating well the risks. The danger is clear: if the new churches become overly identified with any given politician, movement, or regime, they risk losing when and if their patrons lose, and of suffering by association as they suffer. This has begun to happen.

Max Weber ([1919] 1978) addressed this issue in his famous speech "Politics as a Vocation." Speaking just after the end of World War I to a German audience searching for guidance and a moral anchor, Weber was anxious to underscore the distinction between what he called an *ethic of ultimate ends* (good or evil, building the Kingdom of God) and an *ethic of responsibility*. In his view, politics required an ethic of responsibility, because such an ethic forces actors to take account of consequences. In contrast, working in politics with an ethic of ultimate ends endangered not only politics but the ultimate ends as well. He wrote:

> He who seeks the salvation of his soul and of other should not
> seek it along the avenues of politics, for the quite different tasks of
> politics can only be solved by violence. Everything that is striven
> for through political action operating with violent means and
> following an ethic of responsibility endangers the salvation of the
> soul. If, however, one chases after the ultimate good in a war of
> beliefs following a pure ethic of absolute ends, then the goals may be
> damaged and discredited for generations, because the responsi-
> bility for consequences is lacking. (222)

Earlier in the same text, Weber spoke of the Sermon on the Mount and its ethic of peace:

> By the Sermon on the Mount, we mean the absolute ethic of
> the gospel which is a more serious matter than those who are fond
> of quoting these commandments today believe. This ethic is no
> joking matter, and the same holds for this ethic as has been said
> of causality in science: it is not a cab which one can have stop-
> ped at one's pleasure: it is all or nothing. (224)

The fourth and final theme is the potential contribution of evangelicals to the creation and strengthening of civil society and social capital, and in this way to democracy. The concepts of civil society and social capital are notoriously elastic, and efforts to define and delimit their scope have fueled seemingly endless debate. The reality of the matter is equally diverse and open-ended. Whatever civil society or social capital may mean, there is general agreement that a vast range of groups and kinds of behavior are included. I limit myself here to a few specifications that may be helpful.

Part of the rediscovery of civil society in recent years has involved a renewed appreciation for the role that religion, churches, individuals, and religiously inspired, sponsored, or financed groups of all kinds can play in society and politics. Many scholars have returned to the work of Tocqueville, who was so impressed by the role religion played in the United States in the 1830s, so different from what he knew in France. For Tocqueville, the significance of the relation of religion to American democracy lay in its indirect character. The society was notably religious, despite (or perhaps because of) the absence of any established religion. Tocqueville situated the American pattern of religion within a broader collection of what he called "mores": manners, styles of social interaction, family patterns, ideas about equality and hierarchy, and reinforcing links between civil and political associations that together gave American democracy its special character. In the absence of an established church, religion achieved influence through indirect means. Working through congregations and independent of state power, religion provided Americans with a generative base for norms of participation, equality, and liberty, as well as concrete spaces for putting them into practice. Tocqueville wrote:

> Religion, which, among Americans, never mixes directly in the government of society, should therefore be considered as the first of their political institutions; if it does not give them the taste for freedom, it singularly facilitates their use of it . . . On my arrival in the United States it was the religious aspect of the country that first struck my eye. As I prolonged my stay, I perceived the great political consequences that flowed from these new faces. ([1835] 2000; vol. 1, pt. 2, chap. 9, 280–82)

Tocqueville suggests a few pointers of particular relevance to our cases. The skills he mentions are very specific: literacy, speaking in public, making connections outside the locality. In her work on congregations in the United States, Nancy Ammerman suggests that congregations are prime spaces for acquiring such civil skills and for building social and civil capital. She writes: "If social capital is the basic stuff of organization and connection, civic capital is the repertoire of skills and connections necessary for political life. Beyond association and trust, civic skills involve especially the arts of communication, planning and decision making" (1997, 364). Congregations are a growing and increasingly diverse source of such community involvement. Moreover, "congregations are able to expend social capital in service to the community because they are recognized as legitimate places for investment by people with social capital to spend" (367).

The central point is that religious groups both generate and attract such skills. In contemporary Latin America, as elsewhere, churches and church-related or sponsored groups of all kinds are part of a broad spectrum of groups increasingly prominent in society and politics over the last twenty years: neighborhood groups, human rights groups, women's associations, survival organizations, business federations, cooperatives, cultural groups, old and new trade unions, and the like. Added to the sporadic growth of real local government, this proliferation of organizational life has created a host of new public spaces—figuratively as venues for getting together, and literally in the form of new buildings and meeting rooms everywhere visible. That many of these movements fail, as they do, does not mean that nothing is left. Activists may migrate, and skills and energies turn up somewhere new and unexpected. Anyway, the key question is not so much the group itself as the possibilities of action and skills and their transfer to other areas. Indeed, strong, tightly structured groups may do less to promote the skills and the social capital of interest here than those with weak ties that make possible connections and information flows across groups (Granovetter 1973; C. Smith 1998).

Conclusion

I conclude with a few summary observations about where we are now in scholarship on evangelicals and democracy. Needless to say, the relations of religion, society, and politics are highly dynamic and constantly changing. The same is true for the methods and theories that scholars use to approach and make sense of that reality. Even what we take as "relevant facts" has changed. In a very real way, scholarship is always behind the curve, struggling to keep up with and make sense of the innovations being created all the time in all societies and traditions. This is as it should be.

Having acknowledged that fact, it seems to me that the work collected here pushes the debate ahead in very positive ways. As a group, the authors have taken a decisive step beyond Cold War dichotomies and simple deductions from texts or doctrine. They do not play the numbers game, but look instead to the meaning and structure of church growth. They have also pushed analysis fruitfully beyond attention to conventional dichotomies like tradition and modernity. In this sense, the research is more focused and realist than, say, that associated with the University of Chicago Fundamentalism Project. At the same time, the authors nuance the meaning of politics beyond candidates and elections, including these but going much further.

Together, these positive characteristics add up to a much more realistic understanding of religion, of politics, and of the possible relations between them, and take us well beyond the astonishment and disapproval so often found in early scholarship about "the politicization of religion," as if the political involvement of religion were some kind of temporary confusion, an aberration to be corrected as "development" and the growth of science proceeded on their appointed paths. Such a characterization inappropriately conflates the separation of church and state (for example in the United States, where it has never been absolute) with the separation of religion from politics, which has never been on the table, much less in the past fifty years. In Latin America, religion (in this case the Catholic Church) was pushed and pulled to the center stage of public action in the 1980s by a powerful combination of new ideas, effective leaders, and populations eager to make sense of their situation and find moral sanction and allies in their search for solutions. As circumstances changed, religion has, not surprisingly, moved off center stage. But moving off center stage does not mean moving entirely out of the public sphere. Hopes that the restoration of democracy would bring a thorough depoliticization of religion have already been disappointed.

Why expect religion to be depoliticized in Latin America, when religious issues and groups flourish in politics all around the world, not least in the United States? At issue is not depoliticization or abandonment of the public sphere, but rather a shift in who speaks and what exactly they say. The issue before us is not how religion and politics are to be separated: that is an illusion. The challenge, practical and theoretical, is rather to understand points of interaction and synthesis, and to make sense of the inevitable role religion and religious individuals and themes will play on the public stage.

With respect to the possible and actual contribution evangelicals may make now or in the future to consolidating and defending democracy in Latin America, I think one has to say that for now the jury is still out. The period of time is short, the record is mixed, both across cases and within them, with the explicitly political and the civil society spheres often working at cross-purposes. Anyway, democracy and democratic consolidations obviously depend on a lot a more than religion. What we can say is that there have indeed been positive contributions and some clear learning from mistakes. The end of the Cold War has helped, and there is some clear adaptation to playing the political game with the very present danger, of course, of being played by it. Religious political parties seem unlikely to have much success: as Tocqueville suggested long ago, the more fruitful and long-lasting contributions are indirect.

The pluralization of religious voices has immediate consequences for democracy. In a plural environment, it is in everyone's interest to maintain an open civil society with guarantees of free speech and equal access to institutions and to public spaces. The continuing erosion of Catholicism's monopoly status thus bears on a host of traditional issues from censorship and education to subsidies and representation in government commissions, committees, and public platforms. Pluralization also suggests that building and sustaining a new role will require groups to play the old politics more skillfully and more consistently than in the past. This means sustaining of grassroots democracy while working on allies and connections and assuming a realistic bargaining stance to politics. Groups need to bargain for better terms with everyone and enter into alliances only with great care and caution. Allies, connections, resources, and the shield they provide remain of critical importance. The point to bear in mind is that groups and collections of activists remain a vital presence, above all at the local level. They have been central to the construction of popular movements, and have energized urban politics throughout the region. Is this failure, or do we need a different measure of success?

There are several themes or topics, absent from most of these chapters, that need to be addressed by future publications:

1. Attention to transnational movements and transnational phenomena generally.
2. A broad comparative frame of reference, to set developments in Latin America against comparable changes in a range of cultures, religious traditions, and political situations; Latin American experience has much to teach and much to learn from others.
3. A focused look at the mass media, especially television, which are so important and so ubiquitous in Latin America.
4. To the extent possible, the collection of comparable attitudinal and membership data, for example through surveys and more information on the dynamic of actual beliefs and practices.

This is obviously a research agenda for a generation, and for reasons of time and space I limit myself here to comments on the first two. Systematic attention to transnational movements, associations, and connections would make a considerable contribution to understanding the changing role of evangelicals in Latin American society and politics. Any list of such phenomena would include at least the following: NGOs, educational and media networks, church federations, publications, regional meetings, migration, and transnational church memberships. All these do a lot to move ideas, people, and resources continuously across national boundaries.

In villages and urban neighborhoods throughout Latin America it is common to encounter Dutch, French, German, Canadian, Swiss, North American, and other agencies, groups, and experts, all with some religious connection, financing and helping to run an enormous range of programs from bee keeping to schooling, from laying water piping to promoting inoculations and supporting health clinics. There is a material structure to religious change, a material structure comprised precisely of contacts and connections like this. It is possible to track these, to track the career of a pamphlet or video.

A broad-ranging comparative analysis is also important. Many of the issues of interest here have been explored at length in an extensive literature on the United States, not only about fundamentalist but also about the African American churches and the civil rights movement, antiabortion movements, religious media conglomerates, and interfaith coalitions of all kinds, including those focused on housing, hunger, peace, migrants and migration, labor, ecology, and many more. Such work also underscores the strength of the localism at the core of many evangelical churches (Warner 1993) and the fact that this very strength may work against the construction of big, permanent, politically effective movements. There is also a wealth of relevant historical scholarship, such as Hatch's (1989) wonderful work on the nineteenth-century explosion of popular religion and popular preaching in the United States, which he refers to as "storming heaven through the back door." There is much to learn from these experiences, as well as from the wealth of scholarship on Islam, or on religion and politics in South and Southeast Asia, or Africa, work that examines many themes of great interest and highlights important commonalities, including the role of the mass media and the explosion of "unofficial" churches and popular preaching.

In short, this book sets us on a fruitful path and gives us much to work with as we continue to try to keep up with an ever-changing reality.

References

Adams, Abigail Elizabeth, 1999. "Engendering Evangelical Culture between Highland Guatemala and the United States." Ph.D. diss., University of Virginia.

Aguiló, Federico. 1994. "La cuna olvidada de sendero." *Cuarto Intermedio* 34 (November):31–45.

Ammerman, Nancy. 1997. *Congregation and Community*. New Brunswick, N.J.: Rutgers University Press.

Anfuso, Joseph, and David Sczepanski. 1984. *Efraín Ríos Montt: Siervo o dictador?* Barcelona: Editorial Clie.

Annis, Sheldon. 1987. *God and Production in a Guatemalan Town*. Austin: University of Texas Press.

Bardeguez, Jorge. 1998. *Los evangélicos y las cuestiones públicas en el Pacífico Nicargüense*. Managua: CAV-CIEETS.

Barrett, David, and Todd Johnson. 1999. "Annual Statistical Table on Global Mission." *International Bulletin of Missionary Research* 23(1):24–25.

Bastian, Jean Pierre. 1986. *Breve historia del Protestantismo en América Latina*. Mexico City: CUPSA.

———. 1990. *Historia del Protestantismo en América Latina*. Mexico City: Casa Unida de Publicaciones.

———. 1997. *La mutación religiosa de América Latina*. Mexico City: Fondo de Cultura Económica.

Bautz, Wolfgang, Noel González, and Javier Orozco. 1994. *Política y religión. Estudio de caso: Los evangélicos en Nicaragua*. Managua: Friedrich Ebert Stiftung, CIEETS.

Bebbington, David. 1989. *Evangelicalism in Modern Britain*. London: Unwin Hyman.

Beckford, James A. 1999. "The Management of Religious Diversity in England and Wales with Special Reference to Prison Chaplaincy." *MOST Journal on Multicultural Societies* 1(2).

Benjamin, Medea, and Maísa Mendonça. 1997. *Benedita da Silva: An Afro-Brazilian Woman's Story of Politics and Love.* Oakland, Calif.: Institute for Food and Development Policy.

Berryman, Phillip. 1984. *The Religious Roots of Rebellion: Christians in Central American Revolutions.* Maryknoll, N.Y.: Orbis.

Blancarte, Roberto. 1993. "Religion and Constitutional Change in México, 1988–1992." *Social Compass* 40(4):555–69.

Blondet, Cecilia. 1991. *Las mujeres y el poder. Una historia de villa el Salvador.* Lima: Instituto de Estudios Peruanos.

———. 1993. "Poder y organizaciones populares: Estrategias de integración social." In *El poder en el Perú*, ed. Augusto Alvarez, 189–201. Lima: Apoyo.

———. 2001. "Lecciones de la participación política de las mujeres." JCAS Occasional Paper no. 9. Osaka: n.p.

Bogenschild, Thomas E. 1992. "The Roots of Fundamentalism in Liberal Guatemala: Missionary Ideologies and Local Response, 1882–1944." Ph.D. diss., University of California, Berkeley.

Bourdieu, Pierre. 1989. *O poder simbólico.* Lisboa: Difel.

Brooke, James. 1990. "Another Chapter Due in the Strange Story of Peru's Election." *New York Times*, April 15, 1990, p. E2.

Brusco, Elizabeth. 1993. "The Reformation of Machismo: Asceticism and Masculinity among Colombian Evangelicals." In *Rethinking Protestantism in Latin America*, ed. Virginia Garrard-Burnett and David Stoll, 143–58. Philadelphia: Temple University Press.

Buarque, Cristovam. 1992. *A Revolução na esquerda e a invenção do Brasil.* São Paulo: Paz e Terra.

Burdick, John. 1993. *Looking for God in Brazil.* Berkeley: University of California Press.

Campos, Erick. 2001. "Transformemos a Guatemala." *Prensa Libre*, March 9.

Cantón Delgado, Manuela. 1998. *Bautizados en fuego.* South Woodstock, Vt.: Plumsock Mesoamerican Studies.

Casanova, José. 1994. *Public Religions in the Modern World.* Chicago: University of Chicago Press.

CEG (Conferencia Episcopal de Guatemala). 1998. *Comunicado del consejo permanente de la conferencia episcopal de Guatemala acerda de la entrada en vigencia del códo de la niñ y de la juventud.* Guatemala City: n.p.

Chávez Toro, Carlos. 1997. "Gilberto Siura sale al frente de quienes atacan sus célebres leyes: Se me han prendido." *VSD, La República* [Lima], September 5, pp.10–11.

Chiappari, Christopher Louis. 1999. "Rethinking Religious Practice in Highland Guatemala: An Ethnography of Protestantism, Maya Religion, and Magic." Ph.D. diss., University of Minnesota.

Cleary, Edward. 1997. "Introduction: Pentecostals, Prominence, and Politics." In Cleary and Gambino 1997, 1–24.

Cleary, Edward, and Hannah Stewart-Gambino. 1997. *Power, Politics, and Pentecostals in Latin America*. Boulder, Colo.: Westview Press.

Coleman, James. 1988. "Social Capital in the Creation of Human Capital." *American Journal of Sociology* 94:95–120.

Comisión para el Esclarecimiento Histórico. 1999. *Guatemala, memoria del silencio*. Guatemala City: n.p.

CONEP (Consejo Nacional Evangélico del Perú). 1991. "Evaluación del proceso electoral 1990." Lima: n.p.

Coronel, José. 1996. "Violencia política y respuestas campesinas en Huanta." In Degregori 1996b, 29–116.

Corten, André, Jean-Pierre Dozon, and Ari Pedro Oro, eds. 2003. *Les nouveaux conquérants de la foi: Une église brésilienne á prétention universelle*. Paris: Karthala.

Cortés, Benjamín. 1989. *Reforma y conquista: América Latina 500 años después*. Managua: CIEETS.

Cotler, Julio. 1994. *Política y sociedad en el Perú: Cambios y continuidades*. Lima: IEP.

Cox, Harvey. 1995. *Fire from Heaven: The Rise of Pentecostal Spirituality and the Reshaping of Religion in the Twenty-first Century*. Reading, Mass.: Addison-Wesley.

Cruz, Angélica. 2000. "A nova esquerda." *Noticia e Opiñiao*, October 10. www.no.com.br.

Dahl, Robert. 1971. *Polyarchy: Participation and Opposition*. New Haven: Yale University Press.

Defensoría del Pueblo. 2000. *Elecciones 2000: Supervisión de la defensoría del pueblo*. Lima: Defensoría del Pueblo.

Degregori, Carlos. 1996a. "Ayacucho después de la violencia." In Degregori 1996b, 15–28.

———, ed. 1996b. *Las rondas campesinas y la derrota de sendero luminoso*. Lima: IEP.

de Gruchy, John. 1995. *Christianity and Democracy*. Cambridge: Cambridge University Press.

De la Jara, Ernesto. 1998. "1980–1998: Violencia política y derechos humanos." *Ideele* 113 (November):4–12.

Del Pino, Ponciano. 1996. "Tiempos de guerra y de dioses: Ronderos, evangélicos y senderistas en el valle del río Apurímac." In Degregori 1996b, 117–88.

Demerath III, Nicholas Jay. 2001. *Crossing the Gods: World Religions and Worldly Politics*. New Brunswick, N.J.: Rutgers University Press.

D'Epinay, Cristian Lalive. 1968. *El refugio de las masas*. Santiago: Editorial El Pacífico.

Diamond, Larry. 1996. "Toward Democratic Consolidation." In Diamond and Plattner 1996b, 227–40.

———. 1997. "Introduction: In Search of Consolidation." In *Consolidating the Third Wave Democracies*, ed. Larry Diamond, Marc Plattner, Yun-han Chu, and Hung-mao Tien, xv–xlix. Baltimore: Johns Hopkins University Press.

———. 1999. *Developing Democracy: Toward Consolidation*. Baltimore: Johns Hopkins University Press.

———. 2002. "Elections without Democracy: Thinking about Hybrid Regimes." *Journal of Democracy* 13(2):21–35.

Diamond, Larry, Juan Linz, and Seymour Martin Lipset. 1989. *Democracy in Developing Countries: Latin America*. London: Lynne Rienner.

Diamond, Larry, and Marc Plattner. 1996a. Introduction in Diamond and Plattner 1996b, ix–xxxiii.

———, eds. 1996b. *The Global Resurgence of Democracy.* Baltimore: Johns Hopkins University Press.

Diaz, Miguel. 1991. "El evangelio de Cambio 90: Los protagonistas de una tempestuosa alianza política y religiosa." *La Revista Domingo de La República,* June 9, pp. 10–12.

Dines, Alberto, Florestan Fernandes Júnior, and Nelma Salomão. 2000. *História do Poder: 100 años de política no Brasil.* Vol. 2, *Ecos do parlamento.* São Paulo: Editora 34.

Dodson, Michael. 1997. "Pentecostals, Politics, and Public Space in Latin America." In Cleary and Stewart-Gambino 1997, 25–40.

Drogus, Carol. 1997a. "Private Power or Public Power: Pentecostalism, Base Communities, and Gender." In Cleary and Stewart-Gambino 1997, 55–75.

———. 1997b. *Women, Religion, and Social Change in Brazil's Popular Church.* South Bend, Ind.: University of Notre Dame Press.

Ebel, Roland. 1972. "Political Modernization in Three Guatemalan Indian Communities." In *Community Culture and National Change,* ed. M. A. L. Harrison and R. Wauchope. New Orleans: Middle American Research Institute, Tulane University.

Ebel, Roland, Raymond Taras, and James Cochrane. 1991. *Political Culture and Foreign Policy in Latin America: Case Studies from the Circum-Caribbean.* Albany: State University of New York Press.

Falla, Ricardo. 1994. *Massacres in the Jungle: Ixcán, Guatemala, 1975–1982.* Boulder, Colo.: Westview Press.

Fernandes, Reuben César, Pierre Sanchis, Otário Velho, Leandro Carneiro, Cecilia Mariz, and Clara Mafra. 1998. *Novo nascimento: Os evangélicos em casa, na igreja e na política.* Rio de Janeiro: Mauad.

Fischer, Edward F., and R. McKenna Brown. 1996. *Maya Cultural Activism in Guatemala.* Austin: University of Texas Press.

Flores Galindo, Alberto. 1988. *Buscando un Inca.* Lima: Editorial Horizonte.

Fonseca, Alexandre Brasil. 1997. "Além da evangelização: Interpretações a respeito da presença das igrejas evangélicas na mídia brasileira." *Cominicação e Política* 4(2):81–116.

———. 1998. "A maior bancada evangélica." *Tempo e Presença* 302:20–23. Centro Ecumênico de Documentaçãoe Informação (CEDI).

———. 2003. *Evangélicos e mídia no Brasil.* Bragança Paulista, Brazil: EDUSF.

Fonseca, Juan. 2000. "Entre el conflicto y la consolidación: Protestantismo y modernización en el Perú (1915–1930)." Licenciatura thesis, Pontificia Universidad Católica del Perú, Lima.

Fortuny, Patricia. 1994. "Cultura política entre los protestantes en México." In *Cultura política y educación cívica,* ed. Jorge Alonso, 397–427. Mexico City: Porrua.

Freston, Paul. 1993a. "Brother Votes for Brother: The New Politics of Protestantism in Brazil." In *Rethinking Protestantism in Latin America,* ed. Virginia Garrard-Burnett and David Stoll, 66–110. Philadelphia: Temple University Press.

————. 1993b. "Evangélicos e política no Brasil: Da constituinte ao impeachment." Ph.D. diss., Universidade Estadual de Campinas, Brazil.

————. 1994. "Popular Protestants in Brazilian Politics: A Novel Turn in Sect-State Relations." *Social Compass* 41(4):537–70.

————. 1995. "Pentecostalism in Brazil: A Brief History." *Religion* 25:119–33.

————. 1996. "The Protestant Eruption into Modern Brazilian Politics." *Journal of Contemporary Religion* 11(2):147–68.

————. 1999. "Neo-pentecostalism in Brazil: Problems of Definition and the Struggle for Hegemony." *Archives de Sciences Sociales des Religions* 105:145–62.

————. 2000. "The Political Evolution of Brazilian Pentecostalism, 1986–2000." In *Imaginaires, politiques, et pentecôtismes*, ed. A. Corten and A. Mary, 287–305. Paris: Karthala.

————. 2001. *Evangelicals and Politics in Asia, Africa and Latin America.* Cambridge: Cambridge University Press.

————. 2004. *Protestant Political Parties: A Global Survey.* Aldershot, England: Ashgate.

Gálvez Borrell, Víctor, and Alberto Esquit Choy. 1997. *The Mayan Movement Today: Issues of Indigenous Culture and Development in Guatemala.* Guatemala City: FLACSO.

García, Carlos. 1992. "5 de abril: Golpe bajo a la democracia." *Ideele* 37 (May):10–11.

García Sayán, Diego. 1988. "Presentación." In *Democracia y Violencia en el Perú,* ed. Diego García Sayan, 11–18. Lima: CEPEI.

Garotinho, Anthony. 2001. *Virou o carro, virou a minha vida.* Rio de Janeiro: Soma.

Garrard-Burnett, Virginia. 1989. "Protestantism in Rural Guatemala, 1987–1954." *Latin American Research Review* 24(2):127–42.

————. 1998a. *Protestantism in Guatemala: Living in the New Jerusalem.* Austin: University of Texas Press.

————. 1998b. "Transnational Protestantism." *Journal of Interamerican and World Affairs* 40(3):117–25.

Gaskill, Newton. 1997. "Rethinking Protestantism and Democratic Consolidation in Latin America." *Sociology of Religion* 58(1):669–91.

Gerth, H. H., and C. Wright Mills. 1946. *From Max Weber: Essays in Sociology.* Oxford: Oxford University Press.

Gills, Barry, Joel Rocamora, and Richard Wilson. 1993. *Low Intensity Democracy: Political Power in the New World Order.* London: Pluto Press.

Giumbelli, Emerson. 2000. "O fim da religião: Controvérsias acerca das 'seitas' e da 'liberdade religiosa' no Brasil e na França." Ph.D. diss., Museu Nacional, Universidade Federal do Rio de Janeiro.

Goldin, Liliana R., and Brent Metz. 1997. "Invisible Converts to Protestantism in Highland Guatemala." In *Crosscurrents in Indigenous Spirituality: Interface of Maya, Catholic, and Protestant Worldviews,* ed. G. Cook, 61–80. Leiden: Brill.

Goto, Rafael. 1993. "Los evangélicos conquistando ciudadanía." *Caminos* 43 (December):8–9.

Granovetter, M. 1973. "The Strength of Weak Ties." *American Journal of Sociology* 78(6):1360–80.

Greenberg, Linda Joan. 1984. "Illness and Curing among Mam Indians in Highland Guatemala: Cosmological Balance and Cultural Transformation." Ph.D. diss., University of Chicago.

Grenfell, James. 1995. "The Participation of Protestants in Politics in Guatemala." Master's thesis, Oxford University.

Grompone, Romeo. 1991. "Fujimori: Razones y desconciertos." In *Elecciones 1990: Demonios y redentores en el nuevo Perú*, ed. Carlos Degregori and Romeo Grompone, 19–67. Lima: IEP.

Gutierrez, Tomás. 2000. *El "hermano" Fujimori: Evangélicos y poder político en el Perú del '90*. Lima: Ediciones AHP.

———, ed. 1996. *Protestantismo y política en América Latina y el Caribe*. Lima: CEHILA.

Haber, Paul. 1997. "Social Movements and Socio-Political Change in Latin America." *Current Sociology* 45 (January):121–40.

Hatch, Nathan. 1989. *The Democratization of American Christianity*. New Haven: Yale University Press.

Haynes, Jeff. 1997. *Democracy and Civil Society in the Third World*. Cambridge: Polity.

Hernández Castillo, Rosalva. 2000. "Los protestantismo indígenas de frente al siglo XXI. Religión e identidad entre los mayas de Chiapas." *Religiones y Sociedad* 4(8):57–74.

Huntington, Samuel. 1991. *The Third Wave: Democratization in the Late Twentieth Century*. Norman: University of Oklahoma Press.

———. 1996. "Democracy's Third Wave." In Diamond and Plattner 1996b, 3–25.

IENPG (Iglesia Evangélica Nacional Presbiteriana de Guatemala). 1982. *Apuntes para la historia*. Guatemala City: Iglesia Evangélica Nacional Presbiteriana de Guatemala.

INDEF. 1998. *Directorio de las iglesias Protestantes en Nicaragua*. Managua: n.p.

Inocencio, Juan. 1998. "Una experiencia misiológica protestante en el sur del Perú: Eduardo Francisco Forga, Arequipa, 1901–1906." Master's thesis, Facultad Evangélica Orlando E. Costas, Lima.

Ireland, Rowan. 1999. "Popular Religions and the Building of Democracy in Latin America: Saving the Tocquevillian Parallel." *Journal of Interamerican Studies and World Affairs* 41(4):111–36.

Isbell, Billie Jean. 1992. "Shining Path and Peasant Responses in Rural Ayacucho." In Palmer 1992b, 59–81.

Jeffrey, Paul. 1998. *Recovering Memory: Guatemalan Churches and the Challenge of Peacemaking*. Uppsala: Life and Peace Institute.

Jenkins, Philip. 2002. *The Next Christendom: The Coming of Global Christianity*. New York: Oxford University Press.

Jonas, Susanne. 2000. *Of Centaurs and Doves: Guatemala's Peace Process*. Boulder, Colo.: Westview Press.

Justino, Mário. 1995. *Nos bastidores do reino: A vida secretada igreja universal do reino de Deus*. São Paulo: Geração Editorial.

Klaiber, Jeffrey. 1990. "Fujimori: Race and Religion in Perú." *America* 163 (September):33–35.

———. 1997. *Iglesia, dictaduras y democracia en América Latina.* Lima: Fondo Editorial de la Pontificia Universidad Católica del Perú.

Lehmann, David. 1996. *Struggle for the Spirit.* Cambridge: Polity.

Lessa, Carlos. 2000. *O rio de todos os Brasis: Uma reflexão em busca da auto-estima.* Rio de Janeiro: Record.

Levine, Daniel. 1995. "Protestants and Catholics in Latin America: A Family Portrait." In *Fundamentalisms Comprehended,* ed. Martin Marty and R. Scott Appleby, 155–78. The Fundamentalism Project, vol. 5. Chicago: University of Chicago Press.

———. 2000. "The News about Religion in Latin America." In *Religion on the International News Agenda,* ed. Mark Silk, 120–42. Hartford: Center for the Study of Religion in Public Life, pp..

Levine, Daniel, and David Stoll. 1997. "Bridging the Gap between Empowerment and Power in Latin America." In *Transnational Religion and Fading States,* ed. Suzanne H. Rudolph and J. Piscatori, 63–103. Boulder, Colo.: Westview Press.

Linch, Nicolás. 1999. *El renacimiento de la política como esperanza.* Lima: Instituto de Defensa Legal.

Lively, Jack, and Andrew Reeve. 1997. "The Emergence of the Idea of Civil Society: The Artificial Political Order and Natural Social Orders." *Democratization* 4(1):63–75.

López, Darío. 1998. *Los evangélicos y los derechos humanos: La experiencia social del Concilio Nacional Evangélico del Perú 1980–1992.* Lima: CEMAA.

Lumsdaine, David H., ed. 2008. *Evangelical Christianity and Democracy in Asia.* New York: Oxford University Press.

Machado, Maria das Dores Campos, and Fabiana Figueiredo. 2002. "Gênero, religião e política: As evangélicas nas disputas eleitorais da cidade do Rio de Janeiro." *Ciencias Sociales y Religión* 4:125–48.

Machado, Ziel. 1997. "Sim a Deus, sim á vida: Evangélicos redescobrindo sua cidadania." Master's thesis, Pontifícia Universidade Católica de São Paulo.

Madrigal, Ligia. 1999. *La evolución de las ideas: El caso de los protestantes en Nicaragua, 1856–1925.* Managua: UNAN-CIEETS.

Mariano, Ricardo. 1999. *Neopentecostais: Por uma nova sociologia do pentecostalismo brasileiro.* São Paulo: Loyola.

Mariano, Ricardo, and Flávio Pierucci. 1992. "O envolvimento dos pentecostais na eleição de collor." *Novos Estudos Cebrap* 34:92–106.

Mariz, Cecília. 1996. "Pentecostalismo e a luta contra a pobreza no Brasil." In *Na força do espírito: Pentecostais na América Latina: Um desafio às igrejas históricas,* ed. Benjamin Gutiérrez and Leonildo Campos, 169–89. São Paulo: Pendão Real.

Martin, David. 1990. *Tongues of Fire: The Explosion of Protestantism in Latin America.* Oxford: Blackwell.

———. 2002. *Pentecostalism: The World Their Parish.* Oxford: Blackwell.

Marty, Martin, and R. Scott Appleby, eds. 1993. *Fundamentalisms and the State.* The Fundamentalism Project, vol. 3. Chicago: University of Chicago Press.

Matamoros, Bartolomé. 1984. *Historia de las asambleas de dios en Nicaragua.* Managua: Distribuidora Viva.

McSherry, J. Patrice. 1998. "The Emergence of 'Guardian Democracy.'" *NACLA Report on the Americas* 32(3):16–25.

Mendoza, Raúl. 1999. "Lo que faltaba . . . Una ley contra la vagancia." *Revista Domingo, La República* [Lima], September 19, pp. 16–18.

Míguez Bonino, José. 1983. *Protestantismo y liberación en América Latina*. San José: DEI.

———. 1999. *Poder del evangelio y poder político*. Buenos Aires: Kairos.

MINUGUA (Misión de Verificación de las Naciones Unidas en Guatemala). 2000a. *Los linchamientos: Un flagelo contra la dignidad humana*. Guatemala City: n.p.

———. 2000b. *Situación de la niñez y la adolescencia en el marco del proceso de paz de Guatemala*. Guatemala City: n.p.

Moisés, José Álvaro. 1995. *Os Brasileiros e a democracia*. São Paulo: Ática.

Mondragón, Carlos. 1991. "México: De la militancia revolucionaria al letargo social." In *De la marginación al compromiso: Los evangélicos y la política en América Latina*, ed. R. Padilla, 61–76. Buenos Aires: FTL.

———. 1994. "Mentalidades y proyectos de evangelización ecumenica en América latina en la década de los años veinte." *Revista de Historia del Protestantismo Nicaragüense*, 4:15–22.

Nicaráuac. 1981. *Revista del Ministerio de Cultura de Nicaragua* 5 (April–June):93.

Novaes, Regina. 1986. *Os escolhidos de Deus*. Rio de Janeiro: Marco Zero.

———. 2001. "A divina política: Notas sobre as relações delicadas entre religião e política." *Revista da USP* 49:60–81.

Oficina de Derechos Humanos del Arzobispado de Guatemala (ODHAG). 1999. *Guatemala, Never Again!* REMHI (Recovery of Historical Memory Project). The Official Report of the Human Rights Office, Archdiocese of Guatemala. Abridged English translation. Maryknoll, N.Y.: Orbis. [Originally published as *Guatemala: Nunca Más*, 4 vols. Guatemala City: ODHAG, 1998.]

Österlund, Markus. 2001. *Politics in the Midst of Terror*. Helsinki: Finnish Society of Sciences and Letters.

Otzoy, Antonio. 1997. "Traditional Values and Christian Ethics: A Maya Protestant Spirituality." In *Crosscurrents in Indigenous Spirituality: Interface of Maya, Catholic, and Protestant Worldviews*, ed. G. Cook, 261–69. Leiden: Brill.

Oxhorn, Philip. 2001. "When Democracy Isn't All That Democratic: Social Exclusion and the Limits of the Public Sphere in Latin America." North-South Agenda paper 44. Coral Gables, Fla.: North-South Center, University of Miami.

Padilla, René, ed. 1991. *De la marginación al compromiso: Los evangélicos y la política en América Latina*. Buenos Aires: FTL.

Palmer, David Scott. 1992a. "Introduction." In Palmer 1992b, 1–14.

———, ed. 1992b. *Shining Path of Peru*. London: Hurst.

Paz y Esperanza. 1999a. *Déjame que te cuente: Testimonios desde las "nuevas" fronteras de misión*. Lima: Ediciones Paz y Esperanza.

———. 1999b. *Probados por el fuego: Testimonios de coraje y esperanza tras las rejas*. Lima: Ediciones Paz y Esperanza.

Peck, Dudley. 1970. "Practices and Training of Guatemalan Mam Shamans." Ph.D. diss., Hartford Seminary Foundation.

Petersen, Douglas. 1996. *Not by Might, nor by Power: A Pentecostal Theology of Social Concern in Latin America.* Oxford: Regnum.

Peterson, Anna L., Manuel A. Vászquez, and Philip J. Williams, eds. 2001. *Christianity, Social Change, and Globalization in the Americas.* New Brunswick, N.J.: Rutgers University Press.

Pierucci, Antônio Flávio. 1989. "Representantes de Deus em Brasília: A bancada evangélica na constituinte." *Ciências Sociais Hoje:*104–32.

Pierucci, Antônio Flávio, and Reginaldo Prandi. 1996. *A realidade social das religiões no Brasil.* São Paulo: Hucitec.

Pixley, Jorge, and Jerjes Ruiz. 1992. *Con fe Viva.* Managua: CBN.

Putnam, Robert. 1993. *Making Democracy Work: Civic Traditions in Modern Italy.* Princeton: Princeton University Press.

————. 2000. *Bowling Alone: The Collapse and Revival of American Community.* New York: Simon & Schuster.

Ranger, Terence O., ed. 2008. *Evangelical Christianity and Democracy in Africa.* New York: Oxford University Press.

Reis, Fábio Wanderley, and Guillermo O'Donnell. 1988. *A democracia no Brasil: Dilemas e perspectivas.* São Paulo: Vértice.

Riis, Ole. 1999. "Modes of Religious Pluralism under Conditions of Globalisation." *MOST Journal on Multicultural Societies* 1(1).

Roberts, Kenneth. 1998. *Deepening Democracy? The Modern Left and Social Movements in Chile and Peru.* Stanford, Calif.: Stanford University Press.

Romero, Eduardo. 1994. "Observing Protestant Participation in Peruvian Politics." *Latinamericanist* (Spring):6–10.

Rooy, Sidney. 1992. "La evangelización protestante en América latina." *Boletin Teológico* 24(47/48).

Rudolph, Susanne Hoeber. 1997a. "Dehomogenizing Religious Formations." In Rudolph and Piscatori 1997, 243–61.

————. 1997b. "Introduction: Religion, States, and Transnational Civil Society." In Rudolph and Piscatori 1997, 1–24.

Rudolph, Susanne Hoeber, and James Piscatori, eds. 1997. *Transnational Religion and Fading States.* Boulder, Colo.: Westview Press.

Sader, Emir. 1995. *O anjo Torto.* São Paolo: Brasiliense.

Saes, Décio. 2001. *República do capital: Capitalismo e processo político no Brasil.* São Paulo: Boitempo.

Sanchíz Ochoa, Pilar. 1998. *Evangelismo y poder: Guatemala ante el nuevo milenio.* Seville: Universidad de Sevilla.

Schäfer, Heinrich. 1991. *Church Identity between Repression and Liberation: The Presbyterian Church in Guatemala.* Geneva: World Alliance of Reformed Churches.

Schneider, Hermann Gustav. 1998. *La mosquitia.* Managua: CIEETS.

Scotchmer, David. 1986. "Convergence of the Gods: Comparing Traditional Maya and Christian Maya Cosmologies." In *Symbol and Meaning beyond the Closed Community: Essays in Mesoamerican Ideas,* ed. G. H. Gossen, 197–226. Albany: Institute for Mesoamerican Studies.

————. 1989. "Symbols of Salvation: A Local Mayan Protestant Theology." *Missiology* 17:292–310.

———. 1993. "Life of the Heart: A Maya Protestant Spirituality." In *South and Meso-American Native Spirituality*, ed. G. H. Gossen and M. León-Portillo, 496–525. New York: Crossroad.

Scott, Luis. 1991. *Salt of the Earth: A Socio-political History of Mexico City Evangelical Protestants (1964–1991)*. Mexico City: Kyrios.

Sennett, Richard. 1988. *O declínio do homem público*. São Paulo: Companhia das Letras.

Shah, Timothy. 2003. "Evangelical Politics in the Third World: What's Next for the 'Next Christendom'?" *Brandywine Review of Faith and International Affairs* 1(2):21–30.

Smidt, Corwin. 1999. "Religion and Civic Engagement: A Comparative Analysis." *Annals of the American Academy of Political and Social Science* 565(September): 176–92.

Smith, Christian. 1994. "The Spirit and Democracy: Base Comunities, Protestantism, and Democratization in Latin America." *Sociology of Religion* 55(2):119–43.

———. 1998. *American Evangelicalism: Embattled and Thriving*. Chicago: University of Chicago Press.

Smith, Dennis A. 1991. "Coming of Age: A Reflection on Pentecostals, Politics and Popular Religion in Guatemala." *Pneuma* 13(2):65–81.

Smith, Dennis A., and James Grenfell. 1999. "Los evangélicos y la vida pública en Guatemala: Historia, mitos y pautas para el futuro." *Voces del Tiempo* 31:25–34.

Smith, Michael. 1992. "Shining Path's Urban Strategy: Ate-Vitarte." In Palmer 1992b, 127–47.

Soares, Luiz Eduardo. 1993. "A guerra dos pentecostais contra os Afro-Brasileiros: Dimensões democráticas do conflito religioso no Brasil." *Comunicações do ISER* 44:43–50.

Starn, Orin. 1996. "Senderos inesperados: Las rondas campesinas de la sierra sur central." In Degregori 1996b, 227–69.

Steigenga, Timothy. 1996. "Religion and Politics in Central America: The Religious Determinants of Political Activities and Beliefs in Costa Rica and Guatemala." Ph.D. diss., University of North Carolina, Chapel Hill.

———. 1999. "Guatemala." In *Religious Freedom and Evangelization in Latin America: The Challenge of Religious Pluralism*, ed. P. Sigmund, 150–74. Maryknoll, N.Y.: Orbis.

———. 2001. *The Politics of the Spirit: The Political Implications of Pentecostalized Religion in Costa Rica and Guatemala*. Lanham, Md.: Lexington Books.

Stepan, Alfred. 2000. "Religion, Democracy, and the 'Twin Tolerations.'" *Journal of Democracy* 11(4):37–57.

Stokes, Susan. 1995. *Cultures in Conflict: Social Movements and the State in Peru*. Berkeley: University of California Press.

Stoll, David. 1982. *Fishers of Men or Founders of Empire? The Wycliffe Bible Translators in Latin America*. London: Zed Press.

———. 1990. *Is Latin America Turning Protestant? The Politics of Evangelical Growth*. Berkeley: University of California Press.

———. 1993. *Between Two Armies in the Ixil Towns of Guatemala*. New York: Columbia University Press.

————. 1994. " 'Jesus Is Lord of Guatemala' ": Evangelical Reform in a Death-Squad State." In *Accounting for Fundamentalisms: The Dynamic Character of Movements*, ed. Martin Marty and R. Scott Appleby, 99–123. The Fundamentalism Project, vol. 4. Chicago: University of Chicago Press.

Tedlock, Barbara. 1992. *Time and the Highland Maya*. Albuquerque: University of New Mexico Press.

Tillich, Paul. 1967. *Systematic Theology*. Chicago: University of Chicago Press.

Tocqueville, Alexis de. [1835] 2000. *Democracy in America*. Trans. and ed. Harvey C. Mansfield and Delba Winthrop. Chicago: University of Chicago Press.

Touraine, Alain. [1994] 1996. *O que é a democracia?* Petrópolis, Brazil: Vozes. (Originally published as *Qu'est-ce que la democratie?* Paris: Fayard.)

Valderrama, Cecilia. 1992. "Evangélicos en la política peruana." *Signos de Vida* 1 (September):18–20.

Varella, Drauzio. 1999. *Estação Carandiru*. São Paulo: Companhia das Letras.

Vargas, Esther. 1998. "Una ley contra la tentación: El congresista Alejandro Abanto y su guerra contra la minifalda." *La República* [Lima], February 22, pp. 26–27.

Ventura, Zuenir. 1994. *Cidade partida*. Rio de Janeiro: Companhia Das Letras.

Verástegui, Ricardo. 1992. "Iglesias: Voces de esperanza para tiempos de oscuridad." *Caminos* 39 (April):6–7.

Warner, R. S. 1993. "Work in Progress towards a New Paradigm in the Sociological Study of Religion in the United States." *American Journal of Sociology* 98(5): 1044–93.

Weber, Max. [1919] 1978. "Politics as a Vocation." In *Weber: Selections in Translation*, ed. W. G. Runciman, trans. Eric Matthews, 212–25. Cambridge: Cambridge University Press.

————. [1922] 1996. *Economía y sociedad*. Mexico City: Fondo de Cultura Económica.

Willems, Emile. 1967. *Followers of the New Faith*. Nashville: Vanderbilt University Press.

Wilson, Everett. 1997. "Guatemalan Pentecostals: Something of Their Own." In Cleary and Stewart-Gambino 1997, 139–62.

Wilson, John. 1975. "La obra morava en Nicaragua." Licenciatura thesis, San José, Costa Rica, Seminario Bíblico Latinoamericano.

Witte, John, Jr., ed. 1993. *Christianity and Democracy in Global Context*. Boulder, Colo.: Westview Press.

Woodberry, D. Robert. 1999. "Religion and Democratization: Explaining a Robust Empirical Relationship." Paper presented at the annual meeting of the Religious Research Association, University of North Carolina, Chapel Hill, November.

Wuthnow, Robert. 1992. *Rediscovering the Sacred: Perspectives on Religion in Contemporary Society*. Grand Rapids, Mich.: Eerdmans.

Yashar, Deborah J. 1997. *Demanding Democracy: Reform and Reaction in Costa Rica and Guatemala, 1870s–1950s*. Stanford, Calif.: Stanford University Press.

Zub, Roberto. 1993. *Protestantismo y elecciones en Nicaragua*. Managua: Nicarao-CIEETS.

————. 1996. *Oficio y modelos pastorales*. Managua: CIEETS-Visión Mundial-INDEF.

Index